Global Masculinities – a new series from Zed Books

SERIES EDITOR: MICHAEL S. KIMMEL

Men face common issues – the balance between work and family, fatherhood, defining masculinity in a globalizing economy, health and reproduction, sexuality, and violence. But they are experiencing these all over the world in very different contexts and are coming up with different priorities and strategies to address them. This new international series will provide a vehicle for understanding this diversity, and reflect the growing awareness that analysis of masculinity will be greatly impoverished if it remains dominated by a European/North American/Australian matrix. A number of regional and thematic cross-cultural volumes are planned.

The editor, Michael S. Kimmel, is a well-known educator concerning gender issues. His most recent book, *Manhood in America: A Cultural History*, was published in 1996 to significant acclaim. His work has appeared in dozens of magazines, newspapers and scholarly journals, including the *New York Times Book Review*, the *Harvard Business Review*, the *Nation* and *Psychology Today*, where he was a contributing editor and columnist on male-female relationships. His teaching examines men's lives from a pro-feminist perspective. He is national spokesperson for the National Organization for Men Against Sexism (NOMAS) in the States.

Already published

Robert Morrell (ed.), *Changing Masculinities in a Changing Society: Men and Gender in Southern Africa*

Bob Pease and Keith Pringle (eds), *A Man's World? Changing Men's Practices in a Globalized World*

Frances Cleaver (ed.), *Making Masculinity Matter! Men, Gender and Development*

In preparation

Adam Jones (ed.), *Men of the Global South: A Reader* (forthcoming Autumn 2006)

About this book

This challenging book of essays outlines the great complexity, variety and difference of male identities in Islamic societies.

From the Taliban orphanages of Afghanistan to the cafés of Morocco; from the experience of couples at infertility clinics in Egypt to the trials of Iraqi conscripts, these essays illustrate how the masculine gender is constructed and negotiated in the Islamic Ummah.

The collection goes far beyond the traditional notion that Islamic masculinities are inseparable from the control of women. The essays outline an experience of the relation between spirituality and masculinity quite different from the prevailing Western norms. Drawing on sources ranging from modern Arabic literature to discussions of Muhammad's virility and Abraham's paternity, Islamic Masculinities portrays ways of being in the world that intertwine with non-Western conceptions of duty to the family, the state and the divine.

This innovative and illuminating book will be of major interest to students of culture, gender and sociology, and will provide new insights even to specialists in the Middle East and Islamic Studies.

LAHOUCINE OUZGANE | editor

Islamic masculinities

Zed Books

LONDON | NEW YORK

Islamic masculinities was first published by Zed Books Ltd, 7 Cynthia Street, London N1 9JF, UK and Room 400, 175 Fifth Avenue, New York, NY 10010, USA in 2006

www.zedbooks.co.uk

Cover designed by Andrew Corbett
Set in Arnhem and Futura Bold by Ewan Smith, London
Index: <ed.emery@britishlibrary.net>
Printed and bound in the United Kingdom by Biddles Ltd

Distributed in the USA exclusively by Palgrave Macmillan, a division of St Martin's Press, LLC, 175 Fifth Avenue, New York, NY 10010.

A catalogue record for this book is available from the British Library.
US CIP data are available from the Library of Congress.

ISBN 1 84277 274 0 hb
ISBN 1 84277 275 9 pb

ISBN 978 1 84277 274 4 hb
ISBN 978 1 84277 275 1 pb

Contents

Acknowledgements

I wish to thank Robert Molteno, Michael Pallis and Anna Hardman for their contributions to the production of this book. I am grateful to Michael Kimmel, who has commented on this work with care, enthusiasm and speed; his faith in and support of this project have been invaluable.

I would also like to thank Ryan, Ben and Joni for their unwavering love.

Edmonton, August 2005

Islamic masculinities: an introduction

LAHOUCINE OUZGANE

In the last three or four decades, scholarly attention to gender issues in the Middle East and North Africa has been focused almost exclusively[1] on a quest to understand femininity: what it is and how it is made and regulated – with Muslim women's oppression, the question of the *hijab*, and the practice of female genital mutilation receiving most of the scrutiny.[2] Some of the most significant literature on this subject includes Fatna Sabbah's *Woman in the Muslim Unconscious* (1984), a detailed critique of the complex and contradictory messages which the Islamic legal and erotic discourses inscribe on the female body; Fatima Mernissi's *The Veil and the Male Elite* (1987), an indictment of the ways in which numerous Hadiths (or sayings of the Prophet) have been manipulated by a male elite to maintain male privileges; Fedwa Malti-Douglas's *Woman's Body, Woman's Word* (1991), a study of the relationship of woman's voice in Arabo-Islamic discourse to sexuality and the body; Leila Ahmed's *Women and Gender in Islam* (1992), a study (the best so far) of the development of Islamic discourses on women and gender from the ancient world to the present; and Marnia Lazreg's *The Eloquence of Silence* (1994), an analysis of gender relations in Algeria from pre-colonial times to the present.

By contrast, studies of Islamic masculinities are surprisingly rare. At a time when masculinities studies is experiencing a tremendous boom in the West, masculinity in Islamic cultures has so far remained an under-examined category that secures its power by refusing to identify itself. Except for *Imagined Masculinities: Male Identity and Culture in the Modern Middle East* (2000), there are very few studies that render Muslim men visible as gendered subjects and that show that masculinities have a history and are part of gender relations in Muslim cultures. Although most of the essays are reprints, Mai Ghoussoub and Emma Sinclair-Webb's *Imagined Masculinities* is thus the first serious collection that addresses the different aspects of being and becoming a man in the modern Middle East. The book examines some widespread rites of passage by which male identities are constructed and desirable versions of masculinity achieved: male circumcision, a boy's expulsion from the women's *hammam*, military service, and the Palestinian rituals of resistance to the Israeli army.

Two other books on the subject of Islamic masculinities are limited to examinations of homosexuality and homoeroticism in Islamic cultures and classical Arabic literature, respectively. In one form or another, the twenty-two essays (fourteen of which are written by the editors themselves) of *Islamic Homosexualities: Culture, History, and Literature* (1997) make the point that 'Before the twentieth century, the region of the world with the most visible and diverse homosexualities was not northwestern Europe, but northern Africa and southwestern Asia' (Murray and Roscoe 1997: 6). The collection offers 'historical, anthropological, and literary studies and texts documenting the conceptions and organizations of homosexual desire and conduct in Islamic societies' (p. 4). As its title indicates, *Homoeroticism in Classical Arabic Literature* (1997), on the other hand, examines the prevalence and significance of 'homoerotic motifs in early 'Abbàsid poetry, courtly letters, political satire, shadow plays, and dreambooks, from the eighth to the fourteenth centuries and from Persia to Andalusia' (Wright and Rownson 1997: xiv).

Islamic Masculinities adopts a social constructionist perspective and is premised on the belief that men are not born; they are made; they construct their masculinities within particular social and historical contexts. Thus, masculinities in Islamic contexts emerge as a set of distinctive practices defined by men's positionings within a variety of religious and social structures.

As for the term 'Islamic' in its title, the book does not propose to offer an essentialist definition of what a Muslim man or woman is. The experiences of masculinity described in the articles collected here are not uniform, not generalizable to all Muslim men. Besides, one should be particularly uncomfortable with the use of the word 'Islam' as a category, especially when it is deployed in the West, for the reasons Edward Said explained at length in *Orientalism* (1978) and, more recently, in *Covering Islam* (1997): '"Islam" defines a relatively small proportion of what actually takes place in the Islamic world, which numbers a billion people, and includes dozens of countries, societies, traditions, languages, and, of course, an infinite number of different experiences' (Said 1997: xvi).

Indeed, all too often, 'Islam' is an easy catch-all term, an Orientalist construct which thrives even more today than in the nineteenth century. As the essays in this collection attest, gender and patriarchy lie at the heart of the ongoing crisis of Arab and Muslim society, thought and politics, all of which lay claim to 'Islam' in one way or another. So the challenge I faced when putting together this book was how to allow a discussion of such issues productively and honestly without fuelling Eurocentric, anti-Arab, anti-Islamic bigotry.

The essays

The book is divided into three distinct sections. The first, 'Masculinities and religion', opens with Durre S. Ahmed, in 'Gender in Islamic spirituality: a psychological view of "low" fundamentalism', examining the significance and place of the masculine and the feminine in the hyper-masculine Pakistani state, where masculinity has less to do with the visions and teaching of Islam and more to do with the pursuit of patriarchal power agendas in the name of Islam. The author argues that, in Islam, male and female represent the highest level of symbolic union with the divine, but in the modern Pakistani state, with its professionalization of the *ulemas* and the Islamization of the army, the feminine has receded and vanished from secular and religious consciousness, making it possible for us to view modernization itself as actually a form of masculinization.

In 'The smile of death and the solemncholy of masculinity', Banu Helvacioglu conceptualizes different forms of masculinity as sexually, culturally, religiously and intellectually marked performances which men, women and children reproduce in innumerable facets of life. Her chapter focuses on death rituals conducted following an earthquake in Turkey in August 1999. To enable the author to come to terms with the inexplicable nature of death, the first part of the article is written as a narrative allowing Banu – spectator, participant and co-producer of these rituals – to view the action through the lens of a child, a woman in mourning and a woman exhibiting constantly alternating masculine/feminine protests. In order to anchor the story in a historical and social context, the second part of the article explains Islamic dimensions of masculinity in relation to universal and particular aspects of nation-building, social and familial bonds, state-centred perspectives and rigid gender codes. The conclusion reads death, loss and tragedy as momentary chances to embrace life with gender-specific laughter.

The next two chapters explore the topic of masculinity in the lives of two foundational prophets: Muhammad and Abraham. Ruth Roded's 'Alternate images of the Prophet Muhammad's virility' argues that, from the advent of Islam and through the centuries, Muslims and non-Muslims have constructed the virility of the Prophet Muhammad in various ways as a function of religious, social, political and psychological factors. The early believers regarded Muhammad as the last and most complete of a long line of prophets going back to the Old Testament. Thus, he was a human being called to a mission by God but characterized by human sexuality much like David or Solomon. Classical Muslim scholars assiduously studied every aspect of Muhammad's life, including his physical attraction to women and his sexual relations with his wives and concubines. Western Christians, emanating from a culture that valued celibacy, could

3

not comprehend this aspect of the Prophet's life, regarding it as one of the main proofs that Muhammad was a false prophet. Muhammad's 'licentious behaviour' was a central theme of the Christian polemic against Islam from medieval times. The Enlightenment, the Romantic movement and colonialism modified but did not totally eliminate this disparaging view. Frequently, it was replaced with a parallel stereotype of a sexually free and active Muslim. From the mid-nineteenth century, Muslims in various parts of the world have attempted to respond to European attacks on Islam and its Prophet for legitimizing and encouraging sensual behaviour. Internalizing European values, they sought to prove that the Islamic sources had been misunderstood and in fact Muhammad led an austere life and preached a moral religion. Some augmented this defensive approach with counter-attacks on Christianity and European society. A very few Muslims, drawing upon their own society and culture, accepted Muhammad's virility as a sign of his humanity and admirable qualities. This made him more comprehensible to the ordinary man but also an outstanding leader.

Najat Rahman's 'The trial of heritage and the legacy of Abraham' is very suggestive in its analysis of the scriptural texts and in its consideration of how some contemporary writers use re-reading 'to make space for hopes that ideologically ritualized readings exclude'. The chapter offers an intriguing depiction of Abraham as a figure caught in a 'double-bind' between the imperatives of divine command and communal duty, particularly as these forces converge in Genesis 22, the 'binding of Isaac', which Rahman takes as a key site for 'patriarchal demarcations of identity'. As it excludes Sarah, recalls the banishment of Hager, and threatens to sacrifice the future of the son, this episode reveals the dynamic construction and undoing that take place in the biblical story of Abraham. Such formulations of identity are then explored in the work of Mahmoud Darwish and Assia Djebar, two writers who call attention to the discontinuities of this shared heritage in an effort to respond to and guard against all nationalist and fundamentalist exclusions.

The essays in the second section, 'Masculinities and the Palestinian–Israeli conflict', consider the legacy of Abraham in its current political context. Celia Rothenberg's '"My Wife is from the Jinn"': Palestinian men, diaspora and love' explores the ways in which some Palestinian male villagers experience the cultural politics of diaspora and return through a popular, serialized magazine story entitled 'Zowjati min al-jinn' published in Arabic by the magazine Fausta. The story reflects the experiences of young men who return from the diaspora, fall in love with foreign, even Israeli, women, and do not uphold their necessary responsibilities and roles in the village, in contrast to analyses of explicit discourses of masculinity which

4

emphasize men as protectors of family honour, providers for the family needs, and fighters or martyrs for the Palestinian nationalist cause.

Rob K. Baum's chapter 'Chasing horses, eating Arabs' argues that, in an attempt to cater to the tastes of its Western audiences, the film *Wedding in Galilee* exploits the exotic Orientality of Palestinian bodies, both male and female, while generalizing and equating Arab male sexuality with the 'politics of dispossession' and leaving us with the overriding image of Arab masculinity as one of cultural and personal impotence.

Daniel Monterescu's 'Stranger masculinities: gender and politics in a Palestinian–Israeli "third space"' concludes this section by looking at the dilemmas of Palestinian Arabs in the mixed town of Jaffa. The chapter locates its analysis of the practices and conceptions of Palestinian *rujula* in the wider network of institutions and ideologies that govern the lives of men with one citizenship and multiple hybrid identities.

'Masculinities and social practice', the final section of the book, brings together five essays that consider the dynamic social processes that construct masculine identities in five different locations. Don Conway-Long, in 'Gender, power and social change in Morocco', finds that, for Moroccan men, masculinity is relational: it is defined by the men's perception of the relations between men and women. His chapter describes the ways in which men in the 1990s perceived ongoing shifts in gendered power, the appropriateness of traditional divisions of labour, the impact of globalization on their own position, and, ultimately, the ways they experienced and responded to the process of social change.

In 'Masculinity and gender violence in Yemen', Mohammed Baobaid studies Yemeni conceptions of masculinity through a look at the different forms of violence Yemeni women undergo on a daily basis. Patriarchal power structures, the chapter suggests, are founded on the repression of the feminine, a theme running through other essays in this collection.

Achim Rohde's 'Opportunities for masculinity and love: cultural production in Ba'thist Iraq during the 1980s' examines several cultural productions under the Ba'th regime to discuss the place and significance of gender relations in modern Iraq. In the context of its war against Iran and in an attempt to construct subjects fit and willing to serve the state, the Iraqi regime introduced several 'improvements' in the status of women designed to fashion them into masculinized subjects and more easily to police both the public and private spheres of life.

Asifa Siraj's 'On being homosexual and Muslim: conflicts and challenges' gives voice to a group of men who speak freely about a topic that continues to be taboo for the majority of Muslims. Though still tentative, the narratives are none the less compelling, capturing the religious, social and familial forces that continue to shape the identities of this marginalized form of masculinity.

Finally, in 'The worms are weak', Marcia C. Inhorn argues that male infertility is the single most common cause of infertility worldwide. Yet, globally, women bear the major social burden of childlessness. In this chapter, Inhorn implicates patriarchy in the gendered asymmetry that accompanies infertility, particularly in the non-Western world. By focusing specifically on the case of male infertility in Egypt – where sperm are popularly referred to as 'worms' and male infertility is glossed as 'the worms are weak' – Inhorn argues that the social dilemmas faced by women with infertile husbands cannot be understood without reference to patriarchy in its local Egyptian form. She then analyses a series of four 'patriarchal paradoxes' in Egypt, involving issues of procreative blame, diminution of gendered identities, untoward marital dynamics and asymmetrical embodiment of new reproductive technologies. Despite the stigma that surrounds male infertility, infertile Egyptian men experience various forms of privilege in their marriages, social relations and treatment experiences, often to the disadvantage of the wives who love and support them.

Islamic Masculinities tries to grapple with the question of what happens to critical men's studies theories when they are brought to bear in conjunction with the challenges of gender research in parts of the Muslim world. Although gender theories can be productively deployed to understand Islamic masculinities, we have to bear in mind that the Muslim world is diverse and ever-changing. We also need to take into consideration local realities, religious and political agendas, the consequences of Western colonialism and imperialism, and the marked effects of globalization. But while the collection reminds us that all masculinity studies must be grounded in historical, cultural and geographical contexts, this attention to and recognition of the diversity of masculinities must not divert our attention from men's social dominance both in the Muslim world and everywhere else.

Islamic Masculinities is necessarily selective and does not claim to cover every possible aspect of Islamic masculinities, but I hope that the essays will stimulate further discussion and research because so much of the literature on gender in Islam over the last twenty or thirty years has been written and read with Muslim men as an unmarked category. The study of gender in relation to Muslim societies has almost always meant a study of women's lives, women's roles and the representation of women in literature. The pervasiveness of this approach has led to a relative neglect of constructions of masculinities within Muslim societies. The present collection is designed to help fill that gap.

6

Notes

1 In a parody of this preoccupation, Fedwa Malti-Douglas (1991: 3) writes: 'The Arab woman is a most fascinating creature. Is she veiled? Is she not veiled? Is she oppressed? Is she not oppressed? Were her rights greater before Islam? Are her rights greater after Islam? Does she have a voice? Does she not have a voice?'

2 In the West, this attention to the practice of female genital mutilation in some Muslim countries often overlooks other forms of female oppression, such as back-breaking labour, economic depency on men and prostitution, realities which are often exacerbated by or are a direct result of Western economic imperialism. Such a concern may also serve as an alibi, as a way of pointing the finger at the pain and suffering of Muslim (and other Third World) women while at the same time overlooking other forms of pain and other forms of marginalization that Muslim women and men face in the West especially after 11 September 2001; it can also serve to divert attention away from the real gender inequities that prevail in the West itself.

References

Ahmed, L. (1992) *Women and Gender in Islam*. New Haven, CT: Yale University Press.

Ghoussoub, M. and E. Sinclair-Webb (eds) (2000) *Imagined Masculinities: Male Identity and Culture in the Modern Middle East*. London: Saqi Books.

Lazreg, M. (1994) *The Eloquence of Silence: Algerian Women in Question*. New York: Routledge.

Malti-Douglas, F. (1991) *Woman's Body, Woman's Word: Gender and Discourse in Arabo-Islamic Writing*. Princeton, NJ: Princeton University Press.

Mernissi, F. (1987) *The Veil and the Male Elite*, trans. M. J. Lakeland. Harlow: Addison-Wesley.

Murray, S. O. and W. Roscoe (eds) (1997) *Islamic Homosexualities: Culture, History, and Literature*. New York: New York University Press.

Sabbah, F. A. (1984) *Woman in the Muslim Unconscious*, trans. M. J. Lakeland. New York: Pergamon.

Said, E. W. (1997) *Covering Islam*, rev. edn. New York: Vintage.

Wright Jr., J. W. and E. K. Rownson (eds) (1997) *Homoeroticism in Classical Arabic Literature*. New York: Columbia University Press.

ONE | **Masculinities and religion**

1 | Gender and Islamic spirituality: a psychological view of 'low' fundamentalism

DURRE S. AHMED

This chapter is part of a continuing exploration of the psychology of two broadly conceived types of Islamic fundamentalism, namely 'high' and 'low'.[1] 'High' Islamism pertains to those who are well educated by modern standards, including in the sciences, but who nevertheless subscribe to a narrow, literalist and violent vision of Islam. As such, they contradict the popular, widely held belief, particularly in the secular Muslim world, that fundamentalism is a lack of rationality which can be inculcated only through systems of modern education reflecting a strong scientific bias (Hoodbhoy 1991). Clearly, this is not the case: witness 11 September 2001. Whether it be Osama bin Laden, or the alleged leader of the aeroplane attacks in the USA, Mohammad Atta, increasingly there are many Islamists highly trained in scientific disciplines ranging from engineering to medicine, to architecture and nuclear physics.[2]

I have examined this type of 'high' fundamentalism in a separate and detailed analysis, including its roots in certain key psycho-philosophical aspects of modernity (Ahmed 2002a; see also Ahmed 2001a). To the extent that increasingly it is the 'high' fundamentalist who provides either the inspiration or, frequently, financial and technical support to his not so well educated brothers who comprise 'low' fundamentalism, modernity and its problems and prospects remain central to understanding the phenomenon as a whole. Given that, high and low, almost all Islamists tend to have repressive and brutal attitudes towards women; broadly speaking, they are similar in terms of socio-political attitudes and impact. At the same time, given the relative lack of exposure to science and other key consciousness-changing technologies such as literacy,[3] 'low' fundamentalism exhibits certain differences in psychology regarding gender.

Of course, the psychologies of both types of Islamists are deeply inter-linked and these are not starkly separate categories/individuals. Given their similarities in terms of outcome (violence, misogyny), these are ultimately differences in *style.* In the case of 'low' Islamists, the differences are more evident at the local/national level, in this instance in Pakistan. Contextualizing them at different levels offers deeper insights, from different angles, into ultimately the same phenomenon. To this end, whereas the analysis of 'high' fundamentalism was primarily located within a critique of modernity, the present one also incorporates an Islamic idiom related to doctrine and gender. Put another way, while both remain connected to modernity, taken together they may represent certain global and local dimensions of Islamic fundamentalism. The first part of this chapter delineates the theoretical underpinnings of the analysis. The second discusses some of the key factors in the rise of 'low' Islamism in Pakistan and the attendant psychological implications for Islamist masculinity.

The psychological/theoretical framework

The connections with modernity of the present analysis are at a dual level. The first has to do with the feminist critique of viewing it as an implicitly 'phallogocentric' ('masculinist') project which is saturated in the 'Cartesian masculinization of thought' (see Bordo 1985). At the same time, I locate myself in the work of Carl Jung and particularly of James Hillman, in what is referred to as Archetypal psychology/theory. Its relevance lies, first, in the significance given by Jung to the role of religion in psychology. Second, apart from being a post-Jungian amplification, there are close connections between Hillman's ideas and an important intellectual tradition within Islam. For Hillman, after Jung, 'the second immediate father of archetypal psychology is Henry Corbin (1903–78), the French scholar, philosopher ... principally known for his interpretation of Islamic thought' (Hillman 1983).[4] This paper also utilizes Murata's work on gender and Islam. Additionally, it is implicitly contextualized in writings on the significance of the 'symbolic imagination' in, among others, the work of Gilbert Durand, Henry Corbin, Mircea Eliade and Paul Ricoeur. As a whole, this body of work signals that

> We should not be surprised ... to find that, in the last half century, developments ... resulting from Freudian psychoanalysis and Jungian depth psychology have converged with a new orientation of the old history of religion discipline. Thus, with Mircea Eliade, Henry Corbin and Georges Dumezil ... to cite only a few authors ... reflections on the phenomenon of religion have broken away from etiological reductions within purely historical, social contexts to enter the territory of a more anthropological field – one centered on the properly religious function of the creative imagination. (Durnad 1987; see also Joy 1987)

In the present context, words such as 'creative imagination' or the 'Imaginal' do not refer to flights of fancy but to a complex epistemological framework. Whether in Ricoeur's notion of a 'poetics of experience' and the dynamic centrality of metaphor, or in Eliade's view that the soul-stifling aspects of modernity can be countered only through awakening the imagination which is innately predisposed to perceive the sacred/symbolic, imagination is conceptualized in a manner that can enable an articulation and understanding of religion and religious experience.

Post-Jungian psychology The (post)Jungian view of the human psyche is based on the paradigmatic significance of myth in both religion and human behaviour. The earliest expression of religion, mythology, is today considered a 'primitive' precursor to psychology. To this extent, like the ancient pantheons (and every civilization had one), our psyche is inherently 'polytheistic'. As experienced by us, in our outer and inner thoughts/emotions/behaviours, ranging from lust to compassion, to love, despondency, ambition and infinitely more, we inhabit a dense and diverse inner reality, not too different from the gods and their complex, multi-level exploits and expressions. In the same way as even today, different festivals honour different gods or aspects of a single deity, different 'gods' enter and exit in continuous flow within us, expressing the varied nature of, for example, love, vengeance, sexuality. As such, our changing moods, obsessions and concerns reflect an inherently polyvalent, polycentric, 'polytheistic' psyche. Forming a sort of web of inner meaning, this ancient notion of archetypes, as reintroduced in modern depth psychology by Jung, refers to the foundations of our basic assumptions about life/relationships and the controlling images that determine the course of our lives.

From within this framework, the issues of gender and socialization, at one level, take on marginal importance. As is evident, the gods, whether Greek or Indian, present a range of masculinities, from Zeus to the bisexual Dionysus. Each archetype represents an attitude, a *style* or structure of consciousness, uniquely *embodied* but expressed primarily as symbol(s). Thus, to study human behaviour is to study its relationship with the symbolic, not only as it appears in mythology and religion, but also in art, drama, epic, music, dance, architecture and other cultural manifestations.

The literal and symbolic When we discuss fundamentalism today, a common refrain is that the symbolic is taken as literal. While this is indeed the fact, the proposed counter-method is actually more allegorical and is not the same as an understanding of the symbolic. The symbolic, in this context, differs from its counterpart in, for example, modern anthropology or semiotics. In archetypal theory, symbols have a certain 'affective' power, can never be fully explained in terms of what they evoke and will always have an element of ambiguity, that is, an individually unknowable, transpersonal element. The attendant aspect of mystery is what we call(ed)

13

a 'sense of the sacred', and which is connected to that ultimate mystery: death. As something that we all will experience but know nothing about, death, by definition can be 'known' only in terms of the symbolic imagination. In so far as it forms the bedrock of the enterprise of religion, our understanding of what life 'means' (or doesn't) is closely linked to how we understand death. Thus, as Corbin put it, symbols say that which *cannot be said in any other way* (Corbin 1987: 14–15, 38–77). In short, phenomenologically, the symbolic is both a psychological, physical (literal), as well as transcendental/metaphysical reality. It was these notions of the symbolic and its virtual absence in modern sensibility that Norman O. Brown was referring to when he said that 'the thing to abolish is literalism ... truth is always poetic in form, not literal but symbolic' (1986: 244). Brown's concern has been similarly echoed by others such as Jung and Eliade who see the primary malaise of modernity as its loss of the symbolic/imagination.

For something to be symbolically true, at some level, it has to be literally true. Death, for example, is a literal fact, but from the perspective of many religions it is largely a symbolic affair, a transformation, a re-birth. To talk of the loss of the 'sense' of the symbolic, then, is not to say symbols have ceased to exist. Given their (trans)personality, they remain as such, but interpreted, and manifest, at increasingly literal levels – which basically means a narrowing of the spectrum of their meaning till eventually all multiple possibilities of interpretations are excluded in favour of just one. But the 'power' of the symbol remains.

For example, the (post)Jungian critique of psychology sees modern psychology as repressive and abusive towards the 'feminine' side of the psyche. As a logical concomitant of the Cartesian split between 'mind' and body, the body is regarded as inferior, 'feminine' in contrast to the rational 'mind' which can be considered 'masculine' in its overvaluation of *logos* and notions of will-power, detachment, instrumentalist rationality, control. Given this dominance, other attitudes which are more intermediate, ambiguous, imaginal, metaphoric, having to do with *eros* and relatedness, can be considered 'feminine'. From the point of the modern Freudian/Cartesian 'ego', this feminine domain and the psyche's diversity as a whole are useless, threatening to its 'consciousness'. When they surface, as they must being a part of life, and erupt from the 'unconscious', they are considered abnormalities, 'pathology', and treated accordingly. Thus, in the West, the first two 'diseases' to be 'discovered' were hysteria and schizophrenia. The first is primarily associated with women, and the second with diversity and multiplicity of personality.

The point is that, first, culture itself can be 'read' symbolically. Second, that whether at the individual or the cultural/collective level, in spite of an absence of the sense of the symbolic, the archetypal power of the symbolic itself lives on, and powerfully at that. Thus, as used in this psycho-symbolic-sacred sense, culture becomes a crucial concept, not only as archetypal canvas but also as a diagnostic one.

Religion and sexuality From the Jungian perspective, gender does not have to do with just literal, outer manifestations of genital sexuality, but also, more importantly, it is a psychological–symbolic construct. For example, in contrast to Freudian literalist reductionism and its tendency to view dream images such as a dagger or a pointed object as symbols of 'nothing but' the male genitals, the Jungian may regard them also as certain attitudes of consciousness which could be normatively termed 'masculine'. As evident in the hero archetype, they could refer to the idea of rational intellect, a 'penetrative' insight, an attempt to 'see through' a situation, mastery, detachment, abstraction, clarity of thought. (It was this literalist reduction of Freudian thought which led Jung to remark, only half in jest, that the penis is 'nothing but a phallic symbol'.)

Similarly, a hollow object may be a symbol of a different set of psychological qualities: relatedness, receptivity, inwardness, more contemplative, reflective and less action-oriented. To the extent that men and women literally embody these genitally based metaphors, they may exhibit individual predispositions. But to consider this, as Freud did ('anatomy is destiny'), exclusively as literal is to fall into gender reductionism. In short, masculine and feminine are also *attitudes*, potentially available to both sexes and, as such, do not have to do just literally with man and woman.

To the extent that the concept of 'masculine' is meaningless without its feminine counterpart, any statements about the latter can substantively imply a view of the former. As one proceeds, this seeming shift in focus will at times be evident. It is remarkable that whenever there is an attempt to 'Islamize' what is in any case a pre-existing and predominantly Muslim society, much of it has to do with the behaviour and bodies of women. Given that such socio-political movements are rarely inspired, led or followed on a large scale by women, to that extent they indicate certain deep-rooted psychological issues within the Muslim male psyche regarding women, gender, sexuality and the relationship of these with religion.

Considering that Jung's extensive forays into comparative religion and spiritual alchemy form major conceptual underpinnings to his work, his ideas about the symbolic dimensions of gender have parallels not only in Gnostic Christianity but in almost all traditions which view the body in both physical and symbolic terms. All mythologies abound with sexual metaphors, simultaneously expressing religious concepts. In these and

15

almost every spiritual tradition, the human being is a microcosm, 'the little world', representing the macrocosm or the 'great world', the universe (O'Flaherty 1980). The micro/macrocosm theme is similarly present in the monotheisms, of humans being made in the likeness of God.

Sexuality and spiritual experience have traditionally been linked in the literature of mysticism, the great spiritual current running beneath all religions. Terms such as 'rapture', 'passion', 'union', 'ecstasy', 'ravish', occur frequently in mystical texts. Many so-called 'esoteric' (to the westerner) psychologies in the East, including the perspective of certain types of yoga, Tantra and Sufism, would say that sexuality is really unexpressed and unfulfilled religious experience (Bataille 1998). These connections between religion and gender are all present within Islamic doctrine and practice.

Elements of doctrine and practice in Islamic mysticism

Perhaps more than most religions, the division between the exoteric and esoteric is vividly present in Islam. That is, there is the *shariah* as codified, textual law and the more informal, also textual but overwhelmingly orally transmitted idiom of the 'path' or 'way' of mysticism (*tariqah*). Both can be considered as *engendering* certain attitudes of the soul/psyche, in this case masculine and feminine respectively, but always as interrelated aspects of a unity, human or divine.

At a basic level, one's sense of self is inseparable from the body, which is a crucial element of understanding this gender/self/spirit connection, literally and symbolically. As in other mystical traditions such as Tantra, which does not perceive sexuality in primarily negative terms, male and female in Islam, and their sexual union, represent the highest level of a symbolic union with the divine. The positive role given to sexuality in Islam finds its fullest expression not only in the life of the Prophet but also in the Sufi poetry and the theme of love as 'realized gnosis', which, as Nasr says, 'dominates its [Islamic] spirituality', and in which 'God appears as the beloved and the female as a precious being symbolizing inwardness and the inner paradise' (Nasr 1980).

It is within such a psycho-spiritual framework, for example, that Henry Corbin has discussed the complex metaphysics of writers such as Ibn al Arabi and Rumi and an important dimension of their vision of the divine: 'a mystic obtains the highest theophanic vision in contemplating the image of feminine being, because it is in the Image of feminine being that contemplation can apprehend the highest manifestation of God ... The spirituality of our Islamic mystics is led esoterically to the apparition of the Eternal Womanly as an Image of the Godhead' (Corbin 1987: 159–60).

The 'inner', hidden nature of mysticism is, at one level, inherently 'veiled', and by definition cannot be revealed outside of initiation. As Hillman has pointed out: 'initiation as a transformation of consciousness about life involves necessarily a transformation about sexuality'. He adds that absence of initiation and of mysteries in modern Western culture is one main reason for its preoccupation with sexuality (Hillman 1972: 64). Thus, by implication and necessity, one can choose not to discuss further the rites and practices in different types of Islamic mysticisms and their relationship to gender, masculine and feminine.

What is more important is to be aware of a rapacious modern consciousness which lacks a sense of the sacred and is behind the modern demand to 'know' such matters 'clearly', simply on the basis of 'knowledge for its own sake', rather than of the divine. Keeping in view the adage 'those who speak do not know and those who know do not speak', one leaves the reader to draw his/her own conclusions. However 'elitist' this may sound, it is not too far different from many types of depth psychologies and their analytic/therapeutic techniques, which also rely on a certain implicit elitism of intellectual and cultural awareness. Given individual human variation and diverse social/cultural/political/economic contexts, even the secular world of knowledge remains an 'elitist' enterprise. Jung himself was of the view that the goal of his brand of analytical psychology/therapy, 'individuation', was not for everyone.

But beyond these deeply personal and private dimensions to this expression of Islamic spirituality, one can nevertheless briefly refer to other aspects of Islamic mysticism and relate them to certain features of contemporary Islamic masculinity and culture.

'Feminine' and 'masculine' Islam To the extent that mysticism can be considered the 'inner', 'private' and 'hidden' dimension of religion, it can be regarded as its feminine expression. As the counterpoint to a more public, outer, moralistic, codified expression of religiosity, its doctrines and practices tend to focus more on the experiential dimension of the divine, rather than cerebral explanation. This is perhaps why its modern academic study reflects the Cartesian split in seeing this area as 'subjective' ('gnosis'), by definition, 'anecdotal' or 'soft' data as opposed to the 'hard' (phallic) facts of scriptural texts and commentaries.

Differentiating these two broad types of religious expression is not to suggest the superiority of one over the other. Even sternly monotheistic religions such as Judaism and Islam have within them a divinity of inherently multiple facets – 'masculine' and 'feminine'. For our purpose, these dimensions are different archetypes, styles of relationship with and of the Divine, which, like the mythic pantheon, are actually much more nuanced

17

than would appear under the broad and general category of, for example, the Divine Feminine or the Hero or the Wise Old Man. But these can be articulated in detail only when the basis of these broad gender distinctions is established. Most important is that, however broadly conceived, these need to be given due significance in the contemporary discourse on Islam. As will be discussed below, to the extent that today mysticism has been marginalized in both academia and religion, one can say that Islam's 'feminine' dimension has been suppressed.

The 'feminine' nature of mysticism aims psychologically to 'de-masculinize' human consciousness, feminizing it to the extent that heroic attitudes such as mastery, control, action and a narrow material notion of rationality must take a back seat to a more contemplative, passive-receptive attitude. 'In relation to God – we are all – men and women alike, basically feminine. Macho insights reveal nothing of God' (Ong 1981: 63). The religious 'feminization' of the psyche exists across cultures, from the shamanastic religions, to Hinduism, Judaism, Buddhism, Christianity (Hillman 1984). When it comes to Islam, the word itself has profound connotations of 'submission', 'surrender'.

Sapiential Islam As a feminine expression of the religious impulse, mysticism has long been powerfully present in Islam in what Murata (1992: 3) and others have called its 'sapiential tradition'. Popularly known as Sufism, Jung (1984: 336) referred to it as Islam's 'secret backbone' and, as Nasr (1999) points out, it is even today a vast and living tradition. As other scholars have noted:

> the massive theological superstructure that Muslims elaborated during
> the first three or four centuries following Muhammad's death was a
> replica of the Christian one: but its sternly ethical and philosophical dry
> vision never satisfied the Muslim soul [...] so it was that mysticism soon
> appeared within the confines of Islam in the guise of Sufism, to enlist the
> enthusiastic support of the masses [...] in the feminine emotionalism of
> Islamic mysticism [...] In the end, Sufism defeated and routed the *ulemas*.
> (Reincourt 1989: 197–203)

The triumph of Sufism was not without violence, and mystics such as Hallaj and Suharwardy are legendary in Islam because of the terrible violence directed at them.

Sufism is itself a vast and nebulous arena having a range of styles and expressions. Within its enormous rubric, one dimension emphasizes the cultural/imaginative as music, dance and poetry, which play a major role in ecstatic Sufism all over the Muslim world and has firmly become part of its local culture. From across Africa and the Middle East to Central Asia, South Africa and Indonesia, there are innumerable places where this expression of ecstatic abandonment has a central place and Pakistan is no exception to this form of 'low' or 'folk' Islam. But this abandon is, yet again, just one end of a spectrum in Sufism, at the other pole of which are the extremely sophisticated metaphysics of Sufis such as the Andalusian Ibn al 'Arabi and the Persian poet and philosopher Jalaluddin Rumi. Both, incidentally, were accused of heresy and threatened by orthodoxy.

Gender and Islam The nature of gender relationships in sapiential Islamic cosmology, theology and spirituality as explored in depth by Murata, is based on a perception of profound similarities between Islamic frameworks and the Taoist concepts of *Yang* (masculine) and *Yin* (feminine) as two fundamental principles of existence, namely, the Active and Receptive respectively. Together they are conceptualized in the circular symbol divided by a sigmoid line with each half containing the other; *Yin/Yang* constitutes 'the Great Ultimate'.

Based on a system of correspondences and the relationship between these two principles, Islamic and Chinese philosophy can be seen as deeply similar in their approach to the three interrelated levels of the metacosm, macrocosm and microcosm – or God, the cosmos and the human being. It is impossible to attempt to summarize the complex dimensions of these gendered ideals as conceived and articulated over many centuries in Islam, and Murata's work remains a milestone on the subject of gender relationships in traditional Islamic thought. Since the main focus is an understanding of contemporary Islamic masculinity, one can briefly touch upon some of the ideas in terms of broad generalizations, bearing in mind that simplifications are inevitable when talking of what is in reality a highly sophisticated, vast body of metaphysical thought developed over more than a millennium across different languages and cultures.

Similar to many other traditions, the male and female dyad in sapiential Islam is part of a larger intellectual and philosophical framework based on a system of polarities, and is in turn based on a recognition of the centrality of complementary relationships. The ultimate aim of this type of polar thinking is to establish the idea of Unity (*Tawhid*) which in fact manifests itself principally through the dialectics of polarity. Thus, male and female, masculine or feminine, are not so much literally man and woman as they are qualities within a human being. One can note the similarities between this and Jungian concepts, which is not surprising, given the extensive references in his writings to Chinese philosophy (but not Islam).[5]

In Islamic theology, God is ultimately indeed beyond gender. But to

19

the extent that humans 'reflect' different attributes of God who created male and female, 'at another level there is an implied androgyny to the Divine Nature' (Nasr 1980: 69). (One can note in passing that compared with the other two monotheisms, Eve in the Qur'an is neither a secondary creation, nor is she responsible for the fall from Paradise, and, as such, Islam rejects the notion of original sin.)

Within this system of polarities, the proverbial 'Ninety-Nine' names of Allah, God's Attributes, can be broadly classified as Names of Grandeur and Majesty (*Jalal*) and those of Beauty and Graciousness/Compassion (*Jamal*). The former can be considered as 'masculine' and the latter 'feminine'.

> The differences between the sexes cannot be reduced to anatomy and biological function. There are also differences of psychology and tempera-ment, of spiritual type and even principles within the Divine Nature which are sources *in divinis* of the duality represented on the microcosmic level as male and female. God is both Absolute and Infinite. Absoluteness and Majesty, which is inseparable from it, is manifested directly in the mascu-line state and Infinity and Beauty in the feminine. (Nasr 1980: 69)

Beyond the broad categories of masculine/*Jalal* and feminine/*Jamal* attributes of Allah, many commentators have pointed out the significance of the names *al-Rahim* and *al-Rahman*. Referring to different aspects of Mercy, Graciousness and Compassion, they are derived from the same root (*rhm*) as the Arabic word for 'womb'. *Al-Rahim* and *al-Rahman* are perhaps the most well-known names of Allah given that, with one exception, every chapter of the Qur'an begins with them. Apart from statistically being the most often repeated name of God, *al-Rahman* is the one name made synonymous with Allah in the Qur'an. In short, the 'feminine' connota-tions emerging from *al-Rahman* and *al-Rahim* – Mercy, Grace/Graciousness, Compassion – dominate all others, forming a significant dimension to the Islamic idea of God.[6]

It must be reiterated that what have been presented here are generaliza-tions regarding a fraction of an elaborate system of cosmology, theology and spiritual psychology vis-à-vis gender. One should also keep in view that while the focus has been on the feminine as an essential counterpoint to the masculine, it is not to imply that the latter is all negative and the former purely positive. In keeping with the principle of polarity, both feminine and masculine have their own positive and negative dimensions. And in keeping with yet another principle close to Islam, that of balance, taken to exclusive extremes, both can turn into negativities. Yet, at another level, and important for our purpose, the overall significance of the feminine is indisputable:

the Feminine is not opposed to the Masculine [...] but encompasses and combines the two aspects, receptive and active, whereas the Masculine possesses only one of the two [...] This intuition is clearly expressed by Rumi: Woman is a beam of the Divine Light/She is not the being whom sensual desire takes as its object/she is Creator, it should be said/she is not creature. (Corbin 1987: 159–60)

Ulemas-culinists, money-theists, and other 'low' fundamentalists

The Islamic state and masculinity Itself a literalization of religion, from its inception the Pakistani state has had to confront questions of religious identity-politics. And whereas questions of gender per se may not have been prominent in the formulation of identity, the emergent profile and the status of its women indicate its largely negative and hyper-masculine nature. Masculinity in Pakistan today has less to do with the visions and teachings of Islam and more with literalism and the pursuit of patriarchal power agendas in the name of Islam.

As a consequence of factors involving national and international politics, the last fifty years have seen a sort of 'modernizing' of Islam that is actually a 'masculinization' to the point of overwhelming its mystical–feminine expressions. Till recently, the latter had traditionally co-existed in what is a culturally and geographically diverse and widespread 'house of Islam', including in the sub-continent.

As the feminine 'face' of Islam, Sufism for centuries was Islam's 'hidden backbone', but with the advent of the modern state which chose to promote orthodoxy for its own gains, Islam was given an 'official' face: one part comprising the emergence of a 'professionalized' *ulema*/priesthood, something alien to the spirit of Islam; the other manifest in the 'Islamizing' of the armed forces and their grip on power. This composite of militaristic machismo and *ulemas*-culinized theology reflects, as a whole, a consciousness that is primarily aggressive, violent and interested only in power machinations. Till recently and in some ways even today, it is alternatively expressed by the military and the mullah and eventually by both as in the case of the dictator Zia-ul-Haq, and later the Taliban, who were raised mostly in Pakistan.

Shortly after the creation of Pakistan, politically-motivated orthodox groups initiated a series of violent protests against communities regarded as heretics and apostates, demanding that they be declared 'non-Muslims'. An analysis of the rituals and beliefs of one such 'heretical' community indicates that the more 'feminine' an expression of Islam, in doctrine, ritual, practice and interpretation, the more violence it evokes in attempts to marginalize and annihilate it (Ahmed 2002b).

21

Such violence can emerge only from within an extreme and exclusively masculinist environment in which the feminine has been theologically and psychologically obliterated/denied to the extent of being rendered wholly 'other', that is, unconscious. When confronted by It, either symbolically as in certain communities, or literally as in the form of a woman, the response is horror/fear of that which seems alien and which then must be eliminated.

Whether superficially or deeply modernized, and even if somehow untouched by modernity, the hyper-masculinity of a psycho-theological consciousness ensures that such individuals have an overwhelming, externally focused view of God. Moreover, unlike the mystical feminine perspective, such a view, and relationship, is with a God known and experienced only *after* death, and then, too, the direction is towards a literalized feminine: *houris*.

Cultural vandalism and Saudi money-theism As a psycho-theological project, efforts at hereticizing, decrying, stifling and marginalizing the mystical dimensions of Islam are intended not only to repress (and oppress) its feminine dimension but to obliterate the magnificent rainbow of its mystical tradition(s) renowned especially for music, poetry and dance. The 'monochromatic bigotry of modern Islam' (Wilson 1988: 30) has emerged in Pakistan as a result of a steady, state-sponsored, empowerment of Deobandism which found its soulmate in Saudi-Wahabi-Salafism. Both tend to be highly puritanical, rigid and literalistic in terms of interpretation. As I have argued elsewhere, this literalism is inspired more by modern modes of thought, rather than a lack of modern education, hence 'high' fundamentalism (Ahmed 2001a and forthcoming). The exclusive emphasis on the material, the rational and the technical, along with other elements of a self-destructive modernity (witness the role of the West in environmental degradation), makes Saudi Islam a similar inwardly and outwardly self-destructive project.

Reflecting the psychological enthronement of *Tawhid*, which is the defining feature of Islam in terms of the Unity of Creation, the singular obsessional goal of Wahabi Islam is to promote its own singular and literal vision of a political and theological 'unity' under its aegis. This is accompanied by a terrifying and monolithic idea of 'God', sans all attributes except those that service goals of brute power and are disconnected from the feminine. Such a mono-theistic vision, better termed as Money-theism, has, for example, (inwardly) destroyed almost all vestiges of Islamic civilization and culture within Saudi Arabia. It ranges from the obliteration of the house of the Prophet and other sites/structures related to him and his companions, to the recent demolition of an Ottoman fort, making way for five-star hotels and other luxury 'development' projects (Wheelan 2002).

This nihilistic, cultural vandalism has been 'exported' on the strength of oil/money for the propagation of a similarly nihilistic Islam and has directly or indirectly contributed to the gradual erosion of local culture and traditions across the Muslim world, from Afghanistan to the Balkans.[7] The mnemonic voids created by Saudi-sponsored/supported cultural erosion then tend to be filled/replaced by Wahabism's singular view of a culturally barren Islam. Thus, a self-reflexive, self-perpetuating movement gains momentum, aimed at making a monolith of a tradition that has been historically and geo-culturally exceedingly diverse.

Inherently bound up with, and reflected in its inner/outer psychological diversity, Islam's geo-cultural diversity was/is its greatest strength. Given the general absence of a Cartesian-based education, the literalist and violent tendency in 'low' fundamentalism in Pakistan is as closely related to poverty and lack of education as it is to the steady erosion of a particular cultural environment(s). In spite of historically low levels of literacy/education in the sub-continent, the popular and intellectual imagination was nevertheless free and active in terms of dance, poetry and other cultural expressions. But with Deobandism backed by Saudi money-theism, and an abdication of intellectual–religious responsibility by the Pakistani intelligentsia/secularists and their own peculiar 'liberal fundamentalism' (Ahmed 2001a), there has been an inexorable momentum towards cultural–spiritual ossification. In tandem, the mysticisms have themselves decayed, and the energy related to them in areas which nourished a culturally rooted sense of identity, dissipated. In short, the feminine has receded and virtually vanished from Pakistani secular and religious consciousness.

The terror within

Inspired by the high ideologue, 'low' or mass Islamism flourishes in a fragmented culturescape, showing similar behaviours, particularly in terms of the body as it becomes the locus of a wholly externalized view of God. Relatively speaking, the 'low' Islamist places even more emphasis on physical, outer aspects, such as beards, veils, clothing and headdress, not to mention an extraordinary preoccupation with various bodily taboos which function more at levels of obsession-compulsion. Psychologically this syndrome is related to the anal personality whose hallmarks are pedantry, parsimony and petulance (Freedman and Kaplan 1967)[8] and an overwhelming desire to control others. The relationship of these psycho-dynamics in the paranoia of mass fundamentalism will be examined shortly. For the moment, one can note a compulsive preoccupation with bodily taboos alongside similar paranoid obsessions around women's bodies and what a woman can or cannot do, as sanctioned on the grounds that 'it is our culture/religion'.

In an atmosphere of cultural nihilism and the suppression of anything close to the idea of 'pleasure' or 'fun', the terrorism of both types prevails, not only in the periodic bloodbaths of sectarian politics but at all levels of life. It ranges from decreeing as 'un-Islamic' events such as kite-flying festivals which are ancient rites of spring (symbols of renewed feminine fecundity), to violent attempts at the suppression of more modern ritual events like the New Year celebrations.

In their zeal to ensure that all become, not so much good as 'correct', Muslims, even home is no longer safe. Beyond the, by now, common incidents of forced entry to disrupt and break up social/cultural gatherings, the television provides an increasing dose of religion. Absurd as it is, since 1990, there has been a nightly news bulletin in *Arabic*. Addressed to a basically non-existent population of Pakistani-Arabic speakers, it is perhaps meant psychologically to reinforce a linguistic connection between the Truth as divinely revealed, and as theo-politically communicated daily by the state.

Just when some are seeking an 'altered state' of consciousness through quiet contemplation, or others attempt to escape into (chemically induced) oblivion, the ear is assaulted by a terror that is relentless in its regularity: the sound of mega-amplified, screeching, pre-pubescent voices of young males, and/or the blood-curdling howls of those masquerading as *muezzins*. Once considered an art-form that took years to cultivate, today one simply recoils at the call to prayer as made from the ubiquitous mosque.

As a whole, the senses are assaulted by an aesthetic and sensory terrorism; for example, in the polluted, decaying, filth-filled cities. This garbage is then presented in different ways as 'art' by those who think it is somehow postmodern and profound to confront the viewer with what may not be so visible in the West, but is self-evident and literally present on a large scale in Pakistan. But one is digressing here into the psycho-cultural domain of 'high' liberal fundamentalism which requires a full-fledged analysis on its own, particularly regarding its masochistic tendencies vis-à-vis the creative imagination.

The hero's shadow

The vast number of young males who primarily comprise mass Islamism can be seen as the collective shadow of the over-inflated heroic ego of modernity. In Jungian terms, the 'shadow' is the inevitable, dialectical counter-archetype of the ego, containing the polar opposite of all that the ego stands for.

24

Increasingly, more and more poverty-stricken parents send their young boys to the *madrassah*, lured not just by simplistic ideas of 'education' but, more importantly, to be relieved of having one mouth less to feed. Trapped between globalizing modernity and an obliterated, vanishing local culture, male rites of passage that are utterly vital for psychological (self-)development become distorted. Thus comes the psychological encounter at an exceedingly young age with an enormous concept like 'God'. Literally and brutally *enforced*, it is inevitably mediated by someone who, by now, is himself a product of this super-speeded-up psychological and cognitive 'development'.

The absence of *eros* and *logos*

The 'education' starts with the foundations of *logos* in language and its building blocks, the alphabet. As research (and personal observation) on literacy primers used in the *madrassah*'s show, the phonetics of each letter are accompanied by corresponding images of weapons whose names begin with the same letter, such as tanks, guns, swords, daggers, bomber aircraft. Art and music are forbidden.[9] The combined impact leads to a psyche that can know nothing else but violence and hatred, setting the stage for what is clinically called the persecutory paranoia of adulthood.

As contextualized in the critique of science and modernity, 'high' Islamism has an overly developed *logos*, leading to literalist reductionism and denial of all that is different, including the psychological absence of *eros*. As a function of relatedness, *eros* has to do with a sensitivity to the interconnectedness of life and its more emotionally nurturing, feminine dimensions. In contrast to the logocentric high ideologue, the 'low' Islamist faces a psychological 'double whammy': youth and poverty ensure that *logos* remains undeveloped. A culturally eroded spiritual environment, along with extreme economic conditions, ensures that the feminine remains inaccessible, hence *both logos* and *eros* remain absent.

The absence of the feminine in 'low' and 'high' Islamist religiosity means the absence of Divine ('feminine') Attributes such as Beauty, Mercy, Compassion, Graciousness, Love, Indulgence, Peace, to name a few. But as a collective 'image', it is the Taliban who become a living symbol of what happens in the absence of the feminine in psycho-cultural-theological consciousness.

For something to be symbolically true, somewhere it must be literally so. This is in the nature of that which is immutable, whether or not we 'hear'/'see' or sense what the symbolic is 'communicating'. To this extent, however faint, or grotesque, the literal remains. The absent feminine in Taliban consciousness, one can note, is self-reflexively related to a *literal*

25

absence of the *experience* of females in the individual lives of many Taliban. As a result of the Cold War, large numbers of Afghan children were abandoned and/or orphaned in an unimaginably harsh, war-torn and poverty-stricken environment. Raised in all-male seminaries, the vast majority of Taliban did not have even the most basic exposure to women,[10] something which most human beings universally have at a young age, even in the most segregated environments.

Whereas the logical function *logos* can be considered a socio-cultural acquisition, the experience of emotional connectedness is simply part of natural life, like the ground beneath our feet; however minimal or rocky, we simply take it for granted. One does not need research evidence to know with certainty that children need care and love. This is *eros*, which in its most fundamental sense is life itself. Whereas Freud narrowed his view of it to focus only on the sexual, the deeper and wider meaning becomes evident in light of the principle of *Thanatos*, death, which is the Freudian postulate for the opposite of *eros*. In the absence of *eros*, physical life mutates into something else.

. A product of mass and prolonged violence, and in the absence of both *eros* and *logos*, once this type of psycho-cultural mutation occurs on a disproportionate and large scale, as it did over more than two decades in Afghanistan, it self-reflexively perpetuates itself through large-scale violence.

Persecutory paranoia Low Islamism's 'double whammy', and factors of poverty, age, absence of parents and the experience of violence at a young age, starkly distinguish it from the high Islamist's background. Whereas the eventual outcome in terms of their violence and misogyny are broadly similar, there are, nevertheless, differences of style. Putting it clinically, there may be a differential diagnosis of paranoia.

Adequate psycho-sexual development requires, above all, a situation of what Erikson (1982) called 'basic trust'. Whereas paranoia as related to homosexuality may develop (according to Freud) due to confusions pertaining to the Oedipal/parental situation, the significance of other, trust-related factors remains the crucial matrix for healthy psychological development. These have to do with what much of humanity takes for granted in the context of childhood/childrearing, having to do with an age when a child's physical survival depends on consistently reliable adult behaviour. Young children need to believe that people in general are well disposed towards them, or at the very least do not actively want to harm them. Similarly, routine activities, such as having food and sleeping, need to occur regularly, at a minimal level, without a child feeling it necessary to take the most elementary precautions against being injured or destroyed (Freedman and Kaplan 1967: 665–75; Davison and Neale 1994: 265).

To this extent, low fundamentalism has less to do with intellectual and cognitive capacities and more with the socio-political-economic environment. As studies on paranoia show, either as infants and/or young children, such individuals were not given the 'usual opportunities as infants to develop basic trust'; they lived through a childhood in which significant persons proved undependable, outright rejecting or simply disappeared or died. Consequently, 'adults who develop the common persecutory form (of paranoia) almost uniformly consider themselves incapable of loving and being loved' (Freedman and Kaplan 1967: 674). It has also been noted that 'adults who develop paranoid reactions under stress have not been able to form or have not been given the necessary intimate close relationship with a loving mother or mother substitute' (ibid.).

The formative years of the Taliban in Afghanistan during more than two decades of a relentless and brutal state of war, and in many ways the similar socio-economics of *madrassah* inmates across Pakistan, can be strongly related to an overwhelming psychological experience of a 'basic trust deficiency'. Persecutory paranoia is especially related to such psychological situations, marked as it is by a deep mistrust of others and a strong tendency to deny one's own hostility which is characteristically projected on to others. There is thus a seamless and self-perpetuating connection between the initial internalizing of a genuinely hostile environment and an externalizing of this hostility on to the world.

Given the feminine void in the socializing of these young males, by the time they reach early puberty, violent and misogynist attitudes have become part of the emergent persecutory paranoia. For example, in a poem from a *madrassah* textbook about a 'Brave Child', a ten-year-old boy kills hundreds of Russians in Afghanistan. As part of a seventh-grade text, a 'letter' from a boy to his mother and sister says: 'If I am killed in battle, celebrate [...] make sure you conceal your body and never wear perfume.'[11]

The enormous void of basic trust, then, is at the heart of the matter in persecutory paranoia, which, in such a context, has nothing to do with initial delusion. In the face of an exclusive and relentlessly inflicted violence by the adult world, the only route to survival is to remain perpetually alert to its dangers. As adults, eventually, 'these relatively infantile defenses take over and become predominant' (Freedman and Kaplan 1967).

In present-day Pakistan, the Taliban and variations on that theme are a steadily growing reality. Given the socio-economics of population and birth rate, the scale of this (still unfolding) tragedy is enormous and its consequences terrifying to contemplate. As an archetype of the times, this

27

motif of a brutal(ized) child-killer is becoming increasingly common, for example, in parts of Africa. In the peculiarly grotesque circumstances of birth/childhood, regardless of biological age, it is unlikely that such a psyche will eventually change and develop further. Disconnected from infancy, especially from its feminine matrix, it becomes disconnected from life itself, in the process, exhibiting (self-) destructive behaviours that are rare even in the larger 'animal' kingdom. Collectively, it signals an enormous crisis, which, while eventually manifest in politics, is driven by a psychological crisis in masculinity, religion, sexuality and love.

Masculinity in crisis

Viagra and other magic bullets The prevalence of paedophilia among those men who have adopted religion as a profession in Pakistan is not unlike its occurrence in the Catholic Church. In a way, both point to a similar psychological malaise. However, differing injunctions about religious celibacy, but especially his inherent paranoia, impel the popular Islamist to demonstrate his 'masculinity' vis-à-vis women in the most macho ways, verging on the grotesque. Beyond the obvious socially negative attitudes towards women, an extreme individual pathology becomes symptomatic of a collective, misogynist, paranoid, religiously rooted, psycho-sexual syndrome. In 1994, an imam of a mosque brutalized his young wife by first placing iron rods in her womb and anus and then subjecting her to electric shocks, leaving her severely burnt and mutilated.[12] Outside the religious world, one of the most grotesque episodes in the nation's history had to do with the alleged murder of more than a hundred adolescent boys by a pederast.[13]

A collective crisis of masculinity, religion, sexuality and love is evident in the nature of advertising directed at the masses. It basically consists of brief, widely prevalent slogans/messages in Urdu and other regional languages, painted/written on the walls of homes and other structures. Their scale and frequency are impossible to ignore and are visible from public roads and thoroughfares. In the last two decades, these advertisements increasingly centre on three themes, reflecting the mix of concerns dominating mass (male) Pakistani–Muslim consciousness. A psycho-cultural reading of these texts indicates that they are primarily addressed to males.

The first is the call to *jihad*, inviting/urging 'men' to join one of the numerous fundamentalist organizations that have proliferated in the country. *Jihad* is primarily an inner, and therefore psychological/symbolic concept, the prerequisite being a subjectivity that is aware of its inner diversity, positive and negative. The inward, subjective primacy of *jihad* is self-evident in the Prophet's referring to this as the 'greater *jihad*' (*jihad-i-akbar*). In contrast, the external, literal form is seen as 'lesser' (*jihad-i-asghar*). But given factors ranging from cultural erosion, shadow rites of passage and the socio-psycho-dynamics discussed earlier, *jihad* has been totally externalized in the service of a persecutory paranoia that is focused on single-mindedly routing out all perceived 'enemies of Islam', everywhere.

The second type of advertisement, on a scale and frequency equal to that of the call to *jihad*, concerns all manner of quick and sure cures for what is euphemistically termed 'male weakness', that is, impotence. Between the popularity of these cures and the modern Viagra, lies the phallic symbol of a nationally and internationally flaccid phallogocentricism. The feminine and *eros* denied/absent, full-filment remains elusive. Yet the need remains. But only as experienced/expressed literally, as in adolescence, mainly through the genitals. Artificially propped up, so to speak, it is expressed in a sexual rage against women's bodies or the despair of a particular sort of depersonalized homosexuality, both experienced and conducted as compulsions. Beneath the self-glorifying, self-gratification of 'handling' all types of guns and weapons, these advertisements for old (and new) 'Viagra' provide a fearful, yet poignant sub-text, to the strident calls for *jihad*.

The third group of advertisements relates to the services of practitioners of healing through magic and other 'spiritual arts', promising, especially, instant fulfilment in love and seduction. The appeal to absolute power and control is summed up vividly by the guaranteed goal of bringing the victim, the 'beloved, at your feet within twenty four hours'. To the extent that the market for this promise of 'love' includes women, *eros* is present, albeit minimally, and in an infantile 'magical' conception, typical of a situation of helplessness and disempowerment. But given the virtual absence of woman/*eros*/mother in the psyche of persecutory paranoia, and the fact that the (by now) biologically adult, 'low' Islamist has consciously tasted (brute) power, the encounter with *eros* can only be brutal.

Occasionally, it surfaces individually in extremely crude and literal ways such as the episode of the imam, or collectively, in the regional cinema and portrayals of women either in fully armed fury and/or, eventually, as extremely vulgar and obscene sex objects. Mostly, it tends to express itself not only in direct physical violence to women but also in terms of a peculiar and crude sexuality, which is perhaps inevitable in exclusively male environments.

Youth by definition is literal, more responsive to the physical, concrete, external; inherently passionate and volatile, 'raging' hormones and all. Given the emergent demographics of a growing and ever younger male population in Muslim countries, the collective manifestation of the hero's

29

shadow and its implications for Islam and women does not bode well for Pakistan's future.

Incidentally, the only advertisements aimed specifically at/for women pertain to different brands of pressure cookers. Therein lies perhaps another symbol of the future.

Conclusion

Within a backdrop of inspiration and support of 'high Islamism' and its psychodynamic sources in modernity, the preceding analysis of 'low' or popular Islamism has drawn from a number of perspectives. These include parallel conceptions of gender in both Islam and Jungian psychology as organizing principles. To this extent, the terms 'masculine' and 'feminine' have been applied to dimensions of the human psyche, the idea of the divine, as well as to different categories of religion. As the 'feminine' side to Islam, the Sufi *silsilahs* can be considered the religion's 'secret backbone', many of which had strong bonds with the creative imagination including local/regional popular culture. High Islamism's influence, as exercised through the state, inflicted severe damage to this backbone, psycho-spiritually cutting adrift an already brutalized, overwhelmingly poverty-stricken population, especially young males.

The different types of cultural terror unleashed by and through mass Islamism indicate a major psychological crisis in self-conceptions of masculine identity, sexuality and religion. The violence of the low Islamist has its roots in a specific type of 'education' and circumstance, namely war and poverty and an absence of restraining cultural factors. Psychodynamically, they form the foundations of what eventually surfaces as persecutory paranoia that is both violent and misogynist.

The differences between 'high' and 'low' fundamentalism are ultimately a matter of style. To the extent that the 'high' ideologue, like so many modern persons, prides 'the mind', his paranoia is related to delusions of grandeur which is much more of a 'mental' condition than delusions of persecution. As clinical evidence suggests, and the socio-historic situation of mass Islamists in Pakistan confirms, persecutory paranoia has very real reasons underlying its 'delusions'. In this case, child abuse is an understatement for describing the impact of war, extreme poverty and parental deprivation on young children.

Given the well educated 'mind' of the 'high' ideologue, its violence is accordingly sophisticated, insidious, covert and systematically thought out in scientific detail. Deeply influenced by the psychology of modernity, different types of 'high' fundamentalisms display not only a masculinist love of violence, weapons and technology, but also generate, as does science, their own predispositions towards literalism. There are similar modern biases towards woman/body/knowledge. The ethos of modernity is also literal, cut off from the feminine in body and consciousness. While emerging from a different psycho-cultural history, it too harbours a Talib(an) within, exhibiting a psyche that is violent and macho. What the West's philosophically and linguistically sophisticated feminist commentators refer to as the 'phallogocentricism' or 'phallocratism' of modernity can be simply called, in the case of the literal Taliban, e(w)recktionism.

As a whole, 'high' fundamentalism inspires, and morally, intellectually, financially and politically supports 'low' fundamentalism. Given the ensuing cultural destruction, 'low' fundamentalism tends to surface and be strengthened. But in the absence of inadequately developed *logos* and *eros*, including an exposure and engagement with the feminine in most aspects of life, mass fundamentalism's violence is even more literal, hence more overt, direct and crude. Together, both types exhibit a crisis of masculinity in religion, sexuality and love.

Notes

1 As originally used by Gellner, the term 'High' Islam and 'Low' (or 'Folk Islam') referred to the puritanical scripturalism of the former and the largely non-literate but more culturally anchored vision of the latter, for example, in the cult of saints etc (*Postmodernism, Reason and Religion*). Whereas I do employ these same categories, Gellner's descriptions do not adequately encompass the developments in Pakistan over the last three decades. Similarly, while recognizing that the term 'fundamentalism' is propagandist and misleading, one is also in agreement with Karen Armstrong that 'like it or not, the word "fundamentalism" is here to stay [...] the term is not perfect but it is a useful label for movements that despite their differences, bear a strong family resemblance' (Armstrong 2000: x). For the most comprehensive study on the subject see the Fundamentalism Project's Marty and Appleby (1995), *Fundamentalisms Comprehended*, summing up their four-volume study.

2 To name a few: Osama (engineering), Atta (architechture), Zawehri (medicine) and the Pakistani Bashiruddin Mahmood (nuclear physics). Similarly, Fatima Mernissi noted many years ago how numerous Islamists were either doctors or engineers.

3 Apart from the writings of Marshall McLuhan, see Ong 1982 and Ong 1981.

4 Some of Corbin's best known work includes *Creative Imagination in the Sufism of Ibn 'Arabi* (1987); *Spiritual Body and Celestial Earth* (1977); *Avicenna and the Visionary Recital* (1980).

5 For details of the limitations to Jung's understanding of Islam as based on an analysis of *The Collected Works of C. G. Jung*, see Ahmed (2000).

6 For a detailed discussion and further sources see Ahmed (2001b).

31

Gender and Islamic spirituality

7 Recalling the Saudi-supported Taliban and their destruction of the Buddhas of Afghanistan, see 'Another "Cultural Massacre"', *Newsweek*, 19 February 2002.

8 See section on 'Personality and Psychopathology'.

9 *Friday Times* (Lahore), 14 February 2003. See also Nayyar (2003).

10 For details on the social conditions and genesis of the Taliban, see Rashid (2000).

11 *Friday Times* (Lahore), 14 February 2003.

12 For details of the case see *Dawn* (Karachi), 1 February 2002.

13 *The Herald* (Karachi), December 1999–January 2000.

References

Ahmed, D. S. (2000) 'Islam and the West: A Psychological Analysis', *Journal of the Henry Martyn Institute*, 19 (1), January–June.

— (2001a) *Masculinity, Rationality and Religion: A Feminist Perspective* [1984], 2nd edn. Lahore: ASR.

— (2001b) 'Hysterics, Harems and Houris: Cultural and Psychological Reflections on Women, Sexuality and Islam', in *Desire and Resistance: Women and Religion*, vol. 4 of HBF, Women and Religion series. Lahore: Heinrich Boell Foundation.

— (2002a) ' "High" and "Low" Fundamentalism: A Psychological View of Masculinity, Modernity and Islam', in Ahmed et al. (eds), *Sex, Politics and the Future of Islam*. London: Zed Books.

— (2002b) 'Violence and the Feminine in Islam: A Case Study of the Zikris', in D. S. Ahmed (ed.), *Gendering the Spirit: Women, Religion and the Post-Colonial Response*. London: Zed Books.

— (forthcoming) ' "High" and "Low" Fundamentalism: A Psychological View of Masculinity, Modernity and Islam', in *Sex, Politics and the Future of Islam*. London: Zed Books.

Armstrong, K. (2000) *The Battle for God*. New York: Knopf.

Bataille, G. (1998) *Eroticism*, trans. M. Dalwood. London: Marion Boyars.

Bordo, S. (1985) 'The Cartesian Masculinization of Thought', *Signs: Journal of Women in Culture and Society*, 11 (3): 441.

— (1987) *The Flight to Objectivity: Essays on Cartesianism and Culture*. Albany, NY: SUNY Press.

Brown, N. O. (1968) 'Response to Herbert Marcuse', in his *Negations*. London: Allen Lane.

Campbell, J. (1975) *The Hero with a Thousand Faces*. Princeton, NJ: Princeton University Press.

Corbin, H. (1977) *Spiritual Body and Celestial Earth*, Bollingen Series. Princeton, NJ: Princeton University Press.

— (1980) *Avicenna and the Visionary Recital*. Dallas, TX: Spring Publications.

— (1987) *Creative Imagination in the Sufism of Ibn 'Arabi*. Princeton, NJ: Princeton University Press.

Davison, G. C. and J. H. Neale (1994) *Abnormal Psychology*, 6th edn. New York: John Wiley.

Durand, G. (1987) 'The Imaginal', in M. Eliade (ed.), *Encyclopedia of Religion*. New York: Macmillan.

Erikson, E. H. (1982) *Childhood and Society*, rev. edn. New York: W. W. Norton.

Fisk, R. (2001) 'Who is Copying Who in the War of Words?', *Independent*, 11 October.

Freedman, A. and H. Kaplan (1967) (eds) *Comprehensive Textbook of Psychiatry*. Baltimore: Williams and Wilkia.

Hillman, J. (1972) *The Myth of Analysis: Three Essays in Archetypal Psychology*. New York: Harper and Row.

— (1984) *In Search: Psychology and Religion*, 2nd edn. Dallas, TX: Spring Publications.

— (1985) *Archetypal Psychology: A Brief Account*, 2nd edn. Dallas, TX: Spring Publications.

Hoodbhoy, P. (1991) *Muslims and Science: Religious Orthodoxy and the Struggle for Rationality*. Lahore: Vanguard and London: Zed Books.

Joy, M. (1987) 'Images and Imagination', in M. Eliade (ed.), *Encyclopedia of Religion*. New York: Macmillan.

Jung, C. G. (1984) *Dream Analysis: Notes of the Seminar Given in 1928–1930*. Princeton, NJ: Princeton University Press.

Law, J. M. (1995) (ed.) *Religious Reflections on the Human Body*. Bloomington: Indiana University Press.

Marty, M. E. and R. S. Appleby (1995) (eds) *Fundamentalisms Comprehended*. Chicago, IL: University of Chicago Press.

Murata, S. (1992) *The Tao of Islam: A Source Book on Gender Relationships in Islamic Thought*. New York: State University of New York Press.

Nasr, S. H. (1980) 'The Male and Female in the Islamic Perspective', *Studies in Comparative Religion*, 14 (1, 2): 67–75.

— (1999) *Living Sufism*. Chicago, IL: ABC International (*Sufi Essays*. Lahore: Sohail Academy, 2000).

Nayyar, A. H. (2003) 'Pakistan: Islamisation of Curricula', *South Asian Journal*, 2.

Neumann, E. (1971) *The Origins and History of Consciousness*. Princeton, NJ: Princeton University Press.

O'Flaherty, W. (1980) *Women, Androgynes and Other Mythical Beasts*. Chicago, IL: University of Chicago Press.

Ong, W. J. (1981) *Fighting for Life: Contest, Sexuality and Consciousness*. Ithaca, NY: Cornell University Press.

— (1982) *Orality and Literacy: The Technologizing of the Word*. New York: Methuen.

Rashid, A. (2000) *Taliban: Islam, Oil and the New Great Game in Central Asia*. London: I.B. Tauris.

Reincourt, A. de (1989) *Woman in Power and History* [1983], 2nd edn. London: Honeyglen.

Segal, R. (1995) (ed.) *The Allure of Gnosticism: The Gnostic Experience in Jungian Psychology and Contemporary Culture.* Chicago, IL: Open Court Publishing.

Wheelan, S. (2002) 'Saudi Government Demolishes Historic Ottoman Castle' <www.wsws.org.28.01.2002>

Wilson, P. (1988) *Scandal: Essays in Islamic Heresy.* New York: Autonomedia Press.

2 | The smile of death and the solemncholy of masculinity

BANU HELVACIOGLU

The main premise of this chapter is that all existing forms of masculinity, including Islamic ones, operate within a negative logic which avoids the simple submission to death and rules out the possibility of an unmediated, incalculable encounter with it.[1] The same logic presumes that death has an intrinsic, secretive kernel coded as an unspoken law, the Law of Death. Although no one knows what the law is, it is protected by innumerable doorkeepers who, as in Camus' *The Plague*, try to save human lives medically and religiously or, as in Kafka's *The Trial*, accuse mankind of an unidentified crime and prohibit entry into the law.

The doorkeepers of the Law of Death have traditionally assumed a male gaze to the dark, secretive, mysterious unknown where one is taken away, disappears or gets lost. The fear of the dark has constructed historically appropriate discourses of light, sun, life, scientific knowledge and different images of Paradise to mediate the ground between the known and the unknown, here and there, this world and the other. The fear of the unknown has been interpellated by doorkeepers whose preaching constructed a make-believe world of the Judgment Day, punishments, rewards, rituals and prayers for forgiveness about one's deeds. Such inventions as sleeping pills for insomnia, sex for easy exit from existential anxiety, have provided human kind with 'technical' facilities to cope with the fear, whereas erotic art transformed fear into desire, and poetry transformed the void into a habitat of senses, feelings, colours and sounds. The eternal irony of this universal fraternity is that the negative logic of death affirms life by denial, renunciation or by means of knowledge, analysis and explanation. One needs to be coded in innumerable layers in life, often in punitive and prohibitive terms, to be prepared for death. Gender coding in this logic is a sure way to direct human existence against loss, disappearance and all the negative values attached to the human psyche.[2]

The story I am about to tell starts with a simple admission that there is no escape from the negative logic of death or a practical way to avoid the doorkeepers. In being circulated within different phases of the eternal loop of masculinity, what I find particularly healthy is the possibility that everything there is to be known and lived will be known and lived after one dies. As for here and now, the least one can do is to laugh at oneself. This gives me an actual possibility, momentarily, in the way in which Kierkegaard talks of possibility: 'In the end it seems as though everything were possible, but that is the very moment that the self is swallowed up in the abyss. Even a small possibility needs some time to become actual. But eventually the time that should be spent on actuality gets shorter and shorter, everything becomes more and more momentary' (Kierkegaard 1989: 66). If the possibility of the unknown takes one into the abyss, then I suggest that one takes momentary laughter into the abyss and brings out the actual smile on the face of death.

Tragedy is comedy

On 17 August 1999 at 3:02 a.m., an earthquake, which registered 7 on the Richter scale, hit Golcuk, a small city renowned for its naval base on the Marmara sea in Turkey (Arlidge 1999: 1). A week after the earthquake, the official death toll was 17,000. Turkish media did not give the number of the missing; it was estimated at 35,000. The difference between the dead and the missing was estimated in an idiosyncratic way which scratches the surface of the relationship between matter, body and the Islamic rules and values concerning death.

In Turkey, where even simple everyday life activities are regulated by laws, there is a rigid, elaborate bureaucracy which governs funeral procedures under 'normal' circumstances. In accordance with the law, the dead have to be registered as dead by a medical report; then the body is taken either to a hospital morgue or a cemetery where the dead person is washed by an imam. Male imams wash male bodies, female imams wash female bodies. Relatives of the dead person can attend the rite. After the dead body is washed, it is wrapped in white cloth, put in a coffin and taken to a mosque where the head imam leads the ritual of praying. During prayer, two rows are formed: in the first, men stand closer to the coffin and follow the head imam's leadership; in the second, women stand behind and pray in the feminine form ascribed by Islamic rules.[3] The next religious ceremony takes place in the cemetery where, under the leadership of the imam of the cemetery, the body is taken from the coffin, laid to rest and the grave is filled with soil. While all this manual labour is undertaken by workers of the cemetery and the male relatives of the dead person, the imam prays and recites special passages from the Qur'an in Arabic. As during prayer in mosques, traditionally, women ought to stay away from the burying procedure, their physical distance being determined by the collective agreement of the family and the imam.

In spite of a national emergency, the state did not change the procedures, which meant that those people officially counted as dead in the earthquake were the 'fortunate' souls whose bodies went through this ordeal on hot summer days. Two weeks after the earthquake, when I went to Golcuk, I came across state officials with notepad in hand, visiting mosques, taking the number of 'religious burials' from imams. In Yalova, a nearby city, the officials constructed a collective graveyard and literally dumped dead bodies without any identification. The number of dead in this graveyard remains unknown. By this account, the missing are individuals and families reported as dead by their relatives, but their bodies have not been coded as dead by medical, religious and state authorities.

My parents, aunt and uncle died in that earthquake. They were staying in their summer houses near Yalova when the earthquake hit. On the first day of the earthquake, phone lines were jammed, roads were closed, and the 'emergency office' established by the Prime Minister was overwhelmed by lack of information. In his first public address, the Prime Minister, Bulent Ecevit, admitted the helplessness of the government and asked people to seek aid from Allah.[4] Being cut off from all means of communication, I used my imagination, pretending to get in touch with my parents by telepathy. My sister, who was also in Ankara, was doing the same. We assured each other that our parents were alive and well. In a funny way, Father was saying the same thing to me and to my sister, almost in the same tone: 'Don't worry; we are fine'. From this 'telepathic' insight communicated to close relatives, the story we were constructing was that the whole family was safe and it was only a matter of time before we would hear from them.

My sister is a clinical psychologist, but in this instance we were our parents' children and aunt's beloved nieces, showing no trace of Freudian neurosis resulting from a forced decision to choose between Mum and Dad as the most loved object.[5] We loved all four of them. For close to ten hours that day, my sister and I created our make-believe world, telling each other not to believe in television, official statements or other rumours. We refurbished our imaginations by making up more detailed stories of our own as to what Mother was saying, where Father was and what Aunt and Uncle were doing.

The bare, naked truth arrived around sunset. Why sunset? Does it have any gender bearing? I do not know. At sunset, I often had long conversations with my father and mother separately, comparing colours, clouds and the condition of the sea. Until the sun set that particular day, I firmly believed that my parents, Aunt and Uncle were alive and they could not reach us because of jammed phone lines. Then, the revelation hit me instantly: if my parents did not call me at sunset, it meant they were dead. Shortly after this inner knowing came the expected call from my cousin, the first person on the site of the earthquake. Her remark on the cellular phone was: 'It is tragic; there is nothing here; here, there is nothing; it is so very tragic'. She could hardly talk, but from this brief conversation we concluded that there was no building left, there was no rescue team, no officials to be found and that it was impossible to reach the bodies of my parents, Aunt and Uncle.

Which one do you love most? My cousin stayed on site, day and night for four days, preventing officials from turning the site into a collective grave-yard and forcing rescue teams to bring my aunt's and uncle's bodies from the rubble. Although their apartments were next to each other, because of the way the building collapsed, we were able to bring my parents' bodies to Ankara with the 'proper' medical report in just over two days. My personal circulation in various phases of masculinities started the moment I put myself in charge of the funeral procedures.

In *The Gift of Death*, Derrida examines the aporia of responsibility in relation to making decisions. He argues that responsibility on the one hand 'demands an accounting, a general answering-for-oneself with respect to the general and before the generality' and, on the other hand, the ethical temptation to absolute responsibility presents itself as irresponsibility in a singular, non-repetitive, silent way. Derrida traces the aporia of respon-sibility in the instant which 'belongs to an atemporal temporality [...] a duration that cannot be grasped [...] apprehended or comprehended. Understanding, common sense and reason cannot seize [*begreifen*], con-ceive, understand, or mediate it'. An instant conceptualized as such also applies to instants of decision whereby, in Kierkegaard's words, 'the instant of decision is madness' (Derrida 1995: 65).

There were decisions to be taken immediately, concerning the selec-tion of the cemetery, the dates of the funerals and the extent to which Islamic traditions were to be applied. Each of these decisions was taken collectively by the family in the context of the incomprehensible ritual of the 'last duty.' In my extended family on the father's side, we are, otherwise, a joyful group of women. My father had four sisters, no brothers, and all except one of my cousins are female. We were all brought up in the same familial Islamic environment and came to know Allah in an intimate way through my grandmother's stories, prayers, unrequited love, generosity, affection and humour. In spite of this bond, in the instant of perform-ing our duty before death, each of us was faced with singular, particular contradictions of our own.

One particular reason I went through different phases of intense mad-ness was that I wanted to perform my last duty to my parents directly, as if they were alive, and the remainder of the family, including my sister, were caught in between the last duty before Allah, the last duty before organized, institutional Islamic rules and the last duty to their loved ones. In an ethical temptation to resist the intrusion of social, religious and cultural norms, I was willing to go to the extremes of irresponsibility, but my parents were also a social construct whose dead bodies were textually interwoven with the history of the Turkish Republic, the common sense of Islamic traditions and the familial modes of love, affection and respect.

In the selection of the cemetery, the obvious destiny proved to be impossible by Islamic rules. Because there was not enough space for four bodies in the family plot, my practical solution was to bury them by the rule of love. Since they all died in their beds, it was all too 'natural' for me to put my parents in one grave, and my aunt and uncle in another. Islam said no. A woman and a man, even if married for more than forty years, cannot be laid to rest in one grave. I accepted the gender segregation and suggested we bury one fresh dead next to an old dead body according to their sex, but then my uncle's blood ties with the family became an issue. Since he was the 'foreigner' in the family, his body was to be treated differently from the rest. To decipher the irrefutable Islamic common sense, it is significant to note that as far as blood relations are concerned, my mother, also an outsider to the family, was nevertheless considered part of the family because, by marrying my father, bearing his children and adopting the family's last name, she became one with the Helvacioglu entity, whereas my uncle with a last name of his own was coded as the foreigner who could not be buried in the same grave with a Helvacioglu man.

When this discussion was taking place, we were consulting my father's only male cousin who, after my father's death, became the patriarch of the extended family. Since it was his first performance, he was uncomfortable, unsure and unprepared. Nevertheless, he was the only person in the whole family who knew Islamic rules. It was important to give a learned decision because to bury the dead in the family plot, we needed to get an official letter of approval from the Directory of Religious Affairs, a state organ in charge of regulating religion. It was forty degrees centigrade and there was considerable anxiety that by the time we decided, there would not be any space left in other cemeteries because of the massive number of dead brought to Ankara. I gave in reluctantly. Four plots were purchased in another cemetery, with a large bribe to make sure the plots were all side by side.

This is my mother and I am the daughter of a holy man If an instant is an atemporal dimension of temporality, in the instant of responsibility before the dead, there are incomprehensible, eternal moments. My parents' bodies were brought to a state hospital morgue through the help of relatives. By this time, friends had become part of the family as well. The more well connected one is to the tentacles of bureaucracy, the more efficiently tasks are performed.[6] In Ankara, a city remote from the centre of the earthquake, the morgues were already full. Rumour had it that elsewhere there was not even a morgue. All this was to comfort us by Islamic submission, that we are fortunate and ought not complain or protest because the worst 'could have been more worst'. The particularly Islamic side to this otherwise universal fatalistic approach is that Islam requires from the believers a blind faith which encourages the unconditional acceptance of an unacceptable condition by relying on the infinity of the worst condition in a cumulative way. In other words, this fatalism does not promise an improvement in the future; the present and the future are constructed from the purview of a doomsday scenario.

On account of this blind faith, I was to be happy that the male members of the family washed my father's body without informing the rest of the family. They confessed that they wanted my mother's body to be washed the same day, but they could not find a female imam because all female imams were on sick leave. No one was able to think straight, which meant that everybody was performing their internalized gender tasks instinctively. The male members were performing the paternal, protective role by being clandestine about my parents' dead bodies in the morgue. They were acting as a shield against the pain of seeing my parents' bodies. I was having fits, in an exemplary mode of what Adler called 'masculine protest'. To over-compensate for my grief at my parents' unexpected death, I started acting aggressively.[7]

In hindsight, the first week of the earthquake was in many respects like a state of war. Not only were the hospital morgues and cemeteries full, but the already dysfunctional political mechanism was also completely paralysed. Moreover, everybody was talking and deciding in the name of Allah. The collective devotion to the transcendental existence of the nation implied that funeral procedures were taking place within a morose setting. Like a soldier, I adopted an aggressive stand as a means of survival, except that I was still my mother's daughter who could not stand leaving her mum in mud. I wanted to wash her and comfort her just as she used to do when I was a kid. My decision to wash my mother in the morgue was taken as the action of a tragic heroine, courageous and self-sacrificing, acting out of an incommensurable love, boldly sacrificing myself to perform my absolute duty to my religion. Caught in between my own desire to be with my mother for the last time and the social construction of my action, I was made to hesitate, to be fearful of my own action.

In the morgue, when I was told that there were no female imams to be found, I gave a sermon about how Allah would have changed Islamic rules in an emergency. Then, like a commander in chief, I told the head imam: I am to wash my mother and he is to help me wrap the cloth and prepare her body for funeral procedures. For a male imam to touch a woman's body is inconceivable, regardless of how impressive my preaching might have been. But my militaristic stand had an impact. Miraculously, a female imam was found in less than an hour. It was my first triumph, which came with a deep sorrow about how submissive the whole society in Turkey is. From the military to imams to university professors, there is a chain of command founded on fear, obedience and a readiness to receive orders.

Masculinity is performative indeed.[8] Inside the morgue, I was my mother's daughter, again doing the most sensible thing, refusing to wear gloves (my mother did not wash us with gloves on), talking to her, kissing and caressing her body and teasing her about the journey she and father took from Yalova to Ankara. I was actually having a good time when I heard Madame Imam ordering me to stay away from the corpse. 'Do not touch,' she said in such a tone that I immediately froze. Above and beyond doubt, she was the commander in chief with the hose in her hand. I was told not to touch not only because my mother was a martyr, but touching the body of a martyr is the worst sin in Allah's eyes. To decipher the irrefutable nationalist Islamic common sense in this instant, one has to remember that the Turkish military has been in a civil war with the PKK, the Kurdish guerrilla group fighting for independence. To reach the height of martyrdom has the resonance of Turkish soldiers who die for the indomitable, indivisible integrity of the Turkish state, military and the nation. According to this belief, the bodies of martyrs have a transcendental value which guarantees a special place in heaven.

I do not know what a soldier does when faced with an enemy soldier. In that room, although Madame Imam was in command, I was in the presence of my mother. My mother would have strongly disapproved of my getting into a fierce argument with Madame Imam, not because she is a religious authority but because my mother always felt uncomfortable in aggressive settings. 'Madame Imam,' I said, 'she is my mother, I love her dearly and I would kindly request that we co-operate.' Without waiting for her response, I started undressing my mother, assuring her that everything was all right and that she need not be upset. Madame Imam agreed, but she ordered me to go out and find a nail polish remover. All her life, my mother took special care of her hands and feet. Her body, brought from under tons of rubble, came with the gift of beautifully manicured fingers and pedicured toes. But Madame Imam could not receive the gift because not only is nail polish a sin, it is also a mortal sin for a woman to be buried with it. I received my mother's body as a gift and gave in to Madame Imam. I assumed my militaristic stance, marched outside, ordered one of the male relatives to find nail polish remover and walked inside to resume my childish and joyful work.

By embracing and kissing my mother's body, I created a singular feminine narcissism in my imagination; turning her uterus into the country I came from, her breasts and lips the last belonging I had for my mother tongue, and her face spoke tranquilly the simple naked truth about death. By the time we wrapped her body, I was convinced that my mother and I had had a happy, joyful relationship in just the way we had always been mother, daughter, friend and muse. Our relationship was not dependent on my father, but neither was it independent of him.

My narcissism was spacious enough to enjoy his presence. I was not to let him go without performing our ritual before journeys: embracing each other for an atemporal duration, giving mutual advice about things not to be forgotten – documents, money, tickets, eye-glasses – wishing each other happy times and the opportunity to travel in Allah's protection: *A Dieu*.[9] My father's body was in a collective room in the morgue. The officials tried to stop me, out of Islamic protective masculine/feminine concern that I would be sick if I saw his body. But, by then, my 'tragic heroine' act was known to a few men, including the head imam, whose special permission gave me a restricted visitation right.

I was not to demand the unwrapping of the cloth. In the head imam's words: 'I believe you when you say he is your father, I respect that. But our religion ... I mean ... you ... well.' The law that the head imam could not spell out clearly was: 'Our religion prohibits a daughter to look at her father's naked body.' To touch my father's naked body was inconceivable. I do not know if there is any religion which permits such an act, but this religion of the head imam was so prohibitive that it did not permit him to speak directly to a woman. I was amazed by how shy, embarrassed and awkward he was. I felt as if my aggressive presence was causing him grave suffering. I realized once again that masculinity in its most segregated, prohibitive mode is the same as feminine subordination, submission and oppression. My masculine triumph to win a restricted visitation right was due to the head imam's feminine, shy curiosity.

My short visit to the collective morgue room was accompanied by the head imam and a few male morgue officials who kept watching me and my father. I kissed my father's face, embraced his body and wished him a joyful journey. At that moment I decided to enjoy myself. I turned to the spectators and told them that I saw a smile on my father's lips. They were like little children, slightly intimidated but curious. A few came and affirmed in Allah's name. I decided to pursue this game and told them that my father was a holy man, at which they nodded and affirmed in a few Arabic statements, which I did not understand. I was rewarded for being the daughter of a holy man. A morgue official told me that he would be glad if I performed his task: to write down my parents' names and attach them to the wrapped bodies.

I must admit: at a young age, my phallic consciousness was shaped by a peculiar, recurring sequence of my mother's no, my father's yes, my mother's yielding to my father's yes and my father's repeating my mother's favourite statement: 'Baba, baba degil, sam babasi' (the father is not a real father, but a father made of pastry). My mother's no and my father's yes were two sides of masculine/feminine authority which would eventually lead to the affirmation of my father's authority. My mother always gave in to that authority. Years later, she confided in me that a father made of pastry was also a husband made of love. I never had a chance to ask them how on earth they managed to create a playground of love and laughter in the midst of strict gender codes shaped by Islamic prohibitions. Yet, there they were in the morgue of a state hospital in the middle of a national calamity, consenting to my childish dissidence.

The playful bond with my father must have been engraved in my unconscious. Months after the funerals I was still sulking; I wanted to wash my father's body before the burial, but my male relatives did not let me. I was inconsolable. Then one night I had a dream: my father was wearing his swim suit from thirty-five years earlier, sitting on a stool in our old bathroom which in real life was fashioned after a mini hamam with a marble water container (kurna) for warm water. I was a child with loose panties, who could barely reach the marble water container, which was closer to my height, and I was throwing water at my father's body. Could this be Lacan's veiled phallus? To me the real authority has always been my sister, not my parents. The next day I happily reported my deed to her. By then, she and I had developed alternating performative tasks of priesthood, listening to each other's confessions, of the wise sage who, by listening, helped the young apprentice develop knowledge of the self, and of the mother/father who repeated the same neurotic, obsessive traits of our parents in self-awareness. She and I had a serious argument as to which swim suit my father was wearing in my dream. Was it the one he wore in the summer we went to Amasra, or the one he wore when we went to that beach in Istanbul? No, not that beach, but the other in Istanbul. To this day I do not know whose solemncholy we inherited.

Bon Dieu, Mr President! The playful relationship with my father is only one side of the otherwise infinitely layered, universal and particular expressions of masculinity. My parents' funeral was on a Friday. A male relative told me that the more crowded the mosque was, the more prayers my parents would receive, and the more points for good behaviour I would get from Allah. He was adamant about his calculation, giving me comparative numbers of total prayers and their proportional value, which would surely take my parents to heaven. To me his remarks meant two things. One, in the age of globalization, this must be a petty bourgeois investment in heaven, collecting prayers individually and multiplying them by the holiest of all holy mosques in the city on the holiest day of the week.[10] Two, in the self-sacrificial universe of any religion, the more one suffers for a greater cause than oneself, the more docile one gets. The holiest mosque and the cemetery are far away from each other. In a city when traffic is always jammed during all hours, our ticket to heaven implied that we ought to fight against distance and time under the hot blazing sun.

Instead of choosing the holiest of all holy mosques, I chose the most spacious at the centre of the city, with a large open plaza, thinking we could have some privacy in paying our last respects. Alas, on a hot summer day at noon, there were at least twenty earthquake funerals taking place at the same time. For the first time in my life, I saw women hitting the coffins with their fists, losing control, hitting their heads and hurting themselves. Advocates of multiculturalism call for tolerance, but I was not to tolerate this self-tormenting group next to my mother's coffin. In a violent setting, the more one tries to escape violence, the more violent one becomes. I wanted my parents' coffins to lie side by side so we can gather and cry in our own familial way, but the head imam, the second imam in charge and distant relatives nearby enforced prohibitive Islamic laws one after another. One, a male and female coffin could not be put side by side. Two, Friday prayer is only for men; my mother's coffin ought to be put aside. Three, I was offending Allah, my parents and relatives. Four, I was obstructing funeral procedures. Five, I ought to be taken away.

Holy places are known for their unexpected miracles. In the middle of a furious fight about to get physical, all the imams started running in panic in the same direction. The President came to the mosque to attend one of the funerals. When the imams left the scene, with the help of my father's friends we managed to put the coffins side by side. But privacy, even in the familial form, was too much to ask for. The presence of the then President Suleyman Demirel implied that the prayers and preaching were unduly long, geared to media coverage, and I was to listen to my parents' names listed among other martyrs of the earthquake through loud speakers. The mosque was so crowded and noisy that I walked from one end of the open plaza to the other, screaming from the top of my lungs and not a single person turned to look at me. That particular moment in the eternal instant of performing my last duty was the climax of madness, doing the unthinkable, screaming in the open plaza of a mosque on a Friday and not being heard or noticed.

Islamic masculinity, will you please stand up?

The mosque gathering was a wholesome but incomplete representation of existing forms of masculinity in Turkey. In our familial gathering, there were women and men over the age of fifty who, in tears and panic, reclaimed my father as their father and older brother. In the meantime my father's sisters were mourning quietly. They lost both their older brother and their sister. My youngest aunt and I embraced each other, not knowing whose loss we were grieving most. At the time, I was not conscious of the fact that, in the same earthquake, I had lost my childhood friends, their parents and children vacationing in the same summer complex.

I received a formal handshake from a stranger, who later turned out to be our paternal lawyer shielding us with his body and using his expertise and connections to protect us from the endless bureaucracy concerning my parents' deaths. Our lawyer also assumed the role of a father, giving me advice about the outcomes of yelling at everybody regardless of rank in government offices. I am still under his tutelage, apprenticing in masculinity and in bureaucracy. The golden rule, I am told, is to look sad, say my parents died in the earthquake and give in to the mercy of the petty administrator. Pity is the surest way to receive 'public service', be it a signature among infinite signatures in the labyrinth of bureaucracy, or an official seal confirming that the death occurred in the earthquake. The silver rule is to recognize that the endemic legitimacy crisis of the state needs to be reproduced in begging for mercy.

What is the difference between a citizen in state bureaucracy and a beggar on the street who looks sad, tells you about her family misfortune and asks for money for Allah's sake? In bureaucracy, the citizen has two options: to beg, using all the means of emotional manipulation, or to steal by means of local patronage networks. Either way it is the victim syndrome, recurring in an eternal loop of the victim victimizing the victimized. There is no way out of the guilty conscience shared between the petty administrator and the victim of the earthquake other than calling for Allah's mercy. In the absence of the state, in whose name all these bureaucratic procedures are undertaken, Allah becomes the only helper to soothe the bad conscience of the state functionary and the citizen.

The smile of death

45

But of course, in my parents' funeral rite at the mosque, the state was present in all its absent grandeur. There were cameramen, policemen, bodyguards and imams, all running after the President, the father of the nation,[11] who was pulling nationalist tricks out of his hat and turning all of us 'victims of an earthquake' into transcendental beings as relatives of people who died for the state. The head imam was preaching about the evils of political Islam, terrorism, traffic accidents, and other sinful acts, which threaten the well-being of our beloved nation.[12] In the meantime, some people who lost their loved ones in the earthquake were cursing at contractors and building companies, declaring them criminals who ought to be hanged. The death penalty, at the time, was a topical issue because of the nationally constructed hysteria about Abdullah Ocalan, the leader of the PKK brought to Turkey to be tried on charges of national treason and murder of 'innocent babies and women'. Hence, within the national imagination, hanging was regarded as the short cut to seek redress for any injustice, be it an earthquake or a war. Missing in this wholesome gathering were a few military officials. Their absence, however, did not make this a civil gathering because the soul of the nation was as religious as it was militaristic.

The spiritual family Writing in 1882 against the principles of blood and soil in German nationalism, Ernest Renan argued that 'a nation is a soul, a spiritual principle' which results from 'the complications of history', 'the common possession of a rich legacy of memories' and finds its expression in the present in 'the common will' and 'the consent on the clearly expressed desire that common life should continue'. In his conception, a nation is a spiritual family founded on memories of sacrifice, devotion and common suffering. These memories leave their mark in the moral conscience (Renan 1996: 57–9). In Turkey, the soul of the nation is deeply religious, patriarchal, misogynistic and militaristic. At the same time, though, this 'spiritual family' is forever schizophrenic and undecided about its past and present. This being the case, the love of the land, state, Islam and nation present a rich medley of paradoxical articulations.

Before attending to each of these, I would like to recall Fanon's (1968) distinction between the official ideology of nationalism and nationalist consciousness. In Turkey, the former dates back to the foundation of the Turkish Republic in 1923 and is referred to as Kemalist ideology, promoted by the military, the state elite and the 'secular, modern' sections of society. Nationalist consciousness, on the other hand, is a much broader category, closer to what Renan calls the moral conscience. In Turkey, nationalist consciousness is articulated by both the left, revolutionary groups of the

1960 and 1970s, and the right, religious groups actively involved in politics in the present conjuncture. The nationalist conscience in the current political/social conjuncture remains an enigma to the extent that it opposes and overlaps with the official state-centred Kemalist ideology. One of the difficulties of isolating Islamic masculinity in this context is that Islam is the bond that unites different nationalist articulations and at the same time it is the contested terrain of political struggle between state-centred groups and Islamicist ones.[13]

Underlying the enigmatic nature of the nationalist conscience is the dictum 'I must come to hate what I love, in the same moment, at the instant of granting this death' (Derrida 1995: 64). This love/hate relationship dates back to the foundation of the Turkish Republic in 1923, which came into existence by granting death to the Ottoman Empire. In the official nationalist ideology of the early Republican years, the Islamic Ottoman tradition was constructed as the hate object. To start anew, cultural reforms were enacted with the net result of changing the alphabet, introducing a new language, and imposing a new lifestyle, which included changes in dress codes, fashion, music, education and the arts (Toprak 1981). All these reforms were enacted by means of laws. What is puzzling in the break from the Ottoman tradition is that, although the abolition of the caliphate was taken as the first step towards the construction of the Turkish state as secular, the means of change remained squarely within the Islamic Ottoman tradition.

More specifically, the Arabic word '*din*', which in Turkish came to be known as religion, also means faith and denotes the moral law. Freedom of conscience in the Ottoman tradition was granted from within the Islamic moral law. The secular Republican state did not abolish the moral, cultural, traditional aspects of Sunni/Hanefi orthodox Islam but instead introduced regulations as the right, lawful way of practising religion. Thus, laws and freedom of conscience came to be enforced from within the moral power of the secular state. To this day, the state and the military maintain their moral power. Any political challenge or resistance to the inseparable entity of state/military is construed from within the pervasive and persuasive moral context of the enemies of the state/military/nation.

If the first continuity from the Ottoman past was to preserve the moral power of the state, the second heritage is to identify the whole civic society with the collective consciousness of a community. The word '*millet*' in Ottoman denoted a religious community, as well as a nation. In the Turkish Republic, '*millet*' came to be known as the secular Turkish nation. With the continuation of the patrilineal, patriarchal Ottoman system, the secular Turkish nation came to be identified as a particular type of a collective whole: the spiritual family. Hence, not only a political challenge is again construed in moral terms as an act of defiance in the family/community, but also it is rehabilitated from within the collective consciousness and moral conscience. Repentance is the most frequently used form of rehabilitation since the 1960s' revolutionary movements.

Serif Mardin, who has written extensively on the social and political constitution of Islam both in the contexts of the Ottoman Empire and of the Turkish Republic, addresses part of this problem in the following way: 'Republican laicism was [...] a Janus like affair: on the progressive side the Caliphate was eliminated in 1924, but on the other, platoon practice in officer training in the 1950s still culminated with the storming of a hill with cries of Allah, Allah' (Mardin 1971: 238; see also Mardin 1977). I am not in a position to explain the common bond between the Sunni Orthodox Islam and the Turkish military, except to note that within the nationalist conscience, the military is constructed as an object of faith, love for the nation and the state. It has a transcendental existence, founded upon a collective belief. The specific articulations of this faith in the military are provided by the politically tailored legacies from the national war of independence in the 1920s. In the post-Cold War era, the Turkish nation still looks up to the military not so much for national defence against foreign invasion (though the possibility of a Greek invasion is always kept alive within the nationalist imagination), but as a transcendental protective power. Moreover, in the current struggle between the secular, modern groups and politically active Islamic groups, the military projects itself as the guardian of secular, Republican, Kemalist principles.

The masculinity of the 'new woman' The enigmatic, complex relationships between Islam, state, nation and the military find their particular expressions in the specific context of gender roles. The problem is the one-sided view which focuses on the pivotal role played by women in the construction of the new nation. On this issue, we are again faced with ambiguities resulting from the problematic aspect of the break from the Ottoman tradition.

On the one hand, the legal, administrative and cultural reforms aimed at creating an ideal, pro-Western, educated, professional woman as the prototype of the new Republic; on the other, traditionally, Islamic gender roles for women remained intact in both the official ideology of nationalism and its different articulations. The predominant discourse on this transformation is that the break from the Ottoman Empire brought a pro-Western, secular attitude at the level of state and society. When the pro-Western, secular character of the Turkish Republic is examined in contrast with Arab Middle Eastern countries, Turkey appears as the champion of women's rights and Arab countries as the site where women's rights remained within the Islamic gender relations (Cagatay and Soysal 1995: 269; Ahmed 1984). This contrast between the pro-Western, secular Turkey and Arab Middle Eastern countries with 'a stronger Islamic identity' creates a false dichotomy whereby Islamic influences in both Turkish society and the official nationalist ideology of Kemalism need to be re-problematized over and over again (Jayawardena 1988; Kandiyoti 1977, 1987, 1991).

In investigating the historical lineage of a repressive gender regime, Kandiyoti refers to men of letters in the nineteenth century. She argues that at the time of the Tanzimat Charter,[14] male novelists were in 'a form of [...] rebellion against Ottoman patriarchy in the family; [they] no longer wanted arranged marriages, controlled and manoeuvred by their older female relatives, they desired romantic involvement and love, educated wives with whom they could have intellectual communication, a social life where the sexes could mingle freely without the fear of scandal and gossip' (Kandiyoti 1991: 310).

Naila Minai makes a similar argument about the most prominent male writers from the Tanzimat period to the early 1900s. She argues that Tanzimat writers published books and articles defending women's rights to go to school and to practise various professions. Following the formation of the constitutional governments in 1876 and 1908, bolder demands were made. Halil Hamit demanded women's suffrage in 1910; Celal Nuri wanted the abolition of polygamy; Ahmet Agaoglu called for women's emancipation along with public education, which he considered the most important prerequisite for progress in the Islamic world. Minai examines these demands for women's rights in conjunction with travel accounts of Arab writers from the fourteenth century, the British women living in Istanbul at the time of Tanzimat, and the personal life of Zeyneb Hanim in Istanbul at the turn of the century. The point where reform-minded male attention to women's rights and the personal accounts of women meet is Pierre Loti's novel *Les Desenchantées* (1906), 'which describes the malaise of a Turkish woman [Zeyneb Hanim] whose brain had leaped to the twentieth century while her body remained imprisoned by medieval customs' (Minai 1981: 47–52).

This schizophrenic split between the mind and body is a heritage of an ahistorical male gaze to both male and female sexuality. In Turkey it has been reincarnated in different disguises since the Tanzimat period. If it were possible to strip layers from the contradictory gender roles and public images of women in Republican Turkey, the characteristic feature of the masculinity of the 'new woman' is the schizophrenic split between her brain and her body. While the brain has been governed by Republican modern values, the body has been repressed by the collective consciousness of the family, community, and by specific national and Islamic values. In that respect, the masculinity of the new woman contains: motherhood as the most sacred status in Islam and motherhood construed from within the Republican ideology, comrade women from both the Qur'anic perspective and that of nationalist independence. As to asexual, professional women, it dates back to an idealized interpretation of the Enlightenment idea of an all-knowing intellect that knows by means of an undiluted virgin reason embodied in the mind. In each of these contradictory articulations, the masculinity of the ideal new woman is at the same time the suppression of male sexuality.

Before attending to this universal–particular construction of masculinity, we need to recall the enigmatic nature of the nationalist consciousness, shaped by the spiritual family of Islam, state, military and nation as a moral collectivity. The pervasive nature of this wholesome familiality is to be found in the left revolutionary gaze of women as well. Fatmagul Berktay draws attention to the recurring theme of the repression of female gender in the context of the revolutionary politics of the 1960s and the 1970s. She notes that the revolutionary discourse has borrowed an Islamic notion, *fitna* (discord), and a national/cultural notion, *baci* (sister), in producing an image of women introducing discord into the revolutionary unity and solidarity as well as unsexed, depersonalized comrades. The net effect of this articulation was to justify the control and supervision of women (Berktay 1995: 252, 260).[15]

There are too many continuities between this specific gender repression and the existing repression in the current political conjuncture. To name the predominant trends: first, the revolutionary unity was maintained in part by strict dress codes for women and in other part by the suppression of male and female sexuality. Any trace of femininity, sexual attraction, dating, falling in love is considered bourgeois. Disciplinary action was taken within the confines of revolutionary solidarity. At present, this has been reincarnated in political Islam in another disguise. It imposes dress codes for women, proper moral codes of conduct within Sharia (e.g. a man does not shake hands with a woman) legitimated within a combative mind-set against corrupt Western values. The militancy of the revolutionary left of the 1960s and that of Islamic groups in the 1990s have striking parallels in guerrilla organizations, in constructing images of self-sacrificial male heroes willing to die for the cause, and militant women as sisters of the wider community devoted to a transcendental destiny.

The second similarity between the 1960s and today is the systematic use of torture under police custody. Those subjected to torture in the past were left on their own to deal with the resulting physical, emotional and psychological trauma. Women and men were expected to be stoic on this issue. Nowadays, youth subjected to torture talk openly about the treatment they undergo. They become news items in the daily press and media in a skilful way so that the public is informed about the existence of torture but somehow it is not perceived from within the collective national conscience. The familial collective body, exhibiting deep emotional and emphatic bonds with the nation, does not take offence or feel injured by the existence of torture. The systemic nationalist silence on torture breaks the existing forms of masculinity. This silence, in fact, introduces another dimension of masculinity founded on the worthlessness of male and female bodies. While all other forms of masculinity give a value to the human body, torture violates all values.

The third parallel between the past and the present is to construct media images of 'terrorist' females. In the 1970s, a woman nicknamed Leila Khalid was portrayed as a militant, trained in military camps in Palestine. Today there are too many of them. Each time such a woman is captured or put under police investigation, the media interview her father who invariably says either that his daughter is innocent and the truth will be revealed in due time or that she should be punished in the way the state deems just.

The endemic problem in this repressive gender regime is the fixed focus on the physical appearance and public performance of women, be it in the form of revolutionary or Islamic dress codes, or in the images of a terrorist woman, a militant Islamic woman. This, on the one hand, contributes to the suppression and manipulation of female sexuality and, on the other, continues to reproduce more contradictory images of masculine women, such as a dangerous terrorist woman, who is also the daughter of a law-abiding man, or a well-educated woman, coming from a well-to-do family and who happens to be a militant's lover.

Whose solemncholy is this? If the gender regime since the 1920s produced an ideal Republican woman and her devilish counterpart as a potential seductress, militant, terrorist and revolutionary type, what types of men did it produce? First, the utmost importance is given to physical outlook produced by men in military uniforms, in Western suits, in revolutionary, guerrilla outfits with the moustache as the sign of masculinity, the salon man of Paris in artistic circles, Islamic spiritual leaders with specifically-grown beards in traditional outfits. Men's outlook has been subjected to self-supervision. In a protest against the revival of the 'Islamic beard and moustache', several secular men shaved their beards and moustaches on behalf of Western, modern values. On the other side, the political rivalry between PKK and Hizbullah led to a peculiar punishment: while one group shaved the beards of rival group members by force, the members whose beards were shaven shaved half of the moustaches of the other group in front of their wives.

Second, as to the national demands put on the ideal man of the Republic, he is obliged to be circumcised, do military service, and be subjected to varying hierarchical ranks in the family, at work and in society. He is also expected to be an obedient son, the breadwinner of the household, the patriarchal self-sacrificial man ready to suffer for a cause greater than himself, be it the nation, Islam or a revolutionary change. At the same time he is to protect the honour of his sister, mother, wife and female comrade. In the absence of an older male, he is to be the paternal figure protecting and supervising the female members of the family. Like the petty administrator in state bureaucracy, the power of these men is always determined by the presence of a grander absence. They are victims and victimizers at the same time.

Third, the ideal, professional man of the Republic is expected to subject himself to the schizophrenic split between his brain and his body. He has to believe in progress, science and professional achievement as a sign of his complete devotion to the national project set by Mustafa Kemal Ataturk. He is also expected to be a complete stranger to his own body and instead subject himself to the conventional regimes of sexual regulation. The well-known conventions include scientific/medical knowledge about male and female reproductive organs, myths about an omni-sexual, over-eroticized female body, myths about free sex in Europe, 'news and information' provided in pornographic magazines, competitive standards set for the size of the penis, and the record number of times a man can have sexual intercourse in one day.[16]

As if unsure of his manhood, the ideal man has to prove himself to himself by taking part in any one or all of these conventional, recreational activities. These conventions produce an over-sexed man in appearance, with an insecure, boyish, shy outlook. Most ideal men are deeply devoted to their mothers.

The ideal man of the Republic is a cultural icon and a product of gender segregation in high schools, military and family. What is Islamic about this man? What needs to be problematized is the complex relationship between language, body and orthodox Islamic practices. Language is a precarious issue in general, and also subject to particular political manipulations in terms of cultural essentialism, authenticity and protection of some sacred traditional values. What is being manipulated in this regard is access to history, memory and sexuality.

The endemic problem in Turkey is the rupture brought by cultural reforms and a series of abrupt changes in language in the 1920s and the 1930s. Turkish grammar does not have masculine and feminine features; instead, genders are described in metaphors. The love for the nation is ambiguous and undecided. The land is our mother (*anavatan*) whose honour, esteem and outlook depend on the exemplary actions of a prototypical, masculine citizenship. The land is also our father because the land, the state and the military are often inseparable. Islam in this undecided stance complicates the situation. In Islam Allah is neither male nor female. As my grandmother used to say, 'Allah does not have a sex, and all there is to know is that Allah loves everybody equally.' Since my childhood, however, Allah has been through several interpretations, translations and transliterations.

The end: go in laughter

Citing from the Qur'an, Fatna Sabbah argues that human beings are imprisoned in the process of birth, life and death, whereas God is above and beyond being born and giving birth. The omnipotence of God is attributed to its infinity in its own rhythm, accompanied by mercy, forgiveness, compassion, generosity, wisdom and all-awareness (Sabbah 1992: 118, 136, 137). Those who, in all-awareness, imprison themselves in birth, imprison their death in fear. I came to this life via my mother's birth canal, aided by my father as the midwife of my mother's delivery. I listened to my father telling the same story over and over again, until I was convinced there was no mystery left in my birth. At the end I accepted their unexpected deaths when I heard my father telling me that there was no need to think any more. 'We are dead,' he said, and I believed him. But I was upset. 'Why didn't you tell me that you were going to die?' I said. 'We wanted to surprise you,' said my mother. 'Are you two still together there?' I asked in surprise. 'Yes,' they said, 'until you let us go.' So I let them go in laughter, reluctantly, in tears, smiles, thinking perhaps they will meet Kierkegaard there. Who knows? 'Possibility is like offering a child some treat: the child straightaway says yes, but then there's the question of whether the parents will give their consent – and as it is with parents, so it is with necessity' (Kierkegaard 1989: 67). So as it is with parents, aunts and uncles, friends, their children and parents, it is with necessity that I embrace life in laughter. Momentarily.

Notes

1 For an explanation of this logic, see Bataille (1992).

2 Elsewhere I investigated the negative logic of death in the context of

masculine conceptions of time, temporality and memory, all of which construe death as loss. The will to death in this logic is to be found in the speed of life and the dizziness caused by socially driven modes of efficiency, productivity, self-discipline on the one hand and by the politically and religiously constructed calls for a return to an 'origin' on the other (Helvacioglu 1999: 98–105).

3 This is the 'modern' rite recognized by the secular state and practised in cities by 'moderns' – the professionals, middle to high income groups, and by those categorized as secular in the political, social rift between Islamicists and seculars in the current conjuncture. Since 1998, there has been an unresolved debate over women praying side by side with men. The debate is often resolved in the actual site of the mosque and the cemetery where, after considerable aggression, the decision depends on the collective consciousness of the particular community involved in the funeral rite.

4 In Turkish there are expressions which concern the all-mighty, all-knowing, forgiving, giving, understanding, helping, reasoning nature of Allah. In this case, the Prime Minister's words *'Allah yardimciniz olsun'* translate as 'May Allah help those who have relatives in the earthquake region'.

5 According to Freud, the question 'Who do you love most, Daddy or Mummy?' accompanies the child throughout life. The child initially enters into the contradiction of an either/or opposition but later in life reaches a satisfying resolution by acknowledging unequal demands from both the mother and the father (Freud 1957: 128).

6 Deniz Kandiyoti explains this situation as follows: 'since the state itself uses local patronage networks and sectional rivalries in its distributive system, citizens also turn to their primary agencies of the state to compensate for or take advantage of inefficient administration' (Kandiyoti 1992: 387).

7 Masculine protest 'means over-compensation in the direction of aggression and restless striving for triumphs'. 'Adler considered the masculine protest to be active in normal as well as neurotic mental life [...] The masculine protest was a feature of women's psychology as well as men's, but overdetermined by women's social subordination' (Connell 1995: 16).

8 Judith Butler argues that gender is performative, which suggests two things. One, that the performance retroactively produces 'the illusion that there [is] an inner gender core [...] when there is no gender "expressed" by actions, gestures and speech'. Two, 'there are clearly workings of gender that do not show in what is performed as gender, and the reduction of the psychic workings of the literal performance of gender would be a mistake'. In psychoanalysis, 'what is exteriorized or performed can be understood only through reference to what is barred from the performance, what cannot or will not be performed' (Butler 1995: 31–2).

9 The two expressions my father used before journeys were *Allahaismar-ladik* and *Allah'a emanet*, both of which translate as *A Dieu*.

10 'Devoid of imagination, as the petty bourgeois always is, he lives within a certain orbit of trivial experience as to how things come about, what is possible, what usually happens, no matter whether he is a tapster or a prime minister. This is the way in which the petty bourgeois has lost himself and God' (Kierkegaard 1989: 71).

11 Mustafa Kemal Ataturk, the founder of the Turkish Republic, is regarded as the father of the nation. In the existing political climate, if Ataturk is the transcendental father whose soul and spirit govern the official national ideology, the President of Turkey, Suleyman Demirel, is the father of the nation in a human form. He has the nickname of a father, and acts like a father in social and political settings.

12 Shortly before the earthquake, mosques were given orders to talk about the danger of traffic accidents. The head imam must have been reading the text given to him by an authority. Since the times of the Ottoman Empire, mosques have traditionally been centres of education. In the current climate they are used by the state, politically active Islamic groups and by state-sponsored feminist groups.

13 I examined the parameters of this struggle in 'Allahu Ekber, We are Turks' (Helvacioglu 1996). Here it is important to specify the type of Islam being contested. The majority of the population in Turkey is Sunni and within the Sunni tradition they belong to Haefi school. The minority Islamic groups are Alevis and Bektasis. Alevis make up about 30 per cent of the Kurdish population.

14 The Tanzimat Charter was launched in 1839 with a decree providing for the protection of life, property and honour as fundamental rights. It paved the way for the abolition of slavery and the elimination of concubinage system. The next reform was undertaken in 1856 with the Islahat Charter aimed at formal equality before the law. For further details of these charters and constitutional governments in 1876 and 1908, see Örücü (1996: 92–3).

15 On the question of the relationship between the revolutionary politics and women's issues, also see Sirman (1989: 16).

16 My young friends tell me that cyber-sex is also very exciting.

References

Ahmed, L. (1984) 'Early Feminist Movements in the Middle East: Turkey and Egypt', in F. Hussain (ed.), *Muslim Women*. London: Croom Helm.

Arlidge, J. (1999) 'Slow, Helpless and Disorganized', *Guardian Weekly*, 161, 26 August–1 September.

Bataille, G. (1992) *Theory of Religion*. New York: Zone Books.

Berktay, F. (1995) 'Has Anything Changed in the Outlook of the Turkish Left on Women?', in S. Tekeli (ed.), *Women in Modern Turkish Society*. London: Zed Books.

Butler, J. (1995) 'Melancholy Gender/Refused Identification', in M. Berger et al. (eds), *Constructing Masculinity*. New York: Routledge.

Cagatay, N. and Y. N. Soysal (1995) 'Comparative Observations on Feminism and the Nation-building Process', in S. Tekeli (ed.), *Women in Modern Turkish Society*. London: Zed Books.

Connell, R. W. (1995) *Masculinities*. Cambridge: Polity Press.

Derrida, J. (1995) *The Gift of Death*. Chicago, IL: University of Chicago Press.

Fanon, F. (1968) 'The Pitfalls of Nationalist Consciousness', in his *The Wretched of the Earth*. New York: Grove Press.

Freud, S. (1957) 'Notes Upon a Case of Obsessional Neurosis', in *The Standard Edition of the Complete Psychological Works of Sigmund Freud*, Vol. 7. London: Hogarth Press.

Helvacioglu, B. (1996) 'Allahu Ekber, We are Turks', *Third World Quarterly*, 17 (3).

— (1999) 'An Ankara Chronicle: Fidelity to an Impossibility', in C. C. Davidson (ed.), *Anytime*. Cambridge, MA: MIT Press.

Jayawardena, K. (1988) *Feminism and Nationalism in the Third World*. London: Zed Books.

Kandiyoti, D. (1977) 'Sex Roles and Social Change: A Comparative Appraisal of Turkey's Women', *Signs: Journal of Women in Culture and Society*, 3 (1).

— (1987) 'Emancipated but Unliberated? Reflections on the Turkish Case', *Feminist Studies*, 13 (2).

— (1991) (ed.) *Women, Islam and the State*. London: Macmillan.

— (1992) 'Identity and Its Discontents: Women and the Nation', in P. Williams and L. Chrisman (eds), *Colonial Discourse and Post-Colonial Theory*. New York: Harvester Wheatsheaf.

— (1995) 'Patterns of Patricarchy: Notes for an Analysis of Male Dominance in Turkish Society', in S. Tekeli (ed.), *Women in Modern Turkish Society*. London: Zed Books.

Kierkegaard, S. (1989) *The Sickness unto Death*. London: Penguin.

Mardin, S. (1971) 'Ideology and Religion in the Turkish Revolution', *International Journal of Middle East Studies*, 2: 238.

— (1977) 'Religion in Modern Turkey', *International Social Science Journal*, 29.

Minai, N. (1981) *Women in Islam: Tradition and Transition in the Middle East*. New York: Seaview Books.

Örücü, E. (1996) 'Turkey: Change Under Pressure', in E. Örücü et al. (eds), *Studies in Legal Systems: Mixed and Mixing*. London: Kluwer Law International.

Renan, E. (1996) 'What is a Nation?', in S. Woolf (ed.), *Nationalism in Europe: 1815 to the Present*. London: Routledge.

Sabbah, F. (1992) *Islam 'in Bilincaltinda Kadin* [Woman in the Muslim Unconscious]. Istanbul: Ayrinti.

Sirman, N. (1989) 'Feminism in Turkey: A Short History', *New Perspectives on Turkey*, 3 (1).

Toprak, B. (1981) *Islam and Political Development in Turkey*. Leiden: E. J. Brill.

3 | Alternate images of the Prophet Muhammad's virility

RUTH RODED

Forthright classical Islamic descriptions of the Prophet's sexual life

Classical Muslim scholars collected every detail of Muhammad's life for various reasons. Some wished to extol his virtues; others to enumerate his actions, words and deeds as a norm for believers and a basis for Islamic law and custom. This natural tendency to record the life of the founder could also descend into a scholasticism in which the clothing the Prophet wore or the precise shape of his beard would become the subject of debate. In these frameworks, the sexual performance and intimate life of the Prophet were frankly discussed.

In Ibn Sa'd's collection of biographies of great Muslim men and women of the early years of Islam, for example, eight traditions address the superior sexual performance of the Prophet (Ibn Sa'd 1960–68: 8: 192–3; cf. 1: 374). According to one of these, one night the Prophet made the rounds of all nine of his wives. Others relate that the Prophet had the virility of forty men. The Prophet's sexual fortitude was a divine gift; a dish provided by the Angel Gabriel gave him his unique potency. Whenever Muhammad wanted to have sex with women, he would eat from the earthen pot. The Prophet himself reported that he had been the weakest of people in intercourse until God revealed to him this sustenance.

After a monogamous, companionate marriage to Khadija, Muhammad married some fourteen wives (ibid., 8: 216–18).[1] All sources agree that the young 'A'isha was his favourite and he would spend more nights (and days) with her than her allotted share. This partiality is human, but it also took on a broader meaning when 'A'isha became one of the foremost sources for a large mass of crucial normative information for the Muslims. Thus, 'A'isha would describe her physical intimacy with Muhammad as a background to sexual issues, such as the degree of contact a man may have with his wife when she is menstruating, or to religious questions, such as the unclean objects that nullify the prayer (Anas 1989: 20; al-Bukhari 1973–76: 1: 480).

Although Muhammad married some women for social or political reasons, his physical attraction to others is candidly described in the classical sources. Zaynab bint Jahsh was a pretty woman Muhammad was drawn to, marrying her after she was divorced by her husband (Ibn Sa'd 1960–68: 8: 101, 102, 104; al Tabari 1989: 8: 2, 3, 4).[2] The Prophet also chose the attractive captive Juwayriyya bint al-Harith and married her, although she was allocated to another warrior as part of his booty (Ibn Sa'd 1960–68: 8: 116, 117). Likewise, he selected the comely war captive Rayhana bint Zayd and eventually gave her the opportunity to convert to Islam and become his wife (ibid., 8: 129, 130). Asma' bint al-Nu'man was offered to the Prophet by her father who said she was more good-looking than his wives. When he married her, the other wives were so jealous they tricked her into alienating him (ibid., 8: 143–5). The addition of a beautiful wife or concubine to the household naturally aroused jealousy among the other wives, as in the case of Mariya the Copt, who gave birth to a son by Muhammad.

Although sexuality is interfused in the classic Islamic material, Muhammad often displays a tenderness to women that does not seem to detract from his masculinity. 'A'isha was a child when she was betrothed to him and moved into his house. The Prophet was sensitive to her situation, allowing her to continue playing with dolls and even joined her in play (ibid., 8: 65, 66). He married a number of widows of Muslim men who fell in battle to care for them. His sympathy for the plight of female captives was demonstrated when Safiyya bint Huyyayy was brought to him. Muhammad chose her for himself, but reproached the man who had brought her for his lack of mercy in bringing her past the slain Jewish men (al Tabari 1989: 8: 122).

Virility, then, was only one dimension of masculinity in the eyes of the early Muslims. In the Arab society of the Hijaz and subsequent Islamic empires, manliness was reflected in martial ability, as it has been in so many societies. Men were warriors, but women participated in battle only in rare circumstances. Military exploits were recorded in battle stories (*maghazi* or *ayam al-'arab*), a pre-Islamic Arabic genre that was to influence Islamic literature as well (Roded 1999: 32–47). Honourable lineage (*nasab*) – a long, noble line of free men going back to a prominent ancestor – was also primarily a male virtue, although there are signs of semi-matrilineal descent in the extensive genealogical literature (Roded 1994: 12, 140–1).[3] Most elusive is the pre-Islamic and early Islamic concept of *muru'a*, which derives from the general Arabic term for man (*mar'* or *imru'*). In the narrow sense, it meant the physical and material qualities of man, but, by extension, encompassed moral qualities (similar to *rajul*) and good manners. If *imra'a* was a perfect woman, *mar'* was an eminent man. During the formative centuries of Islamic culture, *muru'a* came to mean a number of positive qualities ranging from chastity and good nature, to dignity and compassion, to good conduct and urbanity.[4]

Muhammad's sexual attraction to women was regarded by the Islamic classical scholars as natural and appropriate for a human prophet. As a man chosen by God to disseminate His message, he had unique qualities that made him superior to ordinary men. One of these was his exceptional virility.

Western European attacks on Muhammad's 'licentious behaviour'

In medieval Europe, the life of Muhammad was considered an important proof, if not *the* proof, against the claim that Islam was a revealed religion. European writers believed and tried to demonstrate that Muhammad was an idolater who spread his religion by violence and by permitting his followers to engage in licentious behaviour, the same behaviour that characterized him.[5]

The Christian West was scandalized in particular by Muhammad's family life and the 'immodesty' of Muslim writers in describing the Prophet's sexual life. The favourite story in medieval Europe was Muhammad's marriage to Zaynab bint Jahsh after her divorce from Zayd b. Haritha. In their view, Muhammad's sexual relations with the wife of his adopted son bordered on adultery and incest. The affair demonstrated that he was incapable of overcoming the temptations of the body. Moreover, he employed a special revelation to justify his actions. In European texts, Zayd was referred to as Saidus and various inaccurate names were ascribed to the woman in question. Further proofs of Muhammad's sexuality were found in selective and inaccurate translations of the Qur'an.

In Christian eyes, Muhammad's sin was compounded when he justified his improper actions with religious arguments. (Christian clergy were certainly guilty of sexual transgressions, but they recognized them as sins and did not try to justify them.) A good example was the case when Muhammad slept with Mariya the Copt in the home of one of his other wives. When the wife finds them and complains, Muhammad swears that he will stay away from her but reneges on his pledge. Then 'he said in his Qur'an' that Muslims can repeal their oaths without punishment (Stowasser 1994: 99–100, 112).[6] The themes here are similar to those demonstrated in the Zaynab story: the Prophet is a slave to his passions, who justifies his behaviour by inventing revelations and turning his behaviour into a rule for his followers. The most important point for Christians was the religious justification for what they regarded as a sin.

The story of the slander against 'A'isha and the subsequent proof of her innocence by divine revelation was grist for the Christian polemic mill (ibid., pp. 94–5).[7] Similarly, inaccurate readings of Bukhari's collection of authentic words and deeds of the Prophet, and perhaps defamation by Arabic-speaking Christians, led to the claim that the Prophet had intercourse with 'A'isha during her menses. Muhammad's large number of wives was further proof of his unbridled sexuality.

Christian European writers devoted a great deal of attention to the domestic side of Muhammad's life. They always interpreted and believed the worst possible situation. These authors, men of religion themselves, feared primarily the legal justification for sexual acts. If men had difficulty facing temptation when they deemed it morally improper, what would happen if these acts were permitted? The Christian authors sometimes fabricated stories to make their claim, but for the most part, they misinterpreted Islamic material. No less important, the Christian clergy who regarded celibacy as a mainstay of their faith were incapable of accepting Muhammad's domestic life. A true prophet simply did not behave in this fashion.

The Enlightenment movement in Europe in the seventeenth and eighteenth centuries should have brought about a balanced approach to Muhammad's life since it was characterized by belief in the power of reason. At the same time, during this period of scientific discovery, the customs of foreign peoples were considered less strange and more worthy of study. French and English scholars began to study original Arabic texts and expressed various attitudes towards the Prophet Muhammad. Although he was still portrayed as a first-class enemy of Christianity, positive evaluations were expressed as well. Traditional Christian attacks on Muhammad, particularly in the area of sexuality, however, were still discernible and continue to inform Western works to this day.

Voltaire's *Mahomet*, published in 1741, is a historical tragic drama, similar to *The Death of Caesar*, written several years earlier. It has been claimed that the play was written not as an attack on Islam and its Prophet but as an oblique critique of the Catholic Church and clergy (Schimmel 1985: 5, 263), but Voltaire himself, in a letter addressed to Frederick King of Prussia, cites the traditional Christian arguments. Moreover, Voltaire admits: 'Mahomet, I know, did not actually commit that particular crime which is the subject of this tragedy: history only informs us, that he took away the wife of Seid, one of his followers, and persecuted Abusophan, whom I call Zopir; but what is not that man capable of, who, in the name of God, makes war against his country?' (Voltaire 1905: 16: 10–11). Voltaire's negative portrayal of Muhammad was not a result of ignorance. He was familiar with accurate and positive material on the Prophet of Islam in his time. *Mahomet*, a five-act play set in Mecca, is a blend of classical tragedy and traditional Christian arguments against Muhammad that originated in the middle ages. Criticism of religious fanaticism does permeate the text, but the major crime is committed by Seid, slave of Mahomet. Mahomet commands Seid, in the name of God, to murder Zopir, his father; then Mahomet has Seid poisoned. From the outset, Mahomet desires his slave girl Palmira, the only woman in the play. In the last scenes, she attacks Mahomet as an impostor, bloody savage, seducer and a tyrant. Anti-clerical or not, Voltaire portrayed Muhammad in traditional Western Christian terms as motivated by a combination of unbridled sexuality and belligerence.

Thomas Carlyle's 'The Hero as Prophet: Mahomet, Islam' was the second of a series of essays *On Heroes and Hero Worship, and the Heroic in History* (1841). A Scottish Calvinist, Carlyle was influenced by the great German philosophers and Romantic authors and was critical of the scepticism of French rationalism.[8] Carlyle's choice of Muhammad as representative of the prophet-hero indicates an appreciation for Islam in sharp contrast to Voltaire. Moreover, Carlyle rejects traditional Christian criticism of Muhammad and refutes it point by point. Nevertheless, Carlyle's religious belief may be discerned in the essay (Carlyle 1841: 4, 5, 6, 15, 20).

Among the accusations aimed at the religion of Muhammad, Carlyle refers specifically to the charge of sensuality: 'Much has been said and written about the sensuality of Mahomet's Religion; more than was just. The indulgences, criminal to us, which he permitted, were not of his appointment; he found them practised, unquestioned from immemorial time in Arabia; what he did was to curtail them, restrict them, not on one but on many sides' (ibid., p. 33).

This reproach, he argues, is in direct opposition to the rigorous demands of fasting, ablutions, prayers and abstinence from wine. Moreover, Muhammad was a poor and hard-working man (pp. 33-4). Carlyle describes Seid as an 'emancipated well-beloved Slave, the second of the believers', and Muhammad's reaction to Seid's death illustrates the Prophet's generosity (p. 35). It is difficult to believe that this is accidental and that Carlyle was unaware of the central role that the story of 'Seid' played in traditional Christian polemics against Muhammad. Another reference is to the sensuality of Paradise in Muhammad's religion. Carlyle argues on the one hand that this was a crude depiction by the Bedouin Arabs that Muhammad modified, and, on the other hand, that it was Muhammad's followers who exaggerated the sensual aspects of the hereafter. Also, in a constrained argument, he states that 'enjoying things which are pleasant; that is not the evil: it is reducing of our moral self to slavery by them that is' (pp. 38-9).

From the mid-nineteenth century, modern oriental scholarship aimed to study Islam and its Prophet in an objective, scientific manner based on

61

critical analysis of newly discovered primary sources. European oriental scholarship was not free from stereotypes about Islam, and the Prophet's virility continued to be a sensitive issue. European scholars were aware of this problem, and some tried to avoid traditional European stereotypes, but the epithets they selected to flesh out the text often reveal their ambivalence towards this aspect of Islam.

At the same time, Orientalist literature and art portrayed the Islamic East as a hotbed of sexuality (Hopwood 1999; Thornton 1994; Kahf 1999). The 'licentiousness' of the Prophet of Islam was expanded to all of his followers. This image was to be one of the most compelling underpinnings of European colonialism.

Modern Muslims' defensive responses

Since the Indian sub-continent was subjected to the longest European conquest, Indians were among the first Muslims to become familiar with European oriental scholarship. Muslim intellectuals regarded these ostensibly scientific studies of the life of Muhammad as even more dangerous than traditional Christian attacks. Indian Muslims were horrified when they encountered European scholarship on Islam in the British educational system in India.[9]

Apparently, the first modern Muslim biography of the Prophet was a series of essays composed by the great Indian reformer Sir Sayyid Ahmad Khan in 1870, in response to William Muir's four-volume *Life of Muhammad from Original Sources* (Troll 1978: 28–31).[10] Sayyid Ahmad was the first of a long line of modern Muslim scholars to refer to, rely on and critique the works of European oriental scholarship. He did not, however, relate to the Prophet's sexuality. His defensive tone, which became prevalent in many modern Muslim biographies of the Prophet, reveals much about the insecurities of modern Muslims and perhaps the cultural balance of power as well.

The Indian Syed Ameer Ali also produced his first biography of the Prophet in response to a Western description of Islam.[11] He developed a work eventually published under the title *The Spirit of Islam* (Ameer Ali 1922).[12] The book was immensely popular in the West where nine English editions were produced between 1922 and 1961 (Ahmad 1967: 87).

The Prophet Muhammad in Ali's view is a great man by modern Western standards. In contrast to the defensive tone of his predecessors, Ameer Ali goes on the offensive. Ameer Ali's response to the traditional accusation of sensuality is an attack on Christian asceticism as misogynist. Countless quotations from the Fathers of the Church reflect their antipathy to women. Following the innovations of earlier Indian Muslim reformists, he underscores the intention of the Qur'an to limit and eventually eliminate polygamy, although it is permissible under certain circumstances (Ameer Ali 1922: 222–7, 229). Referring to the Zaynab affair, he states:

Mohammed had married his devoted friend and freedman, Zaid, to a highborn lady of the name of Zainab, descended from two of the noblest families of Arabia. Proud of her birth, and perhaps also of her beauty, her marriage with a freedman rankled in her breast. Mutual aversion at last culminated in disgust. Probably this disgust on the husband's part was enhanced by the frequent repetition, in a manner, which women only know how to adopt, of a few words which had fallen from the lips of Mohammed on seeing Zainab. He had occasion to visit the house of Zaid, and upon seeing Zainab's unveiled face, had exclaimed, as a Moslem would say at the present day when admiring a beautiful picture or statue, 'Praise be to God, the ruler of hearts!'

The words, uttered in natural admiration, were often repeated by Zainab to her husband to show how even the Prophet praised her beauty, and naturally added to his displeasure. At last he decided not to live any longer with her, and with this determination he went to the Prophet and expressed his intention of being divorced. 'Why,' demanded Mohammed, 'hast thou found any fault with her?' 'No,' replied Zaid, 'but I can no longer live with her.' The Prophet then peremptorily said, 'Go and guard thy wife; treat her well and fear God, for God has said "Take care of your wives, and fear the Lord!"' But Zaid was not moved from his purpose, and in spite of the command of the Prophet he divorced Zainab. Mohammed was grieved at the conduct of Zaid, especially because he had arranged the marriage of these two uncongenial spirits.

After Zainab had succeeded in obtaining a divorce from Zaid, she commenced importuning Mohammed to marry her, and was not satisfied until she had won for herself the honour of being one of his wives (Ameer Ali 1922: 235–6). While recognizing Muhammad's attraction to Zaynab as natural (as opposed to Christian asceticism), Ameer Ali turns Zaynab into a villain. She is proud, condescending to her husband, carping, and she uses her wiles to attain marriage to the Prophet.

From the 1930s, virtually every major literary figure in Egypt composed a modern biography of the Prophet. Egyptian intellectuals' fundamental and underlying ambivalence towards Western civilization and culture was one of the factors that prompted them to return to their religious and cultural roots. They began to realize that European society was neither as secular, nor as rational and liberal as its theoreticians claimed. Like the Indian Muslims before them, Egyptians were shocked to discover that

European attitudes towards Islam, its Prophet and the believers retained many traditional Christian stereotypes of violence and sensuality.

One of the first Western-educated Egyptians to produce a modern biography of the Prophet was Muhammad Husayn Haykal (1888–1956), who began publishing a series of articles in 1932 reviewing a life of Muhammad published in French in 1929 by Emile Dermenghem.[13] The articles eventually evolved into one of the most popular and influential modern Muslim biographies of the Prophet.[14] Haykal sets out his primary aim in the introduction: to defend Islam and its Prophet from Christian attacks, a religious polemic that in his time had been advanced by European colonialism, missionary activities and Orientalist scholarship. Equally responsible for the inaccurate view of the life of Muhammad, in his view, were conservative Muslims whose errors actually contributed to Western assaults. Like Sir Sayyid Ahmad Khan, Haykal intended his book for young educated Muslims who had turned away from Muslim religious authors to read Western works, believing them to be more scientific (Haykal 1935: 20, 28–9, 29–30; 1976: xxv, xlvii, xlviii).

The dominant theme of Haykal's *Life of Muhammad* is a defence of Islam against Orientalist claims regarding the belligerency of the Prophet and his followers as well as their sensuality. The stories of Muhammad's marriage to Zaynab and the wives of the Prophet in general are cited in Haykal's preface as examples of erroneous material attributed to the Prophet alongside the case of the goddesses of Mecca (ibid., p. 34; p. liv). This subject is explored in depth in a chapter on the Prophet's wives that opens with a section on 'The Zaynab Affair and the Orientalists' (ibid., pp. 257–65; 285–98). After describing Orientalist and Christian missionary claims about Muhammad and Zaynab, Haykal admits that these are based on reports in questionable Muslim biographies and books of hadith. If these claims are true, Haykal explains, then they do not constitute a flaw in the character of Muhammad since the rules for regular people do not apply to great men. Moses committed murder and the whole life of Jesus was a violation of natural law. While the 'great men' theme may hark back to Carlyle, the strategy of attacking the heroes of Judeo–Christian civilization is undoubtedly drawn from Ameer Ali.

Such an explanation, in Haykal's view, would be an injustice to history because 'Muhammad was not a man given to passion and desire' (ibid., p. 259; p. 288). True, some Muslim authors in certain periods attributed such things to the Prophet, because they regarded him as outstanding in all realms of human endeavour including sexuality, but this is clearly false. Muhammad's monogamous marriage to Khadija, an older woman, was clearly for love, and he remained loyal to her although polygamy was the norm at that time and despite the fact that none of her male offspring survived. Muhammad's subsequent marriages are explained as a kindness to widows and a consolidation of ties within the Islamic community. Moreover, Haykal, following the Qur'an and the Prophet's example, recognizes the need for polygamy with certain limitations. A 'critical history' of the story of Zaynab, however, reveals that it was not physical attraction that led to the union. Muhammad himself arranged Zaynab's marriage to Zayd to exemplify the ideal of social equality in Islam and to reform inheritance laws. The failure of the marriage resulted from Zaynab's pride and difficult character.

While cognisant of classical Islamic attitudes towards the Prophet's sexuality and Ameer Ali's counter-attack, Haykal has clearly internalized Western Christian negative views of Muhammad's virility. The apologetic tone suggests a defensive stance by Muslims towards the West – a product of military, political, economic and cultural imperialism.

The influence of Haykal's book was enormous. Within three months of its publication, ten thousand copies had been sold, and since then numerous Arabic editions have been produced. The book has been translated into Turkish, Persian, Urdu, Chinese and English (Schimmel 1985: 235–6). Ironically, *Life of Muhammad* has become a leading work in the Islamic canon, replacing to some extent its classical predecessor, the Sira of Ibn Hisham.

Modern Muslims' views of sexuality

Acceptance of Muhammad's sexuality as an integral part of his humanity is most evident in Naguib Mahfouz's allegorical rendition of the life of Muhammad, first published in 1959.[15] As a young man, Kassem=Muhammad is 'crazy about women', unlike the Jesus figure.[16] The sexual instinct, in Mahfouz's view, may defy rationality, but sexuality, like aggression, is an innate human quality (Milson 1998: 101, 103).

The Prophet's first wife, Khadija, named here Kamar or moon, a traditional Middle Eastern symbol of beauty, dominates the chapter devoted to the life of Muhammad. Her relationship with him, a relatively short episode in the early Islamic sources, comprises more than half of the chapter, and even after her death she is an integral part of the action, up to the end.[17] Kassem=Muhammad is immediately attracted to Mrs Kamar's fine qualities – her tenderness and kindness – and her beauty.[18] He is not interested in her money or to exploit her love for him, but rather expresses love, consideration, compassion and longing for her throughout his life, even after her death and his marriage to other women.[19] She is physically attractive, 'beautifully plump, soft and sweet' but demure.

His attraction to his second wife, a lovely girl of twelve or so, is mentioned repeatedly.[20] Mahfouz finds a sensible and human explanation for the Prophet's relationship with the child-bride 'A'isha, so criticized by non-Muslims and apologetically defended by Muslims. The twelve-year-old actually looked older than her age, and we imagine a Lolita-like pre-adolescent rather than a child playing with dolls (as in the early Islamic sources). The Prophet's subsequent marriages are shown as the outcome of his attraction to beautiful women.[21] Although his polygamous marriages are only briefly referred to, this seems to be a structural decision, since there is no attempt to occult the Prophet's numerous wives and give an impression of monogamy, as some Muslim authors of modern siras have done. The classic explanation for the Prophet's multiple marriages, that they were to cement socio-political alliances, is raised; but Mahfouz emphasizes that in this social milieu, no explanation or justification is required, for men are admired for their virility and love of women. Moreover, Mahfouz presents a unique psychological insight into the Prophet's numerous marriages: his incessant search for the love he had enjoyed and lost with his first wife.

Mahfouz does not relate at all to the 'Zaynab affair' and in fact there is no reason he should. In the classical Islamic sources, the story is a marginal exegesis of a Qur'anic verse, appearing in some of the biographical collections as well. In Mahfouz's semi-fictional account of Muhammad's life, the Muhammad figure is a virile man with active sexual drives. There is no need to bring in the Zaynab story to prove this point. Most important, Mahfouz is not defending the Prophet against Western calumnies but rather crafting a view of Muhammad from the social environment in Cairo and from his own psyche.

As the storyteller sums up the life of Kassem=Muhammad, he addresses the hero's attraction to women and his polygamy:

> But the alley did not need any explanation or justification of what happened: the truth was that they admired his character; they admired his virility and love of women many times. In our alley the capacity to love women is a thing men boast of, and it gives a man a prestige as great as or even greater than that of being a chief.[22]

Mahfouz's attitude towards male and female sexuality in his earlier works is similarly humanistic. Despite the ostensible separation between genders – or perhaps because of it – young men become romantically obsessed with distant, idealized images of young women. More mature men are naturally drawn to more realistic sexual escapades. In Mahfouz's view, it seems that men achieve satisfaction and freedom only with free women such as singers and prostitutes. Moreover, the attraction of older men to young women is described as a fact of life with no obvious value judgement.[23]

One is tempted to regard Mahfouz's acceptance of Muhammad's sexuality as a sign of the decline of British and French colonialism in the post-Suez era. This line of thought would posit that the ebb of the West enabled an Egyptian Muslim to affirm the virility of the Prophet and of other Muslims as a natural human attribute without recourse to apologetics. It would dovetail with political interpretations of Mahfouz's work.[24]

Ironically, the Islamist Shaykh Abd al-Hamid Kishk regards Mahfouz's allegory (*Awlad Haratina*) as the height of sacrilege, based in part on the depiction of the Prophet's sexuality.[25] One must give the shaykh credit for trying to analyse Mahfouz's work (even if he does not fathom the principles of the allegory) but some of Kishk's comments raise doubts about his knowledge of the classical Islamic sources. Muhammad's so-called womanizing and multiple marriages are explicitly derived from the classical siras, Qur'anic exegesis and hadith collections.

For Mahfouz, Muhammad is an integral part of his imaginative life and of the Egyptian social milieu. He has taken the life of the Prophet of Islam to a new level, serving as an allegory of philosophical and spiritual ideas. He has achieved these challenging and revolutionary goals precisely by placing Muhammad in a semi-realistic Cairo neighbourhood, much as the Prophet appears in classic Islamic sources among the people of Mecca and Medina. In these human environments, male sexuality is a fact of life.

Conclusion

The four images of Muhammad's virility presented here are, of course, products of the societies and cultures in which they were constructed. The negative Christian polemic against the 'licentiousness' of Islam and its Prophet is in keeping with an almost universal depiction of the foreign other as hyper-sexual. The privileging of celibacy in Christianity since its advent reinforced this trend.

Some Muslims internalized the Western hegemonic discourse of sexuality (with its Christian underpinnings) as the balance of power between East and West shifted. They defended their faith and culture, but in Western terms, as the format and style of their works indicate. Nevertheless, their apologetic efforts attest to a sense of inferiority. Many twentieth-century Muslims who wrote biographies of the Prophet Muhammad aimed at an audience of Western-educated elites who had lost contact with their own religious and cultural roots. Some others, however, attempted to dramatize Muhammad for their countrymen, maintaining a dialogue between classical texts and familiar domestic situations (Roded 2002).[26]

Classical Muslim scholars, writing during one of the political and cultural high points of Islamic history, may have been influenced by Jewish and Christian themes. But they had a fundamental sense of the superiority of their faith. Muhammad was the culmination of a long line of prophets from the Judeo-Christian (and Arab) tradition, although the Muslim mainstream rejected Christian celibacy. Thus, Muhammad's virility became an integral part of his life story.

Naguib Mahfouz is undoubtedly one of the most creative and original twentieth-century Muslim writers, so attempts to explain his work in socio-cultural terms seem to dwarf its genius. Nevertheless, the question inevitably arises to what extent Muslims today may view Muhammad's sexuality in human terms.

Notes

1 For affirmation from Qur'anic exegesis, see Stowasser (1994: 86, 165, n. 5).

2 Stowasser (1994: 87–9) deals with Qur'anic revelation and exegesis on the problems raised by the fact that her first husband Zayd was Muhammad's adopted son.

3 F. Rosenthal, 'Nasab', in *The Encyclopaedia of Islam*, 2nd edn (1993).

4 B. Faris, 'Muru'a', in ibid., vol. 7, pp. 636–8.

5 The first part of this section is based on Daniel (1960: 79–108 and 96–102).

6 66 (al-Tahrim): 1–4.

7 Spellberg (1994), an in-depth analysis of the image of 'A'isha in various classical and modern Islamic sources, deals with the accusation of adultery in pp. 61–99.

8 Carlyle was influenced in his positive evaluation of the Prophet by Johann Wolfgang von Goethe's 'Mahomet Gesang' and *West-Ostlicher Divan* (1819) (Schimmel 1985: 240).

9 Two Western scholars who wrote about the life of Muhammad in the mid-nineteenth century were prominent figures in British Indian public life: Aloys Sprengler's *The Life of Muhammad from Original Sources* was published at the Presbyterian Mission Press in Allhabad in 1851; William Muir, an English missionary in India, published a four-volume *Life of Muhammad from Original Sources* in London from 1858 to 1861.

10 A succinct biography of Ahmad Khan may be found in *The Encyclopaedia of Islam*, 2nd edn, vol. 1 (1986), pp. 287–8.

11 W. Cantwell Smith, 'Amir Ali', in ibid., pp. 442–3.

12 Ameer Ali (1922: 443).

13 Dermenghem's *La vie de Mahomet* was based on an impressive selection of classical Arabic sources, modern Muslim writers (Muhammad Abduh, Sayyid Ameer Ali) and many of the most outstanding orientalist studies of his time (Caetani, Lammens, Massignon). Dermenghem's purpose was to navi-

gate between old-fashioned, traditional views and the hypercritical version of certain modern Orientalists.

14 Muhammad Husayn Haykal, *Hayat Muhammad* (Cairo: Matbaca Dar al-kutub al-misriyya, 1935); *The Life of Muhammad*, trans. Ismacil Ragi A. al-Faruqi (North American Trust Publications, 1976). See also Badawi (1971); Wessels (1972); Smith (1983).

15 Mahfouz (1997). Oddly, the English version is more complete than the Arabic as Stewart noted in the introduction. More recently, he has explicated this view and published the discrepancies: Stewart (2001: 37–42).

16 *Children of Gebelawi*, p. 205/*Awlad Haratina*, p. 318.

17 *Children of Gebelawi*, pp. 206–55, 256, 257, 258, 265, 266–7, 270, 271, 272, 286/*Awlad Haratina*, pp. 320–94, 397, 399, 400, 411, 412–14, 418, 420–1, 443.

18 *Children of Gebelawi*, p. 207/*Awlad Haratina*, p. 321.

19 *Children of Gebelawi*, pp. 228, 221, 251, 253, 266, 267/*Awlad Haratina*, pp. 353, 340–41, 389, 391, 412, 413.

20 *Children of Gebelawi*, pp. 256–7, 263–4, 265, 267–68/*Awlad Haratina*, pp. 397–8, 408–9, 411, 414–15.

21 *Children of Gebelawi*, p. 286/*Awlad Haratina*, p. 443.

22 *Children of Gebelawi*, p. 286/*Awlad Haratina*, p. 443.

23 See: *Zuqaq al-Midaq* (1947; trans. T. Le Gassick, 1966), *Al-Sarab* (1948), *Bidaya wa-nihaya* (1949; trans. R. Awad, 1985), and in particular the 'Cairo Trilogy': *Bayn al-Qasrayn* (1956), *Qasr al-Shawq* (1957), *Al-Sukkariyya* (1957); trans. W. M. Hutchins and O. E. Kenny, *Palace Walk* (1990), L. M. Kenny, *Palace of Desire* (1991), A. B. Samaan, *Sugar Street* (1993).

24 Jareer Abu-Haidar (1985), for example, has argued that the book is actually a parable of authority and power in Egypt and the Middle East.

25 See Najjar (1998: 139–68), summarizing Abd al-Hamid Kishk, *Kalimatuna fi al-Radd 'ala Awlad Haratina* (Cairo: al-Mukhtar al-Islami, 1990).

26 Roded (2002). Hakim does not relate to Muhammad's sexuality.

References

Abu-Haidar, J. (1985) 'Awlad Haratina by Najib Mahfuz: An Event in the Arab World', *Journal of Arabic Literature*, 16: 119–31.

Ahmad, A. (1967) *Islamic Modernism in India and Pakistan, 1857–1964*. London: Oxford University Press.

Ameer Ali, S. (1922) *The Spirit of Islam: A History of the Evolution and Ideals of Islam with A Life of the Prophet* [1891]. London: Methuen.

Anas, M. b. [d. 179/795] (1989) *Al-Muwatta*, trans. A. A. Bewley. London: Kegan Paul.

Badawi, M. M. (1985) 'Islam in Modern Literature' [1971], in *Modern Arabic Literature and the West*. London: Ithaca Press.

al-Bukhari, M. b. Isma'il [d. 256/870] (1973–76) *The Translation of the Meanings of Sahih al-Bukhari*: Arabic-English. Al-Medina: Islamic University Press.

Carlyle, T. (1841) *On Heroes and Hero Worship, and the Heroic in History*. London.

Daniel, N. (1960) 'The Life of Muhammad: Polemic Biography', in *Islam and the West: The Making of an Image*. Edinburgh: Edinburgh University Press.

Dermenghem, E. (1929) *La vie de Mahomet*. Paris: Plon; (1930) *The Life of Mahomet*, trans. A. York. London: George Routledge & Son.

El-Enany, R. (1988) 'Religion in the Novels of Naguib Mahfouz', *British Society for Middle Eastern Bulletin*, 15: 21–7.

Haykal, M. H. (1935) *Hayat Muhammad* (Cairo: Matbaca Dar al-kutub al-misriyya); (1976) *The Life of Muhammad*, trans. Isma'il Ragi A. al-Faruqi. Illinois: North American Trust Publications.

Hopwood, D. (1999) *Sexual Encounters in the Middle East: The British, the French and the Arabs*. Reading: Ithaca Press.

Ibn Sa'd [d. 230/845] (1960–68) *Kitab al-tabaqat al-kubra*, ed. Ihsan al-'Abbas, 9 vols, Beirut.

Kahf, M. (1999) *Western Representations of the Muslim Woman: From Termagant to Odalisque*. Austin: University of Texas Press.

Mahfouz, M. (1989) 'A Journey in the Mind of Naguib Mahfouz. On his 50th birthday, Mahfouz talks to Fouad Dawwash', in M. M. Enani (ed.), *Naguib Mahfouz Nobel 1988, Egyptian Perspectives*. Cairo: General Egyptian Book Organization.

— (1997) *Awlad Haratina*. Beirut: Dar al-Adab; (1981) *Children of Gebelawi*, trans. P. Stewart. London: Heinemann.

Milson, M. (1988) *Najib Mahfuz: The Novelist-Philosopher of Cairo*. New York and Jerusalem: St Martin's Press and Magnes Press.

Najjar, F. M. (1998) 'Islamic Fundamentalism and the Intellectuals: The Case of Naguib Mafouz', *British Journal of Middle Eastern Studies*, 25: 139–69.

Roded, R. (1994) *Women in Islamic Biographical Collections from Ibn Sa'd to Who's Who*. Boulder, CO: Lynne Rienner.

— (1999) *Women in Islam and the Middle East*. London: I.B.Tauris.

— (2002) 'Gendered Domesticity in the Life of the Prophet: Tawfiq al-Hakim's Muhammad', *Journal of Semitic Studies*, 47: 67–95.

Schimmel, A. (1985) *And Muhammad is His Messenger: The Veneration of the Prophet in Islamic Piety*. Chapel Hill and London: University of North Carolina Press.

Smith, C. D. (1983) *Islam and the Search for Social Order in Modern Egypt: A Biography of Muhammad Husayn Haykal*. Albany, NY: State University of New York Press.

Somekh, S. (1991) 'The Sad Millenarian: An Examination of Awlad Haratina', *Middle Eastern Studies*, 7: 49–61; and in T. Le Gassick (ed.), *Critical Perspectives on Naguib Mahfouz*. Boulder, CO: Lynne Rienner, pp. 101–14.

Spellberg, D. A. (1994) *Politics, Gender and the Islamic Past: The Legacy of 'A'isha bint Bakr*. New York: Columbia University Press.

Stewart, P. J. (2001) 'Awlad Haratina: A Tale of Two Texts', *Arabic and Middle Eastern Literatures*, 4: 37–42.

Stowasser, B. (1994) *Women in the Qur'an: Traditions and Interpretations.* New York and Oxford: Oxford University Press.

al-Tabari, M. i. J. [224–310/839–923] (1989) *The History of al-Tabari.* Albany, NY: State University of New York Press.

Thornton, L. (1994) *The Orientalists*, vol. 1. Paris: ACR.

Troll, C. (1978) *Sayyid Ahmad Khan: A Reinterpretation of Muslim Theology.* New Delhi: Vikes.

Voltaire, F. M. A. [1694–1778] (1905) *Mahomet*, vol. 16 of *The Works of Voltaire.* Akron, OH: Werner Co.

Wessels, A. (1972) *A Modern Arabic Biography of Muhammad: A Critical Study of Muhammad Husayn Haykal's Hayat Muhammad.* Leiden: E. J. Brill.

4 | The trial of heritage and the legacy of Abraham

NAJAT RAHMAN

I could conceive of another Abraham – to be sure, he would never get to be a patriarch or even an old-clothes dealer – an Abraham who would be prepared to satisfy the demand for a sacrifice immediately, with the promptness of a waiter, but would be unable to bring it off because he cannot get away, being indispensable; the household needs him, there is always something or other to take care of, the house is never ready; but without having his house ready, without having something to fall back on, he cannot leave – this the Bible also realized, for it says: 'He set his house in order'. (Franz Kafka, cited in Walter Benjamin 1969: 129)

When Kafka expresses the possibility, if not the desire, to textually re-envision the inherited figure of Abraham, he is echoed by contemporary Arab writers contending with Abraham's presumed legacies: nationalism and religious fundamentalism. Kafka envisions an Abraham who would not be easily bound by the various monotheistic traditions and nationalist readings. He would fail to meet the demands of his household and to become patriarch, but he would be none the less diligent in his quest. He would also fail to meet the sacred commands, though he may be always ready, being 'indispensable' to his family. Kafka's Abraham represents a fragile but arresting possibility before it is textually foreclosed. He is a figure, more specifically, of the double-bind, one that demarcates the conflict and suspended difference of the divine commands and the communal duties. Kafka wants to insist on this difficult impasse, since Abraham never manages to establish order in his house. His paternity is already in question in the biblical story, even as it is being consolidated.

Abraham is fundamental for monotheistic, patriarchal demarcations of identity. Hence, a specific examination of Islamic articulations of masculinity, intimately linked to conceptions of patriarchy, nationalism and fundamentalism, requires one to turn to the Old Testament to explore how Abraham is later incorporated and reworked in the Qur'an as Islam attempts to inaugurate its difference from older monotheistic traditions. While masculine identity in all monotheistic traditions seems construed along a father–son nexus, the Qur'an reveals a different emphasis on the relationship between father and son. In introducing Abraham as a rebelling son, Islam reworks the bonds of filiations so that the son is valorized in his faith to his God and not in his submission to his father. The son's questioning of his father's traditional beliefs is encouraged as *ijtihad* or intellectual labour necessary for faith. Abraham nevertheless emerges as a figure of ambivalence – as father and rebelling son – who will become in Islamic readings the father of submission.

Two contemporary literary responses to Islamic and biblical constructions of identity are presented in the latter part of this chapter. The Palestinian poet Mahmoud Darwish and the Algerian writer Assia Djebar are engaged in re-examining their heritage, which they identify as paternal. The Abraham story is revisited, since it combines nationalist and religious constructions of identity and forges collective identity by way of submission to the authority of the father and exclusion of the other. They suggest that this long literary heritage speaks of dispossession, exclusion, and that those predicaments are historically enacted through nationalist and religious readings of inherited myths. They expose nationalist demarcations of identity that have failed and brought on a crisis of collective identity in Algeria and elsewhere where a pluralist past is denied, women are secluded from public life, and any voice of difference is silenced.[1] They reconsider these monotheistic myths before they are foreclosed into monolithic meaning by history to explore new ways of thinking about identity. Djebar invokes the memory of Abraham to recall Hagar's repudiation and the overall exclusion of women. Darwish invokes the father who exiles, who sacrifices the future for the past.

Walter Benjamin introduces the citation of Kafka above when speaking of narrative (Kafka's in particular) as the possibility for the postponement of the future. Benjamin reads the desire for the deferral of closure as a desire for hope (1969: 129). To postpone the future is to defer closure, to foreclose violent formations of identity, and to entertain the possibility of new readings. Perhaps Abraham is the figure that refuses closure as Kafka envisions him and as Darwish and Djebar read him. While he is invoked by Darwish and Djebar as an emblem of paternal heritage predicated on submission, exile and the sacrifice of the son, he is interrogated again to allow for hope, home and future. It is a collective effort of re-reading that would allow for new stories to emerge from old myths.

For what would it mean for Abraham to 'set his house in order'?[2] Why is it necessary to do so before the sacred tasks can be carried out? God proclaims in Genesis 18:20 that he has chosen Abraham precisely because he can keep order in his household and by extension maintain the covenant with God, so 'that he may charge his children and his household after him to keep the way of the lord by doing righteousness and justice;

so that the Lord may bring to Abraham what he has promised him' (New Revised Standard Version 1962). But more importantly, how did Abraham presumably 'set his house in order'? Is it by division? One woman kept, one exiled? One son claimed, one disinherited? These questions can hardly be excluded as outside the parameters of the binding of Isaac (or is it Ishmael?). Is the sacrifice of the son to God or to the other woman? Is not the house already in disorder because of the birth of Isaac and the conflict of inheritance that will lead Sarah to demand the exile of Hagar and Ishmael? The division among the women and their sons carries with it double promises from God on behalf of Isaac and Ishmael. To Hagar, too, God promises that Ishmael will be 'a great nation' (Genesis 21:18). From these familial segmentations will come a separation of nations.

Perhaps one way for Abraham's house to be in order is to guarantee sole inheritance for Isaac. But, then, having put his house in order, Abraham would blindly climb the mountain to disorder again, where, without God's change of heart, his heir seems fated to perish. In fact, the event of the binding of Isaac is marked by disorder. Genesis 22 begins with Sarah's exclusion from this event and from the family of father and son. Sarah, Isaac, Hagar and Ishmael all end up in different places. The Old Testament relates that when Sarah died in Hebron, 'Abraham went in to mourn for her' (Genesis 23:2). As Jon D. Levenson notes, Abraham 'dwells in Beer Sheva, far from Isaac, far from Sarah who is in Hebron, far from Ishmael and Hagar in Egypt. In the end, Abraham is close only to God' (1998: 259). In the Qur'an too, Abraham will have divided houses as he journeys to see his son Ishmael and return to his wife Sarah, although the reason for this 'exile' is less directly attributed to Sarah's rivalry: 'Abraham said: 'Lord make this a secure land [...] I have settled some of my offspring in a barren valley near Your Sacred House, so that they may observe true worship, Lord'" (Dawood 1999: 14:36).[3]

Abraham's house has never been in order, for disorder is written into paternity as the Qur'an also relates. Beyond the general impossibility of ascertaining the certainty of paternity, Abraham himself needed divine intervention to father Isaac; he is already an old man and Sarah has passed her childbearing years. The foundation upon which the claim to paternity is made is never secure. One asks with Carol Delaney: *'Is Isaac his to sacrifice?'* (1998: 22). Implied also in the rendition of Abraham's attempted act of sacrifice is the valorization of paternity over and above any parental claims that the mother, who neither knows nor is asked, can make. His is a paternity predicated not simply on an acknowledged biological relationship, nor a social role based on that relationship, but one, as Delaney states, that 'has meant *the primary, creative, engendering* role [...] The notion of paternity, therefore, already embodies *authority* and power and provides the rationale for a particular constellation of the family and the structure of relations within it' (ibid., pp. 7–8). The valorization of paternity creates a certain family order out of unstable elements where the father's claim to paternity has to be shared with another, where the mother is made absent, and where the future of the son is offered to the past-God. This is the heritage of paternity received as social (and political order) from the myth of Abraham filtered through the various traditional accounts. In such a rendition as the Old Testament's, which launches the 'patriarchal narratives,' the divine and paternal powers of creation and annihilation are henceforth interwoven and the only story that remains, as Delaney points out, 'could only be a story of recognition, that is of acknowledging and submitting to the one true God' (ibid., p. 21).

Why is paternity so important? What order does it uphold? In the Old Testament, paternity guarantees inheritance of home and identity, but through the dispossession of others. The promise of paternity is made in the same breath as the promise of land. God commands Abraham: ' "Leave your country, your family and your father's house, for the land I will show you." [...] Abram passed through the land as far as Shechem's holy place [...] the Canaanites were in the land [...] "It is to your descendants that I will give this land" ' (Genesis 12:1–7). This is a covenant not revealed as such in the Qur'an. Rather, the emphasis throughout is on Abraham's leaving his father the idolater. Even his descendants will be subject to their faith. ' "And what of my descendants?" asked Abraham. "My covenant," said He, "does not apply to the evil-doers" ' (Dawood 1999: 2:125). It is significant that the possession of land does not happen in Abraham's lifetime in the Old Testament. Even his immediate descendants will be without a home, 'sojourners in a land not theirs' (Genesis 12:13). Although they eventually create a new home, this promise is deferred and mediated through divine threats that Israel's inheritance will be broken (Schwartz 1997: 129). The land remains a promise, though a strict, literal nationalist reading has attempted its actualization. 'Almost every promise made to Abraham,' Silvano Arietti points out, 'concerns not the present but the future' (1981: 108). And though Abraham begets Ishmael and Isaac, the question remains: is paternity ever fulfilled? (ibid.). Genesis 22:19 relates that Abraham, after his attempted sacrifice, returned to his men whereupon they set off to Beersheba and lived there. It does not mention Isaac. Although Isaac ultimately resurfaces to hear Jacob, this still leads Delaney to ask, 'Where is Isaac?' The ending of Genesis 22 establishes the patriarchal lineage through Abraham's brother Nahor, 'as if Isaac had ceased to exist' (ibid.).

Abraham's biblical story centres on paternity, on Abraham's desire to have a son who will be the fulfilment of God's promise so that he can be a 'father of nations'. His identity is inscribed in his paternity and is divinely ordained. Even the name of Abraham etymologically denotes fatherhood. The deity of the Old Testament changes Abraham's name from Abram (or 'exalted father') to Abraham (or 'father of a multitude') (Genesis 17:5). Not only is he favoured for his paternity; he is also a father to a heterogeneous (and conflicting) collectivity after God's image in the Torah.

But Abraham himself occupies an ambivalent position in relation to paternity. Both a father and rebelling son in Islam, he is obligated to God at the expense of his own father, his own fatherhood, and his own son. He replaces his father and the visible idols for the invisible One (Arietti 1981: 57). The Islamic rendition of the story of Abraham greatly emphasizes the encounter between Abraham and his own father, going back further into his life than does Genesis. It follows the post-biblical *Midrashim* story, and we encounter a defiant son destroying the idols worshipped by his people. While they decide to burn Abraham, his own father waits among the crowd (Dawood 1999: 37:109). Just as he displaces his father for his faith, so is his own father willing to sacrifice him for his own faith: 'Do you dare renounce my gods, Abraham?' (ibid., 19:46).

Abraham is pivotal to Islam, which traces itself back to him as an originary monotheistic religion, and which considers both Judaism and Christianity to have shared this message of monotheism only to distort it. So Islam claims to be both the new and the old faith. It is precisely to restore people to the faith of Abraham that Muhammad was sent. The Qur'an asserts that 'Abraham was not a Jew, neither a Christian, but he was a pure monotheist (*hanif*) and one who submitted (*Muslim*) to God; certainly he was never of the idolaters' (cited in Delaney 1998: 162). In considering Abraham as a pure monotheist, Islam continues from previous traditions and succeeds in having that status acknowledged still today, as evidenced by the link it makes between Abraham and Muhammad. The parallels between the two prophets in the Qur'an include repeated references to them as breakers of idols.

When Islam delivers Abraham as a youth in search of a God among the gods, it is essentially defying the fatherly conception of the Old Testament where biological fathers are conveniently monotheistic believers (Dawood 1999: 6:75). It reconfigures affiliation and replaces the allegiance to the pagan and biological father with that of God: 'show kindness to [your] parents. But if they bid you serve besides Me deities you know nothing of, do not obey them' (ibid., 29:7). So in having the story of the father, and Abraham as a rebellious son, it accentuates the faith of Abraham. In a sense, Abraham becomes another Adam, but one whose genealogy is of prophecy. And among the prophets, he holds a special status, being linked with a new conception of divinity and due to his line of descendants being one. He made his heritage one of prophecy, so that all the prophets that succeeded him were of his line of descent. And God, the Qur'an relates, took him as a friend.

It is a fragile paternity in a process of consolidation. A father and a son, Abraham is the figure of the patriarch and of heritage. Abraham upholds paternity to such an extent that he is willing to sacrifice his desire for fatherhood to the divine vision. He submits and in his submission he reigns over his desire. The faith of Abraham knows no bounds, and his possession of his paternity is predicated on the selfless abdication of all for the One God. The attempted sacrifice is the act that binds Abraham's identity as patriarch to his excessive faith and binds the heritage given to the son. It furthermore has historically 'bound' our reading of Abraham.[4] Through religious and nationalist readings, he has been received as patriarch and emblem of faith. The binding of Isaac has been the inherited story that demarcates heritage as paternal, faith as submission, where inheritance is possible only through submission to the patriarchal authority and at the same time threatened by that very faith. The Qur'an avoids the pitfalls in the Old Testament, however. For Abraham speaks to his son about his dream and asks him for his judgement: 'He said: I see in a dream, my son, that I sacrifice you, so consider what you see fit. He [the son] answers: Do as you are commanded, you'll find me, God willing, forbearing ... ' (Dawood 1999: 37:102–11).[5]

Abraham becomes the closest image to God, not only fathering the Jews and Arabs but being claimed by all three monotheistic religions, being willing to sacrifice his own son as perhaps the Christian God was willing to do. He is not only the beginning of monotheistic religions, he is also their essence: 'Who but a foolish man would renounce the faith of Abraham? We chose him in this world, and in the world to come he shall abide among the righteous. When his Lord said to him: "Submit," he answered: "I have submitted to the Lord of the Universe"' (ibid., 2:31).

Abraham ultimately promotes dissension rather than community, as Regina Schwartz notes: 'It could have been one community. Sadly enough these revisions succumbed to competition for the status of the true children of Abraham, to the scarcity principle' (1997: 159). Not unlike the monotheistic Old Testament God who cannot recognize all peoples as his own and who cannot give blessings to all, so Abraham can inherit only one son and dispossess the other, and can keep only one woman and exile another. While Abraham stands behind all three monotheistic religions as the past, he may also be the figure of future and promise as

Kafka and the work of Darwish and Djebar implicitly suggest. It is only through opening these myths again to new readings that the possibility of new stories emerges.

The story of Abraham in its many forms remains contemporaneous. It is a heritage of sacred writing that has translated to profane nationalist and fundamentalist configurations of identity. If one is to acknowledge with Schwartz and Delaney that secular ideology has its roots in religious texts, one can further specify that nationalism may have its foundation in the Abraham story. The divine promises to Abraham of land and of paternity over many nations are the key moments in Genesis, a link that nationalism also makes. While the Bible is too heterogeneous to provide unambiguous demarcations of a 'nation' or a 'people', nevertheless it has been too often authorized as 'a manual for politics' (Schwartz 1997: 123).

There is an intimate connection between the development of European nationalism and the widespread reading of biblical narratives as Schwartz indicates: 'this Europe – filled with Bible stories about peoples – was also a Europe on the road to carving itself into new peoples, into nationalisms' (ibid., p. 7). The biblical preoccupation with collective identity is filtered through German nationalism, so that modern nationalism is conceived through the interpretive work and reading of the German versions of biblical narratives:

> In a disturbing inversion, soon nationalism was authorized by the once-holy writ. A text that had once posited collective identity as the fiat of God ('I will be your God if you will be my people') came to posit collective identity as the fiat of the nation authorized by God ('one nation under God'). Where nationalism is not explicitly authorized by God, it replaces God. (Schwartz 1997: 11–12)

The Hebrew Bible has had a tremendous impact on formulations of identity. In its biblical delineation, identity is linked with a unilateral notion of heritage. It is through inheritance, whether of faith or kinship, that collective identity is consolidated to the exclusion of all others. Even the promise of land is one that is inherited through the sacred words; land, like identity, is not to be gained through exchange with others but against them and at their expense. Schwartz attributes the violence in collective identity formation to monotheism where a 'principle of scarcity' permeates. The monotheistic God not only demands exclusive adherence but also confers exclusive blessings not to be shared by all.

A questioning of nationalist paradigms leads necessarily, then, to a re-examination of the cultural paradigms that father modern ideologies. What has strongly carried into the Qur'anic rendition is the obligation of the submissive and obedient son. The binding of the son has led to the binding of a one and 'true' reading. The need remains henceforth for re-reading to make space for hopes that ideologically ritualized readings exclude.

Both Darwish and Djebar are engaged in such an endeavour of reading. In invoking Islamic stories informed by biblical ones, the two writers locate their heritage with Abraham and his ensuing legacy.[6] The paternal figure in their work as emblem of faith and submission predicated on the exile and sacrifice of the son is re-examined to allow for home, hope, and future without exclusion, submission or disappearance. Both of their literary ventures involve an attempt at reconstruction, a work that implies a collective effort. The work of reconstruction through narrative and poetry would allow for new stories to emerge from the old myths.

The patriarchal narratives that forge collective identity by way of submission to the authority of the father and at the exclusion of the other are revisited, since the mythical has always encroached upon the historical and history has always attempted to speak for myth. Already the Qur'an foregrounds the mythic status of Abraham: 'People of the Book, why do you argue about Abraham when both the Torah and the Gospel were not revealed till after him? [...] Indeed you have argued about things of which you have some knowledge. Must you now argue about that of which you know nothing at all?' (Dawood 1999: 3:65). Unlike other prophets who are invoked directly and whose stories are told after they have been named, Abraham is often introduced in relation to his story: 'Tell of Abraham' or 'recount [...] the story of Abraham' (ibid., 6:75, 19:40). And yet the Qur'an has been received as another closed patriarchal narrative.

The family drama of one father, two women and two sons continues to be played out not only in the literary world but in the critical, historical present as well. A father to two peoples, Abraham is the figure who brings together, if not violently binds, myth and history. What is more symbolic of this binding than the violence in Hebron perpetuated by the Jewish settler upon the praying Muslims, a violence that takes place at the presumed tomb of Abraham?[7] These simultaneous claims to the historical paternity of Abraham are predicated on the inherited accounts and myths of monotheism. With the patrimony of Abraham that continues to be claimed and proclaimed historically, is not one ultimately still within the mythic? The myth of Abraham continues to be read as a story of origins that forges collective identities and identifications of home. But these origins are mythic, for Abraham's beginnings, as the accounts relate and as history bears out, are always elsewhere. And yet his tombstone remains a politically contested site in history. And Hebron remains a volatile place.

In seeking to be part of a continuing work of reconstruction that would allow for new figurations of home and identity to emerge from the inherited myths, Darwish and Djebar attempt to find an opening in how history reads myth to reveal its encroachment on myth. Djebar writes:

> For [...] years I had been an uncomfortable witness of the fundamentalist rise in public life [...] I told myself that the only kind of response of which I was capable, as a writer, was to go back to the written sources of our history. I wanted to study [...] this specific period that the fundamentalists were in the process of claiming for themselves, deforming [...] from the standpoint of facts as well as the standpoint of intent. (cited in Zimra 1993: 122–3)

Darwish and Djebar foreground the way in which history has read the Abraham myth to result in nationalist and fundamentalist configurations of identity. Myth, which suggests comparisons and connections out of disparities, provides writers with a world in which everything can be identified with everything else. The realm of myth is revealed to be that of metaphor where identification between history and myth emerges out of seeming difference. History haunts myth and tries to identify with it, for myths also impose a narrative structure on events and desires. And with Darwish and Djebar, poetry and literature bring myth and history together through the heritage selected to expose this structure of identification, a heritage that emerges not only from within the bounds of literary texts but also from the historical readings of them. They seek alternate forms of history that would not settle too quickly the meaning of the old myths and that would overcome readings and enactments of dominant histories.

In Darwish's and Djebar's invocations of Abraham as a figure of heritage, there is an implied suspicion that Abraham, who is doubly bound, reveals a double movement to heritage: not a heritage that emanates from the past and looks towards the future, but one that is arrested in a certain textual bind, in a perfect Benjaminian historical gesture, that turns back to the past while being propelled towards the future. Such a heritage looks upon piling heaps of ruin, as Benjamin envisioned that turning back, and inevitably produces that textual lineage in a narrative binding. And the two writers are well aware that textual production also creates its own progeny.

A dialogue with the father ensues for both writers: 'as you used to carry me my father, I will carry this longing / to my beginning and to its beginning / and I will cross this road / to my end and to its end' (Darwish 1994: 42). For both Darwish and Djebar, that heritage has been paternal because of the textual silencing and historical loss of the mother, figured previously and respectively as land and language, that surer but irrecoverable remainder. The heritage of the transient and ephemeral father, if absent, provides possibility for words and for home but only in displacement. Darwish writes: 'I learned all the words and how to take them apart so I can form one word, homeland' (ibid., p. 327). And as Abraham's chosen deity is intangible, so have Darwish's and Djebar's notions of home been inaugurated in words that respond to textual delineations of heritage that have become historical: 'the countries between my hands are the work of my hands' (ibid., p. 382). Djebar invokes the memory of Abraham to recall Hagar as the one left behind, as that inheritance that has not become part of any tradition and yet continues to be inherited. 'Abraham accompanies Hagar and the child [...] until the site of Mecca, between the two hills of Safa and Merwa. / Then Abraham leaves. There, they are alone / Ishmael is thirsty / Ishmael is going to die' (Djebar 1991: 302). Darwish invokes Abraham as the father who always leaves, the father who could not defend his sons, neither to celestial sacrifice nor to the fears of Sarah: 'And every absence is my father' (1994: 102). Perhaps for both Darwish and Djebar, Abraham is ultimately the site of contestation that remains, a remainder not only through the historical conflicts that are contemporaneous but also through the textual production.

Darwish's poetry often addresses the father or the forefathers; and, often, it has the form of a question, an accounting, or trial as evidenced by his titular question about the departure, 'Why have you left the horse alone?' He does not invoke Abraham directly but addresses him through Ishmael and all the other sons. His poetic voice gathers the sons with whom it identifies: Ishmael, Joseph, Cain and other exiles. The poetic voice also addresses his own father and literary forefathers such as al-Mutanabbi and Imru' al-Qais. When there is no faith, there can be no submission and no silence for the son. Ishmael dialogues with and interrogates the father through the poetic voice: 'Where are you taking me, father? / In the direction of the wind, my son ... / – Who will live in our home after us, my father? / – It shall remain as it was, my son' (Darwish 1995: 32–3). The saddened and sympathetic voice of the son holds the father accountable not to condemn him but to reopen the register of events to reinvent the outcome.

Poetry for Darwish is not only a staging of voices but also a space of survival. It seeks an inheritance that will not dispossess and that will open towards a future. 'I look upon a procession of ancient prophets / as they climb barefoot towards Orshalim / And I ask: Is there a new prophet/for this new age?' (ibid., p. 13). The search for new prophets is an acknowledgement that the old prophets, including Abraham, still loom as ghosts over the place and its absence. The father becomes ghost, ghost of self that haunts the memory of place. The father's departure from his house occupies the question of Darwish's poetic voice: 'Why have you left the horse alone?' Through the paternal response, 'for homes die without their inhabitants', he inherits a notion of home in its absence from the one who left. The voice of the son, which recognized only the departure, learns through dialogue with the father how home cannot be dissociated from a paternal heritage and a paternal failing and from the question and the words. The haunting is not only of the past and its failings, but also of the future and the limits of the poetic endeavour.

Like Darwish, Djebar frames her narratives with the figure of the father, whether it is her Algerian father, the literary fathers of St Augustine and Ibn Khaldun, the French chroniclers or Abraham. Hers is an inheritance usually bestowed on males. Aware of being privileged to receive this heritage of writing, she uses it to interrogate the father figure and to 'resurrect' the silenced voices of women:

> My fiction is this attempt at autobiography, weighed down under the
> oppressive burden of my heritage [...] But the tribal legends criss-cross
> the empty spaces, and the imagination crouches in the silence when lov-
> ing words of the unwritten mother-tongue remain unspoken – language
> conveyed like the inaudible babbling of a nameless, haggard murmur
> [...] How shall I find the strength to tear off my veil, unless I have to use it
> to bandage the running sore nearby which words exude? (Djebar 1993: 218)

Djebar is haunted by the necessity and the impossibility of such a project. She names Abraham explicitly to recall these female suppressed voices, which are marked as discontinuous moments in heritage.

The heritage of Abraham for Djebar is the heritage of Ishmael and his mother: exile and repudiation: 'Hagar the repudiated, because she is the first' (1991: 302). And this heritage is replayed in Islam for her. Political strife embedded in the Islamic community will have its familial roots where patriarchy is impotent, just like Abraham's predicament. The multiple marriages of Muhammad never guarantee any unity or order in the household. She recalls specifically Fatima and her inability to inherit either spiritually or materially from her father: 'There is also her right as a daughter, her share of the inheritance. In this second controversy, she will fight alone' (ibid., p. 78). She conjures Hagar as if to announce a beginning to a tradition of disinheritance. Djebar seeks the source for the legacy of Ishmael who ultimately repeats the repudiation of his father Abraham, upon the injunction of the father. And Ishmael submits.

While Djebar increasingly links the legacy of Muhammad to that of Abraham, locating Islam within this fixed paternal heritage of sacrifice and dispossession, she at the same time recalls Hagar as the body of struggle.

It is precisely the dance of Hagar, as she searches for water for the thirsty Ishmael in the desert, frantically traversing the two hills of Safa and Merwa, that is the added story of Islam and that provides the possibility for inclusion, struggle and survival. It is this dance that stages the fiction and this fiction that allows a voice to emerge through the body. 'The child, in disarray [...] scrapes [...] the sand [...] when finally the water surges forth / finally a source / finally a music / of beginning / Hagar, dances in an abandoned folly, Hagar listens / Hagar stops' (ibid., p. 303). This is not only the supposed beginning of the sacred spring of Zemzem that runs in Mecca to this day, but it is also the commencement of possibility.

Djebar also points to the convergences and separations of traditions inherited. This heritage, encompassing an Islamic tradition predicated upon submission, offers her the opportunity for dialogue through the song of Abraham. In music, one can locate the promise: 'Tradition would seem to decree that entry through its gate is by submission, not by love. Love, which the most simple of settings might inflame, appears dangerous. There remains music' (1993: 169). In her reading of the ballad of Abraham, she sees love in the story of Muhammad towards his wife Khadija (and, in *Loin de Médine*, towards his daughter Fatima), a love rendered secondary to submission if not altogether ruinous in traditional Islam. This is perhaps the divergence of Muhammad from Abraham as the paradigmatic father. It is this inherited cultural moment that will lead both Darwish and Djebar to point to the ruptures of their heritage. In focusing on the father–daughter relationship, Djebar recalls Muhammad's own intervention on behalf of his daughter. 'Fourteen centuries have elapsed: it seems that no father has since, at least within the community of Islam [...] developed such a compelling defence for the tranquility of his daughter!' (1991: 68–9). Djebar's focus on the daughter allows for healing and for inclusion.

Djebar imbricates Abraham's cultural patrimony with a menacing present in an indictment against contemporary Arabia and Algeria: 'Abraham has returned, retracing his steps' (ibid., p. 305). The violent legacy of Abraham, authorized by a blind paternal faith turned law, is in the continual displacement and dispossession of Hagar. Danielle Shepherd's comment on *L'amour, la fantasie* is appropriate as well for Hagar: 'Woman sees herself called upon incessantly to conquer the laws of necessity and to advance regardless of destiny' (1996: 188). The struggle of Hagar, embodied in her frenzied dance, is to survive; and the need for survival still remains. Djebar's endeavour of writing is likewise one of struggle and survival, simultaneously a displacement of the father and a transgression against him. For her, writing is associated with the father, for she learns it from him and against his prohibition (on love letters, for instance).

We return to Kafka who wants to consider Abraham not as an inaugura-
ting figure of paternal authority and submission, nor even as the everyday
man who meets his communal duties, but as a figure of the double-bind
where the demands of the everyday never cease and his devotion to the
divine is neither compromised nor fulfilled. This bind inhabits the centre
of this figure of heritage as a discontinuity. So, ultimately, whether one
shares Kafka's vision of Abraham or not, one certainly needs his inter-
rogation of this figure of heritage. Not unlike Kafka, both Darwish and
Djebar invoke, through Abraham, this arrested vision of myth to point to
its possibilities before its narrative closure. This mythic moment endows
the writers with the ability to abide before the damage of old myths. This
arrested moment further grants an opening for new conceptions of identity
and new masculinities to emerge from the old. It allows at the very least
for a marking of that desire.

Notes

Reprinted from *Men and Masculinities*, 5.3 (January 2003): 295–308.

1 In Algeria, violent conflict ensued after the nationalist government can-
celled the 1992 elections because Islamic fundamentalists won by a landslide.
Supporters of the Front Islamique du Salut, or Islamic Salvation Front, which
presented the only alternative to a corrupt nationalist dictatorship, and those
concerned about their rights under fundamentalists immediately protested.
Civil strife continues in Algeria. In Israel, the mere suggestion of including
Darwish's poetry in the country's high school curriculum threatened to dismantle the government and the second uprising unfolds violently as a result
of one group making nationalist claims at the expense of the other.

2 While Kafka, as cited by Benjamin, attributes the expression 'He set his
house in order' to the Old Testament, the origin of this phrase is uncertain.
The expression cannot be strictly traced to the German versions of the Hebrew
Bible. It seems to be put into play by the two writers based on a verse in
Genesis 22:9, which is the closest biblical phrase to Kafka's and is said in the
context of binding: 'Abraham laid the wood in order, and bound Isaac.' See
Young (1936). Moreover, Benjamin does not cite the source of Kafka's words.

3 One cannot account for all the readings that this episode has generated.
Noteworthy are the readings of Immanuel Kant and Søren Kierkegaard. While
monotheistic religions have read this binding as testimony to Abraham's
faith, it was Immanuel Kant who began in the philosophical tradition a
reopening of this reading based on a notion of universal ethics. Kant argues
that an action that is considered wrong in itself cannot be deemed right as
a result of divine directive. He wants to ground a moral actor not on 'laws
proceeding from another person's act of choice' but on 'inner laws that
can be developed from every man's own reason' and that would constitute
'universal ethics' (cited in Levenson 1998: 260). Søren Kierkegaard's defence
of Abraham in *Fear and Trembling* is a response that underscores the conflict
within Abraham. Kierkegaard insists on the 'dread' that Abraham presumably

experiences, a tension that results both from his faith in God's promise and from his love for his son. If the ethical for Kant is universal and directed from within itself, faith for Kierkegaard is so radically individual that it is incommunicable; it isolates and places the individual above the universal because of his/her unmediated relation to the absolute.

4 I am referring to the work of Darwish and Djebar since the early 1980s.

5 The massacre in Hebron took place on 25 February 1994 at the Cave of the Patriarchs, known as Abraham's tomb. A Jewish settler from Hebron, Dr Baruch Goldstein, entered the mosque where Muslims were praying and opened fire, killing twenty-nine people before he was killed. Nothing immediate is known to have triggered this event, although Hebron is often tense because of the competing religious claims on its sites and because the Israeli settlements are inside the city.

6 Translations of Darwish's poetry from the Arabic are mine.

7 Translations from the French are mine.

References

Arietti, S. (1981) *Abraham and the Contemporary Mind*. New York: Basic Books.

Benjamin, W. (1969) *Illuminations: Essays and Reflections*, ed. and introduced by Hannah Arendt, trans. Harry Zohn. New York: Schocken Books.

Darwish, M. (1994) *Diwan* (complete works of poetry). Beirut: Dar al-'Awda.

— (1995) *Limatha Tarakta al-Hisana Wahidan?* [Why have you left the horse alone?]. Beirut: Riad El-Rayyes.

Dawood, N. J. (trans.) (1999) *The Koran*. New York: Penguin.

Delaney, C. (1998) *Abraham on Trial: The Social Legacy of Biblical Myth*. Princeton, NJ: Princeton University Press.

Djebar, A. (1991) *Loin de Médine: Filles d'Ismaël* [Far from Medina: Daughters of Ishmael]. Paris: Albin Michel.

— (1993) *Fantasia: An Algerian Cavalcade*, trans. Dorothy S. Blair. Portsmouth, NH: Heinemann.

Kierkegaard, S. (1968) *Fear and Trembling*, trans. with introduction and notes by Walter Lowrie. Princeton, NJ: Princeton University Press.

Levenson, J. D. (1998) 'Abusing Abraham: Traditions, Religious Histories, and Modern Misinterpretations', *Judaism*, 47: 259–77.

Schwartz, R. M. (1997) *The Curse of Cain: The Violent Legacy of Monotheism*. Chicago, IL: University of Chicago Press.

Shepherd, D. (1996) '*Loin de Médine* d'Assia Djebar: quand les porteuses d'eau se font porteuses de feu' [Assia Djebar's *Loin de Médine*: When Carriers of Water Become Carriers of Fire], in Sada Niang (ed.), *Littérature et Cinéma en Afrique Francophone: Ousmane Sembène et Assia Djebar*. Paris: L'Harmattan.

Young, R. (1936) *Analytical Concordance to the Bible: Authorized Edition Revised*, 2nd edn. New York: Funk and Wagnall's.

Zimra, C. (1993) '"When the Past Answers Our Present": Assia Djebar Talks about *Loin de Médine*', *Callaloo*, 16: 115–28.

TWO | Masculinities and the Palestinian–Israeli conflict

5 | 'My Wife is from the Jinn': Palestinian men, diaspora and love

CELIA ROTHENBERG

This chapter explores how some Palestinian male villagers experience the cultural politics of diaspora and return, and love and desire. The vehicle for expressing these sentiments is a popular magazine serial entitled 'Zawjatī min al-Jinn', or 'My Wife is from the Jinn', published in Arabic by the magazine Fosta.[1] Claiming to be autobiographical, the story is phrased in the discourse of a young man's relationship with a jinnia, or female spirit. 'My Wife is from the Jinn' emphasizes aspects of Palestinian men's cultural experiences and attitudes not generally discussed in daily life by most men or women in West Bank village settings nor typically visible in public spaces.[2] Indeed, in contrast to analyses of more explicit discourses of masculinity which emphasize men as protectors of family honour, providers for the family needs, and fighters and/or martyrs for the Palestinian nationalist cause (see, for example, Massad 1995; Peteet 1994, 1997), I examine this story for what it may reveal about the less obvious, although equally central, dimensions of contemporary Palestinian men's experiences and morals. This examination is based on evidence gathered during fieldwork for my doctorate in 1995 and 1996 in the village of Artas.

The jinn and politics in the West Bank

'My Wife is from the Jinn' draws on common knowledge for Palestinians in the West Bank, including their knowledge of both the jinn and the politics of everyday life. The discourse of jinn stories in village life, usually related orally, often speaks to issues otherwise commented on only subtly, indirectly, or not at all in daily life (Rothenberg 1998, 2004). While the jinn are mentioned in the Qu'ran, most villagers' knowledge of the jinn stems from the expertise of local sheikhs and tales of the jinn which circulate in village settings. It is thus well known to most villagers that jinn are spirits who live in a world parallel to our own and who, at times, visit ours. When in our world, the jinn may appear as cats, humans or other kinds of animals. Often, a jinn will possess a human, controlling the individual's actions and speech. In other cases, a jinn will maintain a relationship with a human, as is the case in the story discussed here.

A particular political setting frames the publication of this story and the context in which it was read and understood by the Palestinians whom I knew best during my fieldwork. In 1994, the year of the publication of the initial episode, the West Bank was hoping to enter a new era. The signing of the Declaration of Principles in Oslo in 1993 had officially ended the intifada and established the Palestinian National Authority as an interim self-governing body. This transitional phase was scheduled to last five years, intended to introduce an era which, many hoped, would mark the beginning of a lasting settlement with Israel and peace in the region. As the episodes continued to be published, some progress was made in the peace process: in the winter of my fieldwork in 1995–96, a number of Palestinian cities were 'liberated' from the Israelis (Israelis withdrew from within these cities' limits), including Ramallah, Nablus and Bethlehem.

Obviously, as time has passed, full implementation of the Oslo agreement has not taken place and Palestinian frustration and pessimism have increased. Israeli Prime Minister Ariel Sharon's provocative visit to the Temple Mount helped to spark a new round of violence in the area. That brief time of hope and optimism, although just a few years ago, now seems to be a distant memory.

It is not surprising that recent Palestinian literature (including literature translated into English and written in English and Arabic) is characterized by its explicit emphasis on the experiences of Palestinians under military occupation and is often termed 'intifada literature' (Velden 1995: 173).[3] For example, in two short stories, Hanan Ashrawi writes powerfully of the experiences of two mothers and their confrontations with Israeli soldiers (Ashrawi 1993: 180–3). Other intifada literature writers include Fadia Faqir, who, in her novel *Nisanit*, explores the experiences of an Israeli interrogator and Shadeed, a young Palestinian guerrilla fighter. Raymonda Tawil, in *My Home, My Prison* (1983), describes being kept under house arrest in the West Bank. In a similar vein, Kanaana describes how oral 'intifada legends' tend to focus on Palestinian men as heroes who challenge and engage the enemy in deadly battles and Palestinian women as pillars of the family (1995: 153–61).[4]

The tone and subject of '*My Wife is from the Jinn*' stand in distinct contrast to this literature. Perhaps the potential for the dawning of a new era, marked by the end of the first intifada, may have helped to create a context which allows this story to look at Palestinian cultural life as entwined in complex and often surprising ways with foreign, including Israeli, powers.

Artas, the village in which I pursued my fieldwork and primarily gathered interpretations of '*My Wife is from the Jinn*', is located approximately two kilometres south of Bethlehem. Many men in the neighbourhood in which

I lived worked building Israeli settlements in both the West Bank and Israel. They did so because these jobs offered some of the best wages to be found for day labourers. While aware of the moral problematics these jobs pose, the men nevertheless felt they had to bring home the best wages they could to support their families. A few women, particularly older, unmarried women and widows, worked selling vegetables in Bethlehem and/or Jerusalem or sewing clothes in factories or at home.

An underlying theme throughout the *Fosta* story, and one which underpins aspects of the analysis presented here, is that of physical proximity to others, including Israelis, and the possibilities for social relations such proximity entails. Physical proximity and an individual's preferences for some relationships over others allow for the development of reciprocal relationships and friendships important to the lives of women and men (Rothenberg 1998, 2004). The implications of this social geography, including the degrees of physical proximity between humans and spirits, villagers and their relatives in diaspora, and Palestinians and Jews, and the relationships, which develop between these groups, are drawn out here.

On interpretation

The interpretation presented here stems primarily from my conversations with villagers in Artas over the course of fourteen months of fieldwork (July 1995 to August 1996). Only a few Artasis had read the story, as some villagers were not literate and, for many, the magazine was expensive. Thus, many of my discussants in the village included those who were told some of the key points of the story as understood by those who had read it. For those who owned copies of the magazine, *Fosta* was often the only piece of written material besides a copy of the Qur'an in their home. I gained further insights from informal discussions with university students in Bir Zeit and Bethlehem, the majority of whom came from villages. These students were likely to have read parts of the story (few had read all the episodes); my research assistant, other students, or I filled in the details of the story to set the stage for discussions about it.

These discussions helped direct my attention to what young people consider important in the story as well as their particular points of interpretation. This story is part of a public and literate discourse, as opposed to stories of the jinn which circulate orally among friends and family of the possessed in Artas. As such, it is a depersonalized story of a young man no one knows. Removed from an immediate, known village context, the story invited its readers/listeners to make more explicit comparisons to their own lives than stories of the jinn which circulate in the village about a particular person. This story thus provided an opportunity for young people who knew

91

its details explicitly to draw more personal meanings from it than they were able to draw from those stories about other villagers. The popularity of the story reflects the extent to which it draws on common knowledge, sentiment and experience. As cultural studies points out, 'popular fiction does something with what people already know' (Teeffelen 1995: 93).

'My Wife is from the Jinn': *a brief summary* Hassan is a young man who, while studying abroad, decides to return to Palestine. Upon his return, he is immediately imprisoned by the Israelis. While in prison he first catches sight of a beautiful jinnia. After his release from his prison, the jinnia appears to him again and tells him that her name is Ghada. Hassan experiences an inexplicable seventy-day paralysis after meeting Ghada, but awakens without permanent physical or mental damage.

Ghada and Hassan quickly fall in love and decide to marry in the traditional way of the jinn. They do this in spite of the risks their marriage poses, especially for Ghada, who will suffer severe punishment from the Katu, the rulers of the jinn world, if her marriage to Hassan becomes known. After a private marriage ceremony, they spend time together in a paradise-like place, part of the jinn world. They realize while in this garden, however, that they are being watched by black cats, known to be helpers for the Katu. They flee to the human world, where Hassan must stay while Ghada continues to flee.

Hassan learns that he has been gone from the real world for forty days and that his mother has suffered from a kind of paralysis due to her worry from his long absence. Ghada discovers the cause of his mother's illness from knowledge available only in the jinn world and continues to visit Hassan. One day Hassan meets an old man named Omar who explains to Hassan that he, Omar, is actually young, but because of the evil influence of a jinnia named Ghada, he has aged quickly. Hassan severs his connection to Ghada immediately.

One day a jinnia who looks like Ghada appears to Hassan, threatening him. Hassan returns to Omar, hoping for an explanation, only to hear Omar triumphantly exclaim that he is part of the Katu. The jinnia who looked like Ghada reappears to Hassan, explaining that her name is Marah and that she will make him suffer as Ghada is suffering in the prison of the Katu. We further learn that Marah is Ghada's sister. To prove her strength, Marah makes Hassan appear the fool when he and his family go to the home of one of Hassan's female relatives to (unsuccessfully) engage her. Marah then tells Hassan she will help him free Ghada, but he must first find a man named Nur, who lives among humans but is actually a jinn. Hassan must bring Nur to the world of the jinn or be prepared to kill him.

Hassan begins to desire Marah, who eventually seduces him. In the meantime, Hassan and Nur become friends. Nur explains to Hassan that Marah is a guardian of the Gates of Evil. If a man passes through the gates and then escapes with the guard, the man will allow him to become powerful. Passing through the gates is dangerous; Nur and Hassan propose to help one another reach the gates, but from that point each will go his own way to try to escape with the guard and her special powers. When Marah appears next to Hassan, she offers him a choice: he can have Ghada come back to him or he can go through the gates. Hassan chooses to go through the gates. Marah then offers to help Hassan, but he must still help her entrap Nur. At the entrance to the Gates of Evil, Hassan learns that Marah had been in love with Nur, who deserted her to live in the human world.

Diaspora and return

Although the magazine provides neither pictures nor a description of his appearance, Hassan, at least initially, is familiar to many villagers: he spent time in the diaspora but missed his family and decided to return home. As for so many others, his return was not easy; indeed, the moment he stepped off the plane, he was immediately imprisoned by the forces of the occupation. Upon his release he entered, almost simultaneously, his village (after a lengthy absence due to being abroad and then in prison) and (somewhat unusually) the world of the jinn with his marriage to Ghada and subsequent involvement in obtaining her release from the forces of the Katu.

Returnees from the diaspora are well known to have difficulties adjusting and fitting into the social life of their village and accepting the realities of Israeli occupation and infiltration into Palestinian life (Dennis 1998; Kanafani 1995; Khader 1997; Khalidi 1995; Tamari and Hammami 1998). Yet these troubles are rarely discussed forthrightly by villagers, who typically prefer to minimize these difficulties. Yet Hassan's plight as an out-of-place returnee in village life is unmistakable, highlighted by his entrance into the jinn world. Hassan's entry into the world of the jinn may be seen simultaneously as an escape from normal village life, providing a subtle commentary on the difficulties associated with re-entering village life from the diaspora.

It quickly becomes clear that Hassan is a lonely and socially isolated character in the village; in *Fosta* he mentions no human friends and relies only on his sister for occasional help and understanding. While Hassan claims in an early episode that he had begun to fit back into village life (April 1994), a sentence later he tells us that Ghada first appeared to him while he was alone in his room while his family was attending a wedding in the village. It is strange indeed for a young man of marriageable age in a village to prefer to stay home alone instead of going to a wedding. Spending time alone in general is usually frowned upon and, indeed, seen as a dangerous opportunity for the jinn to attack. Time spent alone is also seen as a luxury and thus is rarely permitted by the demands of a young man's family. In Artas, young men are not allowed to disappear without explanation for long periods of time as Hassan does, nor given the freedom to spend hours in daydreams while at home. Their families rely on them for earning a wage and building their homes.

It is well known, however, that the exceptions to these rules are the few villagers who have spent most of their lives abroad and have recently returned to Artas. Often returnees have earned enough money to support themselves for long periods of time in the village without working full-time. They may also choose to be alone rather than to socialize with others in the village because they have lost their sense of belonging – the distance and time apart from their extended families were too great. Further, their exposure to, and possible adoption of, alternative lifestyles and desires set them apart from and may make them morally suspect to other villagers.

The fact that Hassan is an out-of-place returnee may explain not only his isolation and loneliness in village life, but also the source of at least some of his moral failings. Villagers who read the story wonder if Hassan's moral failings as a man and a husband are due to his time away from his village, time spent in the diaspora. Hassan's shortcomings are reminders of the moral failings of those who grow up in places lacking the strict moral code of village life. We may see some of these effects in Hassan: he is a tortured character, filled with self-doubt and given to fits of child-like anger. He demands to know the 'truth' from the jinn who enter his life and is always unsatisfied by their indirect answers. In many matters, Hassan is weak, unable to make up his mind when faced with difficult decisions; he is decisive only after being pushed to make a decision by wounded pride. While under the influence of Marah, Hassan expresses his refusal to marry his relative through an undignified practical joke on her and her family, thereby indicating his (albeit due to the influence of the jinnia) rejection of village social patterns. Hassan reveals his greedy nature – seen in his longing to possess the gold shown to him by Ghada in the jinn world (December 1994) and his decision to traverse the Gates of Evil instead of having Ghada return to him (July 1997). Greed is an undesirable character-istic in a man and is grounds for attack by the jinn. Further, Hassan lacks a well-developed ability to consider his responsibilities to others and act on those duties. As with a village child, Hassan's ability to practise social relations properly is lacking. Hassan, in sum, is not very 'manly'.

Hassan is also a sad figure as a husband to Ghada. He is weak before her, deserts her on account of persuasion by another jinn (April 1995), and carries out acts of infidelity with her sister (November 1995). In contrast, most husbands in Artas believe that it is their responsibility to bring home a wage which supports their family and to deal with their wives and children in moderate and moral ways which are firm without being harsh, but clearly point to their role in establishing certain limits on their family members' behaviour. Thus, husbands will generally decide whether or not their wives may work outside the house and most women will feel obliged to abide by their decision. In many instances, husbands and wives negotiate around issues pertaining to their home and children. Hassan is unable to accept his responsibilities as a husband to a human wife in the village.

Hassan thus has the traits of a failed husband, which may not be so uncommon in daily life for villagers, but are rarely, if ever, discussed outright. Hassan's status as both a returnee/outsider and a man involved with the jinn may allow for the articulation of these sentiments. In a close-knit village, a woman's neighbours may be well aware of her husband's misguided actions (as they are of hers), but neighbours generally attempt to minimize these failings' importance in daily practice. Yet in both the jinn world and within his village as an outsider, there is only momentary escape from the eyes of others – in the jinn world the Katu are omnipresent and one's neighbours are similarly present in village life. Thus, Hassan's failures are known to the members of the jinn world but, unlike villagers in their dealings with one another, the jinn do not 'pretend not to see' his shortcomings. Rather, in the jinn world, as for the outsider in village life, open confrontation as opposed to veiled thoughts and accusations seems to be the norm.

Yet the effects of the diaspora are seen not only in Hassan's loneliness or in his status as a morally suspect outsider. When family members, including husbands and wives, are separated for long periods, their emotional ties to one another may weaken. Most villagers now have loved ones who have lived for years in the diaspora. Maintaining feelings of closeness is often difficult, although far away family members are loved and missed (see Rothenberg 1999). Further, villagers are often deeply disappointed that many family members are unable – or, indeed, choose not – to return to those who love them in the village.

The deleterious consequences of distance for social relations emerge clearly in Hassan's tale: his love for and marriage to Ghada is quickly replaced in the stories as a central theme by his illicit desire for Marah, who claims to be Ghada's sister. Marah's success in seducing Hassan – and his weakness in the face of her determination – are in part due to the fact

95

that Ghada is far away (imprisoned by the Katu), confirming the importance of proximity for maintaining appropriate social relationships. In village life it is rare to have the potentially dangerous consequences of separation so explicitly expressed as they are in Hassan's story; here again Hassan's story of the jinn speaks to what is generally not spoken of directly.

In sum, Hassan is a selfish man who exercises neither his rights nor his responsibilities in village life, hurts those who love him most self-lessly (Ghada, his mother and his sister), and fails in his capacities of son and husband. Why Ghada and Marah continue to be drawn to Hassan in spite of their knowledge of his obvious shortcomings is unclear. Ironically, Hassan's imprisonment, which led to his involvement with Ghada and the jinn world, stems from his selfless decision to return to Palestine; presumably, Hassan, like many young Palestinian men in the diaspora, would not have needed to return. The fact that Hassan does return speaks to his sense of responsibility and a sense of national fidelity. Yet these sentiments are not enough.

Love and desire

While the effects of diaspora threaten some kinds of love, notions of romantic love abound in Artas. Artasis, like villagers throughout the West Bank, watch *The Bold and the Beautiful* (an American soap opera) daily (except during Ramadan when the Jordanian channel does not carry it). Westernized ideas of romance – of choosing one's mate (preferably a hand-some/beautiful stranger), dramatically falling in love and being 'swept away' – are commonly discussed by young people. Hassan's story addresses notions of love and desire that cross group boundaries and lead to far-away and unknown places. In practice, however, in Artas, the majority of young people marry within the village; if a young woman is sent away to marry, she is often fearful for her future happiness, as she will live far from those with whom she has grown up and knows best.

The fact that Hassan fell in love with and decided to marry Ghada, a stranger to village life, forgoing all village practices typically associated with marriage, has numerous repercussions: Ghada is imprisoned by the Katu; Hassan loses his beloved Ghada; Hassan and his family are talked about by the people in the village who heard rumours of Hassan's involve-ment with the jinn and stopped coming to Hassan's home (January 1995); Hassan is tortured by the lure of Marah and the Gates of Evil. In short, Hassan's marriage to his jinnia wife is a bankrupt decision, except for the few moments of happiness he and Ghada shared when they first married (November 1994).

What was the lure of Ghada for Hassan? Ghada is shown in many pictures in *Fosta* as beautiful and is often pictured with long black hair (although she is sometimes seen as blonde), and always with white skin and large eyes. She is tall and slim and wears revealing clothing. Ghada is also bold, visiting Hassan when he is alone in his room and agreeing to marry him when she knew the risks this would pose for her. She is vulnerable to Hassan's doubts that the jinn truly exist and she refuses to state directly that she is from the jinn world.

Ghada in some ways is not so unlike village women. After all, Ghada sees herself as living according to her principles. It is the specifics of her morals, which often, but indeed not always, differ from those of Artasi women. For example, Ghada will not sleep with Hassan until he marries her, she refuses to allow Hassan to kill a rabbit from the jinn world to eat it (a selfish act, in her opinion) and she always keeps her promises. Further, Ghada is honest and does not spare her words when she comments on the weaknesses and downfalls of humans, at times chiding Hassan for his stupidity and selfishness – characteristics, in Ghada's opinion, of most humans. Ghada, like village women, restricts who may see her, appearing only to Hassan among all humans because she feels she can trust him. Yet while issues including fertility and a moral 'cleanliness' are central to women's lives in Artas for establishing themselves as morally upright (Rothenberg 1998, 2004), for Ghada these issues of morality are peripheral (neither she nor Hassan discusses children, and mundane matters such as housework are of no relevance).

Ghada is an essentially foreign being to Hassan. She is more tempting, more beautiful and more difficult to figure out than any women he has ever known. In spite of Ghada's similarities in some ways to village women, it is her foreign qualities that make her so desirable to Hassan. Yet these same qualities make it difficult for Hassan to trust her completely; he episodically doubts her until he finally forgoes her presence completely as a result of the persuasion of the jinn Omar.

These foreign qualities may suggest that Ghada is symbolic not simply of foreign women for the readers of *Fosta*, but Israeli women in particular. In considering the likeness of Ghada to Israeli women, one must consider Hassan's knowledge of Hebrew (highlighted by my discussants as significant). This point underscores the context of Hassan's love affairs in the political context of Israeli occupation. When Hassan is in the hospital for his paralysis (May 1994), we learn that he speaks Hebrew 'very well', although the source of this knowledge is not explained. Speaking Hebrew is great symbolic capital for men (proof that they have worked inside Israel, earned a good wage and are able to 'figure out' Hebrew). Women, however, often view the acquisition of Hebrew with distrust and feel that it represents a moral transgression. Thus, Hassan's fluency in Hebrew strikes a familiar note with his readers – he knows Israeli ways and is not impervious to the moral dilemmas such familiarity often fosters. It is in this context that we must frame his affair with Ghada and, indeed, Marah.

In addition, while distance draws Hassan and Ghada apart emotionally, as it may draw apart villagers and their loved ones in diaspora, it is also important to recall that it was proximity on Israeli-controlled territory which brought them together: Ghada was attracted to Hassan because he, like her, loved the tree in the courtyard of the prison where Hassan was held (Ghada found the tree when she was lost as a child and continued to visit it). Their love was the result of their chance meeting in this place, although they are members of different peoples. Thus Hassan's imprisonment by those with whom he and his family are in close proximity stands in contrast with his experience of falling in love with a jinnia with whom he also shares a space: the possibilities (ranging from persecution to love) for social relations entailed by proximity are made vivid here. Indeed, Hassan becomes so attached to the other prisoners and seeing Ghada that he does not want to leave the prison (April 1994), further demonstrating the possibilities for forming meaningful and deep friendships which stem from proximity.

Like Ghada, Marah is foreign, but, unlike Ghada, she is the kind of foreigner to be feared. Marah is mean, not to be trusted. It is ironic that she appears to be identical to Ghada, for the resemblance is only skin deep. The comparison of Ghada and Marah (foreign sisters who physically resemble one another) speaks to both Palestinian men's and women's impressions in the West Bank of foreign – and in particular Israeli – women, impressions which tend to be extreme. Kind and principled or evil and immoral, foreigners are a constant part of life in the West Bank – they are always nearby – and they infiltrate the moral consciousness of Palestinians in important ways.

More specifically, however, Marah, as the explicit embodiment of anti-virtue and an immoral temptress, is comparable to village women's perceptions of Israeli women's 'loose' ways. Yet the actual exploits of Israeli women are rarely explicitly articulated by village women. In Marah's case, we know exactly what she does. This detailed articulation of Marah's evil acts speaks to jinn stories as vehicles for expressing what is otherwise left unsaid, or spoken of indirectly. Human parallels of Marah – women who are mean and immoral – exist for villagers in daily life. Such women may be Israelis or even women from the village (but always seem to live in a distant neighbourhood). These women, Israeli or Artasi, are the subjects of gossip, their reputations dirtied by the fact that stories about them are publicly known and discussed.

Is Hassan's story, thus, a moral lesson in the dangers of marrying a woman one does not know well and, in particular, risking involvement with Israeli women?[5] Perhaps if Hassan had not been so easily swayed by the lies of the jinn Omar (March 1995) and had been more convinced of Ghada's goodness, the story might have turned out differently, focusing our attention on Hassan's qualities as a man rather than his decision to marry a jinnia and, indeed, on the potentially positive qualities of foreign women. Yet the dangers of the jinn world, symbolic of the dangers posed by the foreign and particularly Israeli world, are none the less clear in the story and cannot be taken lightly. Their opportunity to be close to one another in the prison courtyard may have drawn Hassan and Ghada together, under the externally imposed conditions of imprisonment for Hassan. This situation should be compared to the circumstances of other men who have experiences with the jinn while in prison: Hassan's involvement with Ghada signals social displacement, the experience of power Hassan is subject to.

Further, Hassan's rejection of village life and practices (and the villagers' rejection of Hassan) coupled with the Katu's refusal to accept Hassan into the jinn world, leave the couple with nowhere to go. While the love between Ghada and Hassan may not in itself be an immoral experience, the fact that neither the community of the jinn nor Hassan's village offers the couple a place to live forces the conclusion that the possibilities of proximity, in this case, are limited. Hassan's story may be a lesson that romantic love is an empty choice if it forecloses opportunities to participate in the community or to have a place in village life, an interpretation which focuses our attention not on prescribed preferential marriage rules but on the practices (public performance and maintaining a place in society) which surround and bolster a marriage.

In addition, if television shows such as *The Bold and the Beautiful* inform some villagers' ideas of romantic love, then Hassan's affair with his wife's sister suggests that he is living through an experience very much like an episode of the soap. While romance with a stranger may seem to be an exciting possibility for young people, it is framed by the dangers not only of losing one's place in the village but also of implicating oneself in meaningless affairs with people who do not care about the appropriate responsibilities of a man who is part of a social network. The young people with whom I watched *The Bold and the Beautiful* both giggled over the twists and turns of the characters' love affairs and shook their heads at the ease with which the unions were formed and broken. Social relationships are carefully practised in Artas, maintained through daily acts of reciprocity and respect and controlled through gossip and other acts of honour maintenance. To cut off a tie or treat a relationship with disrespect is a carefully considered decision and, indeed, may not be allowed by those surrounding the individual.

Hassan, having entered the jinn world through his marriage and involvement with the jinn, is outside these village practices, which both protect and control individuals. Hassan's affair with Marah and its implications for his relationship with Ghada and the comment it makes on the weakness of his character as an honourable man and dutiful husband, speak again to the dangers of falling in love with a stranger and disregarding village mores. Foreigners have affairs while married and pursue other dishonourable activities; villagers should be wary of such people's actions, for they contain little satisfaction. Ultimately, this experience of love speaks powerfully to the notion of social boundaries and the idea that proximity is not enough to create the grounds for appropriate relationships.

The love affair between Marah and Nur comes to light after a great deal of scheming which uses Hassan. Nur, it seems, deserted Marah so that he might live among humans. Marah, angry and vengeful, sees Hassan as an opportunity to achieve vengeance with the promise that it would help Hassan rescue Ghada. Here we are again reminded of the contrasts with village life as it should be practised: a woman should not exercise vengeance when deserted by her husband, but rather quietly accept her fate. Of course, an honourable husband should leave his wife only for a good reason: the temptation of a different way of life, as seems to have been the issue in Nur's case, is not sufficient. Just as Hassan succumbed to the temptation of the Gates of Evil, thereby forgoing the opportunity to rescue Ghada, Nur left Marah for his own selfish ends. The temptation of the Other is a powerful force for Nur and Hassan, and has hurtful repercussions for the women they claim to love.

The contrast of these experiences of romantic love with those Hassan experiences with his family are dramatic. Hassan's mother and sister are concerned for his health, and suffer on account of his suffering. His mother visits sheikh after sheikh to help Hassan, but to no avail (and doctors are equally useless). Indeed, the unfortunate woman is cheated out of her money for the sake of useless amulets and charms, a relatively common experience for villagers. Hassan's mother is fearful of the jinnia who she believes has possessed Hassan, while his sister is enthralled by the details of the romance. Hassan's sister is, although only temporarily, his confidante, able to be trusted with important information. The mother and the sister are the only members of Hassan's family we get to know, and then only briefly. Both hope to arrange his marriage to make him happy and both make excuses for him to the villagers to protect him from gossip.

They are close to Hassan as they all live together in the family home, but they do not really know him, a fact of social relations, albeit one rarely discussed. Yet their love for Hassan is reliable. Hassan, however, largely overlooks their love, brushing it aside in favour of his desire for Ghada and his involvement in the jinn world. The love of Hassan's mother and sister, enduring and selfless, is devalued by Hassan who is seduced by the foreign ways and people of the jinn world.

Compared to the complicated emotions Hassan has for Ghada and Marah, his feelings of affection for his mother and sister are straightforward, but lack the immediacy and compelling nature of his feelings for the spirits. Human women, such as Hassan's mother, sister or, indeed, the generic 'relative' whom Hassan was supposed to marry, are bland if morally righteous when compared to the jinnias.

The power of love

'*My Wife is from the Jinn*', through a detailed narration of a Palestinian man's love affair with a jinnia, addresses some important and lesser-known areas of social life, including the experiences of returning from the diaspora and falling in love with foreign women. Villagers in Artas interpreted the story against the experiences of their daily lives – a central aspect of which is the fact that many men in Artas are close to Israelis through their work building Israeli settlements both in the West Bank and inside Israel and the experience of occupation. Village women perceive Israeli women to be largely immoral and suggest that they choose not to learn Hebrew words as Artasi men do. Artasi women implicitly realize the possibilities entailed by their men's proximity to Israeli women on a daily basis.

The story thus suggests what many villagers feel – that the threat of Israel is not solely located in its military oppressiveness. Israel is implicated in the ability of the foreigner to steal the heart of a young village man and persuade him to forgo his place in his village. This disruption of the social fabric of village life is an inverse of the experience of 'losing' one's daughter to an arranged stranger marriage. Women may leave the village, but its public backbone is its young men. To lose such men to the lure of foreign ways is dangerous for the village as a whole and for the young man in particular.

Even if the young men remain in the village, however, they must be participants in the public performances of village life, such as engagement and wedding rituals, and the rights and responsibilities of being fathers and sons. To brush off such roles is to threaten village social mores from within. Television shows which demonstrate alternative lifestyles may provide entertainment but should not actually be lived by villagers, men or women. This power of the foreigner to steal the hearts and/or the bodies of young men who experience desire for the foreigner is intrinsically threatening to the life and future of the village.

The fact that the foreigner who may steal the young man may be symbolic of an Israeli, a close neighbour, reveals another dimension of the power dynamics addressed in the story. Proximity entails a potential for social relations and, as such, is a powerful force for the creation and maintenance of social ties and the disruption of others. The power of proximity is demonstrated through the repressive actions of the Katu who act as a symbolic parallel to human neighbours, Israeli forces and the Palestinian Authority, who attempt to control one's actions. Further, by not granting a place to Hassan and Ghada, the jinn world and Hassan's village demonstrate their ability to control who is allowed to enter their respective worlds and who is not.

Yet the power of proximity is seen not only in attempts to repress it; it is seen in the creation of the possibilities it entails. Ghada's entrance into Hassan's life is such a productive possibility, as is the appearance of *The Bold and the Beautiful* daily on Jordanian television. For Hassan to imagine life without his village so that he may marry Ghada is also evidence of this power. Hassan's experience of love is an experience of power, of the infiltration of foreign sensibilities. This is attested to by the possibility of the lure of the foreign Other and the idea that entering into partnership with that Other may seem to be a promising path to happiness.

Notes

Parts of this chapter have been reprinted with permission from my enthography, *Spirits of Palestine: Gender, Society, and Stories of the Jinn* (Lexington Press, 2004).

1 *Fosta* (this transliteration of the magazine name is used by the magazine itself) is a monthly magazine published in Ramallah and widely circulated in the West Bank. At the time of my research (1995–96), *Fosta*'s publishers estimated that approximately 25,000 copies were sold each month, which may indicate an actual readership of approximately 75,000 to 100,000 for each issue. It is generally sold alongside newspapers, although most people admit that it has a far more sensationalist tone. The magazine is popular with young people; it contains advertisements for clothing stores, regular features on love and marriage, and stories of popular interest.

2 The first episode was published in April 1994 and continued through most of the following two years until July 1996. The story did not appear in the following issues: August 1994, October 1994, February 1995, May 1995, October 1995, February 1996 and June 1996. After the July 1996 issue, the next episode ran in September 1996; the following episode was not published until July 1997. The stories have since appeared in August and September 1997 (but not in October or November 1997). I have not followed the story since

November 1997. These issues provided a significant amount of material for discussion with villagers in the West Bank. The fact that the story has not yet formally concluded is not significant for the analysis of Palestinian men and masculinity provided here.

When I asked if it would be possible to interview the author of *'My Wife is from the Jinn'*, the publishers of *Fosta* answered that the author's identity will be revealed in a press conference when the story reaches completion.

3 Van der Velden discusses a number of Palestinian women intifada writers' works in Arabic (Velden 1995: 172–85).

4 In contrast, Azzam (1990: 54–7) describes a Palestinian father's anxious deliberations over naming his son. Tuqan (1990: 26–40), an older Palestinian woman, describes growing up in seclusion in Nablus in the 1930s and 1940s.

5 Shammas demonstrates images of the Arab male and Hebrew female in Israeli literature, arguing that in this literature, 'as in every minority–majority discourse, most of the engendered inter-racial encounters in this literature take place between an Arab man and a Jewish woman, mostly in the fringe of an impacted reality' (1994: 170; see his references for a selected bibliography).

References

Ashrawi, H. (1993) 'Women on the Hilltop,' in E. Augustin (ed.), *Palestinian Women: Identity and Experience*. New Jersey: Zed Books, pp. 180–4.

Azzam, S. (1990) 'The Protected One' [1967], in M. Badran and M. Cooke (eds), *Opening the Gates: A Century of Arab Feminist Writing*. Indianapolis: Indiana University Press, pp. 54–6.

Dennis, M. (1998) 'America's Uneasy Export: It's a Hard Life For U.S. Muslims in the West Bank', *Newsweek*, 16 March, p. 37.

Kanaana, S. (1995) 'The Role of Women in Intifada Legends,' in A. Moors et al. (eds), *Discourse and Palestine: Power, Text and Context*. Massachusetts: Martinus Nijhoff International, pp. 153–62.

Kanafani, N. (1995) 'Homecoming', *Middle East Report*, May–June/July–August, pp. 40–2.

Khader, H. (1997) 'Confessions of a Palestinian Returnee', *Journal of Palestine Studies*, XXVII (1): 85–95.

Khalidi, M. (1995) 'A First Visit to Palestine', *Journal of Palestine Studies*, 24 (3): 74–80.

Massad, J. (1995) 'Conceiving the Masculine: Gender and Palestinian Nationalism', *Middle East Journal*, 49 (3): 467–84.

Peteet, J. (1994) 'Male Gender and Rituals of Resistance in the Palestinian Intifada: A Cultural Politics of Violence', *American Ethnologist*, 21 (1): 31–49.

— (1997) 'Icons and Militants: Mothering in the Danger Zone', *Signs: Journal of Women in Culture and Society*, 23 (1): 103–29.

Rothenberg, C. (1998) 'Spirits of Palestine: Palestinian Village Women and Stories of the Jinn', unpublished PhD thesis, University of Toronto.

— (1999) 'Proximity and Distance: Palestinian Women's Social Lives in Diaspora', *Diaspora: A Journal of Transnational Studies*, 8 (1): 23–50

Palestinian men, diaspora and love

— (2004) *Spirits of Palestine: Gender, Society, and Stories of the Jinn.* New York: Lexington Press.

Shammas, A. (1994) 'Arab Male, Hebrew Female: The Lure of Metaphors', in F. Gocek and S. Balaghi (eds), *Reconstructing Gender in the Middle East.* New York: Columbia University Press, pp. 167–73.

Tamari, S. and R. Hammami (1998) 'Virtual Returns to Jaffa', *Journal of Palestine Studies*, 27 (4): 65–79.

Tawil, R. (1983) *My Home, My Prison.* New York: Holt, Rinehart and Winston.

Teeffelen, T. (1995) 'Popular Literature and Palestine', in A. Moors et al. (eds), *Discourse and Palestine: Power, Text and Context.* New York: Martinus Nijhoff International, pp. 93–105.

Tuqan, Fadwa (1990) 'Difficult Journey – Mountainous Journey' [1984], in M. Badran and M. Cooke (eds), *Opening the Gates: A Century of Arab Feminist Writing.* Indianapolis: Indiana University Press, pp. 26–39.

Velden, M. (1995) 'Kill the Wall of Silence, O Sword of the Words: Palestinian Women Writers in the Occupied Palestinian Territories', in A. Moors et al. (eds), *Discourse and Palestine*: Power, Text and Context. New York: Martinus Nijhoff International, pp. 173–88.

6 | Chasing horses, eating Arabs

ROB K. BAUM

Urs bil Kalil [*Wedding in Galilee*] is a contemporary, mainstream Arab feature film intended for mass consumption. The tastes towards which the film appears to have been directed are predominantly Western: though directed by a Palestinian film-maker, the film deliberately exploits the exotic Orientality of Arab bodies, both male and female, while generalizing and equating Arab male sexuality with the politics of dispossession. Even the female doll that appears at the wedding feast is passed hand-to-hand, invoking male fetishism of beauty, female interchangeability, and woman's function as decoy and destructive icon for men. Created by the modern, self-consciously rebellious sources that might best know and resist Orientalism, the film produces an overriding image of Arab masculinity founded on cultural and personal impotence.

The language of struggle

Just as Arabic is another barrier to understanding the speech of Arabs (and vice versa), Arabs in Israeli movies are compelled to tread the linguistic grounds of Hebrew-speaking Israelis to communicate with the majority or 'ruling class'.

> The political films, in contrast [to major Israeli films], have the Palestinian characters express themselves, forcefully, in their own idiom. Such a mechanism obliges the spectator – the films are largely aimed at Israeli and Western spectators – to meet the Palestinian characters on the latter's linguistic turf (of course, with the assistance of subtitles) [...] the films do not simply imply the bilingual and even bicultural dimension of Palestinian existence in Israel, but also evoke the linguistic and social dynamics of a classical encounter between dominated people and colonizing society. (Shohat 1989: 253)

In contrast, *Urs'* credits are written in Arabic and French, most of the artists involved are Arabs and, except for a few short conversations between Israeli soldiers, all dialogue is in Arabic. Reversing the daily expectations upon and representations by Arabs in Israel, none of the Arab characters speaks Hebrew, and the Israeli military governor, Bassen, who speaks Arabic to the villagers, is played by a Palestinian actor (the justifiably famous Makram Khouri). On a basic level, communication is surprisingly successful: called upon to intercede with the army when a horse runs into a minefield bordering the road, Bassen rescues the horse, and therefore its grieving owner. Bassen thus expresses both the role of the benevolent Occupier and, by virtue of Khouri's own ethnicity, Israel's material need for an occupied object. In fact, the Hebrew used throughout the film is terse and marginal, and Bassen (though ostensibly Israeli) cannot translate an Arab speaker's eloquent pathos into Hebrew. This would appear a deliberate tactic of the Palestinian film-maker, indicative of the failure of such communication, of a quintessential and insurmountable difference. Resistance to the dominant culture occurs at the point of language, giving place and geographical identity to this marginalized group (avoiding the Derridean sense of a borrowed or displaced tongue). At least at the level of language, the Palestinian emerges whole.

'Palestinian' is a difficult term, connoting a political problem for Israel for fifty years, since the British Mandate ended in 1948 and the small Jewish contingent won its independence and established its own *knesset*.[1] A history of persecution complicates the colonization of this area, particularly as Jewish settlement in Israel does not simulate the colonial expansion of European powers during the seventeenth, eighteenth and nineteenth centuries. Confronted with indigenous rebellions, European colonials could retreat to their own countries, or galvanize the home citizenry to wipe out the colonies. But prior to British rule, both Jews and Arabs lived here; aided by Resistance groups, facing prison or death, Jews immigrated clandestinely to British Palestine. Then, in the 1940s, Jews came as refugees from concentration camps, already nearly erased in their 'home' countries; they had no other place to go. The Zionist state was, in part, established to assuage world guilt in having acquiesced to wholesale slaughter.

During the war, Arabs fled across the borders, abandoning houses and lands. Many attempted to return and take up their lives in an unforgotten but vanished past, promulgating a vision of 'Palestine' now found on old maps and in Arab resistance organizations. Others accommodated themselves to the increased socio-economic opportunities of the new country and, primarily in the northern regions (not within the contested territories of the West Bank), called themselves 'Israeli Arabs'. When the film was made, the concept of an Arab–Israeli peace founded in world summits was more distant than at any time since 1948. Arriving forty years after the war, in the beginning salvoes of the 1987 intifada, this film depicts a range of choices and Arab social 'types': the elderly who survived the war and wearily desire quiet and some kind of peace; angry young men who despise their grandparents for co-optation and seek to rout the establishment;

middle generations (mere children in wartime), politically ambivalent[2] and spiritually impotent, wanting more (or less) for their children than they experienced.

Although inequities certainly exist at the economic level, the Muslim Arab in Israel is not, per se, a social outcast or enslaved worker: sheep and goats still dot ancestrally owned lands; Ottoman houses ring with Arab music in small villages and major cities; Arab children attend schools taught in the state's second official language, or integrate into Hebrew schools. What remains problematic is the self-identified 'Palestinian', the Arab living within Israel's borders but rejecting Jewish claims to self-governance and modern statehood. Many (not all) Palestinians live in the West Bank and Gaza, the Occupied Territories now populated by right-wing Jewish settlers, the site of frequent confrontations between rock-throwing Arabs and Israeli tanks. Since the onset of the current intifada, Arab identity throughout Israel is naturally under negotiation, and Jewish relations with their Arab brethren (by which I mean not only Muslims but also Arab Christians) are shattered. While predicting the outcome of the intifada would be foolish, this movie speaks not only to its time but also to ours, reflecting the conditions of many Arab villagers today. *Urs Bil Kalil* takes place far from the hotbed of Gaza and Hebron, in a northern mountain village near Nazaret (Jesus's presumed home). Here the Arabs depicted have fierce alliances to the political exiles/escapees of the war, maintain their own small social, separatist government under a *mukhtar* (leader), and have little (and then essential) interaction with the Israelis. The movie therefore employs a Palestinian perspective away from 'the front'.

Despite its Palestinian provenance, the film was edited in Paris (as are many Israeli films), and maintains many of the traditional Western associations with the Arab world. These associations may well be a kind of breakthrough for an Israeli audience accustomed to viewing Arabs only as threats, uncomfortable with the idea of eating with Arabs, participating in Islamic rituals, or entering Arab homes. Because these actions are accomplished without incident by the film's 'Israeli' soldiers, the film encourages Israelis to reposition themselves, even briefly, as objects rather than subjects in Muslim/Jewish interaction.

Urs portrays a docile Arab community in opposition to a coarse, fascistic occupying force bent upon consuming the native population. (At this time the Israelis occupied Lebanon.) The only sympathetic Israeli is a single female soldier whose unruly sexuality places her literally inside private feminine Arab custom and the mysteries of Arabic womanhood. Arab female sexuality, super-imposed by masculine prerogatives, is displayed throughout the film as feminine weakness, castrating control, American corruption and

Middle Eastern purity–seductive contradictions. The historically oriental-ized Arab female is not liberated from a sexual context but rooted in it as if in a 'natural' strength, still freely available for the viewer's (male) gaze and (female) imitation. Arab male sexuality follows the customary pattern with its more active and sophisticated inscription of 'normal' desire and equally desirable loyalty between men, in Orientalist parlance simultane-ously heterosexual and homosexual. While proofs of a similar masculine ethic abound in the Occident, Islamic Arab culture[3] does not seem capable of discarding its reputation of female and male licentiousness.

These paradoxes need not (perhaps should not) occur in a film profess-ing accurately to represent indigenes' views of themselves. Directed by a Muslim male seated within Arab culture, the film's construction of female identity and Arabic innocence carries the presumption of 'authenticity'. But in fact the authentic Islamic sexuality expressed by Michel Khleifi's film replicates the major depressing themes of Orientalism. The enemy is Westernized only in relation to the bureaucratic trappings of militaris-tic office, remaining sufficiently Middle Eastern to constitute an(other) oriental Other.[4] In this allegorical romance with the enemy, women are emblematic of a pre-history of conquest where Israeli and Arab men have already conquered their Other. Islamic masculine interaction locates itself in the present conflict in the arenas of women's bodies – channels for male communication, depositories of (vanquished) hopes, oases from the repression of Palestinian rights.

Teshome H. Gabriel identifies three phases in Third World film-making:

1. unqualified assimilation
2. remembrance (nostalgia, folk myth)
3. combative (film as ideological tool) (Gabriel 1989: 30–52).

In Palestinian film-making, however, there has yet been no real move-ment towards assimilation, and the intention of this film is ideological rather than placatory. Israelis are not like Arabs, but hated opponents. The Israeli is an ambiguous, masculine construction: not wholly Western despite his armament, not wholly Eastern despite physical resemblance to Arabs. The Israeli male has a buried, dormant appreciation for common beginnings, yet enters and violates village environs, endangering its cultural fetishes. Since the 1987 intifada, the Israeli has been synonymous with the military, a uniform signifying torture and death.

This Israeli cannot affect the 'true' (symbolic) Palestinian, loyal to the land as to an ideal. Instead, Arab inhabitants alter the perceptions of Israelis through complex negotiations of identity. Arab males behave as their Israeli male counterparts, speaking two languages, wearing two garments, navigating two cultures. Under the ministrations of Arab males at Urs' Palestinian wedding, Islam appears ever more penetrable, humanly compelling and sensual, its men possessed of secret capabilities and sensations. The Arab world personifies an exotic banquet. As the military governor reminisces to his staff: 'You should pray to the God of Israel that he let you taste the food in Aleppo one day.' Ironically, the governor's remarks are made to a young female soldier, and about another conquest. The Arab possesses a taste and culture the Jew can only destroy, not create, defeating the Arab neighbour. In the language of this film, Jews cannot compete artistically but are shallow occupiers, new to the area and not innately its owners. From the Islamic Arab perspective,[5] the Jew does not belong in the Middle East.

The Palestinian position

> Israeli movies about Arabs tend to project Arabs as political, religious and psychical Others, members of an occupied population, and third class citizens (the second class ordinarily formed by Jewish immigration's latest wave). The Palestinian in Israeli cinema is seen largely within combat circumstances, the Arabs are almost always presented in long shot [...] their great numbers, in soldiers and tanks, contrast with their minimal impact on the spectator. They are not privileged with close-ups and are often identified as the enemy through the synecdochic kaffiya on the head and gun in the hands. During the battles, the camera is literally 'on the side' of the Israeli soldiers, virtually suturing the spectator into a pro-Israeli position. (Shohat 1989: 61)

Urs bil Kalil, technically included under the label 'Israeli cinema' despite its Palestinian provenance, belongs to another category of Israeli movie-making in which the Palestinian voice is given prominence and the spectator, too, is 'virtually sutured' into a sympathetic, if not pro-Arabic, point-of-view.

Although Khleifi relocated to Belgium, the award-winning film represents an economically reduced yet physically compelling view of Palestinian life. The Arabs are attractive, articulate, mannerly and communicative, in contrast to the brooding silences, taciturnity and opportunism exhibited by the Israeli soldiers. The village landscape is unfettered and 'natural', especially in comparison with the opening descending shot of the Israelis' imposing municipal building. Even at the wedding (to which the Israelis 'cleverly' invite themselves) the soldiers come as soldiers, emblazoned with the symbols of military life, assault rifles cocked in their jeep, loudly

109

expressing their contempt for the Arab object. The Israelis sit, eat and talk together, wedded to an obdurate superiority.

Feminized by the Israeli social structure, whose national ethic to survive permits alternate narratives but a single conclusion, the Arab men loathe military control but cannot openly resist it: masculinity dooms them to eternal Israeli suspicion. Khleifi remarks Israelis' taste for Arab exotica but collective failure to grasp Arabic itself (if only as a protection). Retaining the essential sexualized corruption of those biologically gendered 'female', Khleifi permits the female characters a range of motion and emotion not available to men; Arab women are thus free to attack Israelis as long as the soldiers themselves remain unaware of it. Arab and Israeli men sit and eat, static forces, their plans grandiose and abortive. Only the women act, preparing for days and nights to come, manifesting a greater psychological strength. Although the entire community is accustomed to the inferior position of an occupied people, the women are additionally trapped beneath their husbands. Located at the bottom, with the least to lose, the women reverse the situation and become those with most to gain. Perceiving what can be safely won in this invasion, they take necessary steps to protect themselves and their helpless men.

Plot lines

Relations between Israeli Jews and Muslim Arabs are at their lowest ebb in these waxing moments of the intifada, and the village languishes under an unreasonable curfew made even earlier during the wedding week. The beautiful fields bordering the village are impassably mined, increasing the sense of isolation and restriction. In private conference with the governor, the male officer conceives a plan to infiltrate the Arab village under the guise of dropping the rigid curfew, to which Mukhtar Abu Adel generously (but not naïvely) responds by inviting Bassen as his guest of honour for the duration of the wedding.

Homi Bhabha's dictum that colonial discourse is an apparatus [whose] predominant strategic function is the creation of a space for a subject people through the production of knowledges in terms of which surveillance is exercised and a complex form of pleasure/unpleasure is incited (Bhabha 1983: 23) is precisely illustrated by the opening plot moves of this movie, especially the decision explicitly to 'exercise a surveillance' of the Palestinian villagers with their permission. The governor's strategy is to cajole the Arabs into participating in their own violation. Beautiful classical music with Arabic motifs climbs a Western scale, deftly illustrating structural dominance, conflict and the possibilities of wedding divergent cultures on Western terms.

The Mukhtar's poetic homebound reverie is broken by the realities of the village to which he returns: women smiling as they quietly work; young men idly watching; a small boy running crazily through tumbled stones. Abu Adel's wife, angry at hosting the tyrants, still comes to respectfully warm and undress her husband; an indolent village girl, legs splayed, sits on the stones combing her hair; a boy amuses himself by chasing a chicken in the courtyard. Israeli soldiers slow their jeep to shout at a group of Arab women walking together. As the ululations of an old woman in the background punctuate the songs of the men in the foreground, a shapely young woman in American denim eavesdrops on the plot of local groups to assassinate the military governor while he is in the village. Old people and children go in to bed early as families continue to sit outside in the legislated near-darkness. Cuts of shadowy groups, a coffee cup and the Mukhtar's deeply scarred face isolate individuals in their own thoughts as evening descends.

Although Abu Adel appears to have sold out to the Israelis, he is morally conflicted. Unlike the whispering men, the Mukhtar has lived through war with the Jews and the dispersal and death of family and friends. Much as he might wish to escape the Occupation and restore personal and cultural virility, he knows the futility of fighting with a stronger opponent. To have been diminished to begging the military governor for the privilege of continuing the wedding under curfew has already significantly weakened the Mukhtar's position in the village and his own sense of self-esteem; as he tells Bassen, 'I have sworn on my life before the whole village' to hold the wedding this month. Now, in accordance with Arab custom, Abu Adel is doubly honour-bound to protect the Israeli soldiers as his guests. The visit is a sacrificial act on behalf of his son, costing him the necessary prestige and power to restrain the cabal from violating the wedding and completely destroying his honour. The wedding ought to bring luck and new life to the village, but brings instead the promise of death.

Opposing forces of Israeli/Arab, Jew/Muslim, male/female and aggressor/aggressed are symbolically signified in the body of the younger sister of the groom Adel, who jealously confronts herself in a full-length mirror in their father's house on the morning of the wedding. Attired only in white underwear, Samaya poses, looking at her naked breasts. In a languorous, unnarrated moment fraught with tension (at any time the door may open; she may be exposed), Samaya carefully dresses herself in her father's kaffiya (headscarf) and black aqal (headcord), an assumption of men's garments and therefore of men's power. Gender, the film seems to suggest, is child's play.

But this scene is a microcosmic development of Khleifi's Orientalist ideology, displaying highly sexualized imagery in short, plot-justified cuts.

Beneath the traditional Arab male dress, the body is unquestionably a woman's, vividly available to the filmic spectator positioned as voyeur. Denied a passive role, the viewer is forced to view the Muslim woman as an erotic object. This happens without the viewer's complicity, without regard to the viewer's own political views. Masculine fulfilment will elude the Arab woman, reduced to the way she wears, and bears, her nakedness. Outside this room, Samaya will never enjoy masculine power, except over other women (but she will briefly taste that pleasure). For this reason Samaya's naked body is only nominally 'Arab' – unlike that of her parents – her colour and features nearly identical to those of the Israeli female soldier from the military office. The women could be sisters, even if their men could never be brothers.

In addition to dressing like a young Israeli woman in American jeans, Samaya defies her father, secretly smokes marijuana cigarettes, tries to seduce her younger brother Hassan into smoking with her and finally seduces Tali, the Israeli female soldier. 'Marry her off,' someone says; 'that'll shut her up, like all the others.' The Mukhtar calls his daughter a traitor; she has learned to capitalize upon her stigma as village temptress. Having overheard the group's secret planning, Samaya threatens to turn them in to her father unless their leader, the ex-convict Ziad,[6] goes with her (to make love). Samaya's uncontrollable sexuality is therefore also the saviour of the entire assemblage.

Screening male/female sexuality

For Palestinian women, marriage means a future of silence, a lifetime of distance from the outside world, similar to the juxtaposition (during the movie's opening scroll of credits) of children playing in the dust as a jet plane rumbles in takeoff. The future is elsewhere, moving in a different direction; here is nothing but the present, a dirty game. Sexuality of women under Islam is constructed for women as receptively innocent and aggressively corrupting. Ladislav Holy writes:

> the product of numerous exegeses of the Koranic text and hadith by medieval scholars and jurists [...] have, in many respects, become more important than the Koran and hadith themselves in shaping the Islamic tradition ... [A]s Mernissi has forcibly argued: 'the whole system is based on the assumption that woman is a powerful and dangerous being. All sexual institutions (polygamy, repudiation, sexual segregation, etc.) can be perceived as a strategy for containing her power.' The woman's power derives from the fact that she is 'endowed with a fatal attraction which erodes the male's will to resist her and reduces him to a passive acquiescent role'. (Holy 1989: 119)

Fatima Mernissi's Freudian reading of the female libido as Islam's un-
holy problem may seem antiquated to modern readers, especially those current in Arab women's writings.[7] Unfortunately, the arrival of Arab feminist
academics does not mitigate the existence and influence of essentialist
concepts. Even the proponents of Arab women's rights may be speaking
of one world while living in another, as when indigenous female anthropologists working in Arab populations must contend with the limitations
of 'good Muslim women' – limitations they are expected to know, if not
possess.[8] Arab female sexuality is a category as dangerously loaded as the
politics of Arab dis/possession: woman is both the possessed and (because
of her intrinsic instability and strange spirituality) the uncontainable. In
postmodern cinema, woman has come to symbolize the land as the site
of Nature under cultivation – or correction. In Israeli/Palestinian politics
(where petroleum is a foreign issue), land is also where history begins.
Land is first wife. Weddings denote the merging of family, increase of
livestock and grazing area, and the ability better to protect oneself and
family from others. The acquisition of a bride for a son is a secondary
rather than primary element in traditional Arab marriage.

Urs depicts traditional undressing and washing of the bride and her
enclosure with other women, a social sequestration to which the bride
must now become accustomed.[9] The gesture of leading the new bride on a
horse enacts the bride's elevation as royalty, and her translation as a horse:[10]
an Arabic symbol of grace and devotion, a carrier of the couple's burdens,
another connection to land. In a Western context, women are 'fillies' or
'mounts', carriers of burdens and family histories. The true Arab stallion
is a double for the Arab man, symbolizing his historical independence,
nomadism and love of beauty. The idyllic image of the wild horse that leaves
no tracks directly opposes that of a heavy tank furrowing the countryside.
Arabs – men and women – exist in, rather than apart from, Nature. Jews
pass through the land in excess, building roads, schools, hospitals, the
military and topological terror. What remains is not the Palestinian Arab's
contribution of Art and Nature, but the service institution – in historical
terms, merely a social trace.

Symbolic elevation of the bride's body to horseback, a poetic allegory
for Arabic love and masculine identity, is depicted in Abu Adel's almost
religious dedication to his beloved animal, whom he kisses before kissing
the bride, whom he asks to 'hold up your head like a proud virgin', and
to whom alone he relates his dreams. When the horse strays into the
minefield, the village is helpless to retrieve him without further endangering human lives; he must be 'rescued' by the Israelis, who can read their
military diagrams and translate maps of death and injury into life-saving

113

steps. Military might is presented as a service for the individual unable to help and protect himself: not only the horse, but also the Mukhtar relies upon the soldiers' ability to translate adequately. Militarism is another language over which to gain mastery yet, unlike Hebrew, one that the Arabs in their state of dispossession cannot acquire. Ella Shohat calls the film a 'modernist "allegory of impotence"' (1994: 10). The one word of Hebrew spoken by Arabs (directly after two small boys discover the horse) is 'Shalom', meaning 'hello' and 'goodbye' but also 'peace', a neatly compressed blessing. Hebrew is equally the language of death and disease: as a child tells us, the field was mined to prevent the Arabs from farming in the spot – planned brutal waste. And children are the most likely to happen upon buried mines, ending childhood in a gory second.

Thrilled at touching a thoroughbred, the boys let loose the Mukhtar's white horse. Boys can achieve what adults cannot, symbolically releasing the village leader's virility in a classic image. The music track signals a difference: the horse stands peacefully in a grove, as if tamed by a word of peace. Underscoring the sensuality of the horse, the boys also discover a woman's naked body, lying still in the field. The man with her moves, but she lies as if dead, her breasts clearly visible in the yellow grass. She is without identity. This sentiment is echoed later, when the groom prematurely ejaculates on to the bridal bed and violently shoves his bride away. Women are exchangeable, spaces standing in for other spaces. But male sexuality, customarily intact, is so feminized by the oppositions of Israeli governance and Arab honour, that it, too, can be irredeemably violated.

Despite the fact that the Israelis are solely responsible for the danger in which the horse now stands, the depiction of the Israeli soldiers is unusually sympathetic in this portion of the film. As involved with the horse as the Mukhtar, they are able to project their true feelings of humanity on to the empty screen of the white animal's body. A 'dumb' animal, the horse becomes the only feasible body of communication between Arab and Jew, ignorance of danger the only possibility of 'running free'. The horse mediates the withheld emotion of the Israelis, who bind back any compassion in stiff regulation uniform.

But allegorical violence is not limited to Muslim/Jewish interaction. In an early scene, an anonymous woman sings a love song in the darkness. Suddenly a rifle fires, and a man shouts at the woman: 'Shut up!' War and violence take precedence over love and passion. Illustrating the combinatory tensions of physical aggression and sexual impotence, which characterize Israeli civil life, another scene depicts an Arab man raping his wife. She has not permitted her husband to touch her for seven months and wants a divorce. Three young conspirators happen upon the woman fighting her attacker, begging for her freedom. Subverting viewer expectation, the men do not constrain the woman, participate in the assault, or even casually permit it to continue (in accordance with Arab custom that demands women's fidelity, the return of female escapees to their attackers, and murder of the victims).[11] Instead, the men deliberately interrupt the attack, placing them curiously on the side of the Arab female as feminized, endangered and needing masculine protection. That protection is ironically what the Israelis pretend to offer, exchanging the hand of one defiler for another. Although the men have prevented this rape, without a radical alteration in the wife's domestic situation she will be subject to other rapes other times. In this world, it is impossible to escape some form of tyranny or patriarchal oppression.

Feminizing the enemy

Death and submission are not the sole available responses to male aggression: two disparate fainting scenes stand out among the displays of Arab female weakness and inferiority. The first is narrated visually, from the point of view of Israeli female Tali, through quickly changing frames, disorienting montage and unfocused lenses. Drinking too much arak (anise liquor) at the banquet, Tali suddenly faints, her glass dropping from her hand as she falls forward. Its breakage clearly recalls the required breaking of glass at Jewish weddings, undertaken by the groom under the chuppah (wedding canopy) as a demonstration of strength and recognition of ethnic sorrows. The drunken Tali is carried quickly into a nearby house and placed in the women's quarter, to which the male soldier follows her, calling Tali's name. Arab women place themselves between the Israelis, shrilly ululating in the darkness. The traditional Arabic call of celebration is used as a warning. Fearfully, the officer turns away. Tali wakes to the women's ministrations and communal blessings.

The following scene arises from *The Arabian Nights*. Everything most feared in the confrontation of the West with Arab sexuality is present in this women's quarter cum cinematic bordello, complete with anointing oils, flowing veils, flickering candlelight, sensual caresses and silent conversations. Eroding the Israeli masculine, women gracefully remove Tali's uniform, garb her in Arab women's robes, smooth her between soft layers of bedclothes. She wakes with breasts unbound, to the magnification of everything in the room: curled hair, whispers, the clank of bracelets, lost glasses, perfumes. Voices in the room fade away; lying sensuously upon the floor, Tali strokes herself. She reaches to touch a woman, only to find herself alone: Israeli sexuality is a gift, a loan, from her Arab sister. The

115

wedding's true bride dances as, standing guard outside, the unseen male soldier sleeps: Israeli virility is a dream. As Tali completes her transformation, the soldier breaks into the boudoir, tearing away the veils. Israeli military presence again saves imperilled femininity from its own iconographic sexuality.

Soldiers in uniform are gendered male in the movie's encounter between Arab and Israeli. Even out of uniform, Israeli women have more socio-economic power than Muslim men. Western audiences sit outside looking in, perceptions and fears of the Other intact. If 'true' Arab nature is to be communicated to Western minds, it must be embodied by Western bodies, an unthinkable experience for Israeli men. How much more so for those who fought in Lebanon. The film relies upon the oriental motif of the feminized as weak, spiritual, accessible and receptive – not the national character of Israeli women – in order to permit a fantasy. Without this lie, there can be no meeting, however allegorical, of Arab and Israeli. Even so, the event must occur in an Arab village, outside the boundaries erected by Israelis, and the 'soldier' must be eliminated with its full load of antagonistic symbolism. Finally, if Tali is genuinely to transform, it must be as a woman freed of national prejudices, a positional shift accomplished partly through her exceeding drunkenness and partly through the medium of Arab women's bodies.

Tali's conversion from straitlaced, buttoned-down Israeli soldier to Arab wife is almost complete. Unlike the young male soldier, who early on comments on the potency of the arak (and eschews it); unlike the older soldiers who share their memories of conquering Lebanon and Syria, and eating in Aleppo and Damascus; the lone female soldier has no experience in the field, as a soldier or with Arabs. Her name (*tali* = dew) is a popular Hebrew name linking her with the natural world and other Israeli women. The movie's first frames show Tali in the office of the military governor, hair tied back, face emotionless and body stiff in official khaki. Upon her arrival at the Arab wedding, her hair is down but the military cap perches precariously atop it; she is the dullest woman present. (All the Arab women at the *haflah* wear dresses and jewellery; their hair and bodies are perfumed.) The conversion to wife and initiation into the domain of Arab sensuality (dark twisting paths, rooms like other rooms opening on to empty spaces) begins with the religiously symbolic act of breaking glass. An older woman, probably a healer, massages Tali's temples and throat with oil, her mouth and – loosening a single button of Tali's shirt – her upper chest, then mouth and lips. The hands expertly loosen the belt and unbutton the uniform, exposing Tali's braless breasts. The filmed moment is frightening and stimulating. Throughout the 'massage' Tali sleeps, devoid of responsibility for anyone's actions including her own. To acknowledge a lesbian encounter with the enemy would utterly shatter the glass separating man and woman, Jew and Muslim, duty and desire.

The movie's plot, with its casual flow of Israeli lies, gluttony and invasiveness, versus Arab hospitality, restraint and helplessness, almost justifies the rape of the foreign woman. Yet despite overt fear of Tali's sexual danger, the threat of rape is minimized, viewers' fears allayed by carefully chosen if unremarked scenes of violence: the near-rape of the Arab woman by her estranged husband; Ziad's refusal of Samaya's advances; Arab women blocking the way of the men as, in the bridal chamber, the groom roughly attempts to penetrate his bride; the survival, unhurt, of the white horse. The infiltration, as such, has gloriously failed: the Israelis are won over – and cast out. Most importantly, Arab men know and respect the bonds of gendered space. Only viewers' eyes, and eventually the will of the fantasizing Israeli soldier, trespass upon the women's encounter.

In these dialogues, the Arab woman remains at greatest risk, as illustrated in the second dizzying scene. The first time we recognize the bride, she is concealed by the women of the village as they dance in a circle about her: as they move aside to frame our view, she stands completely naked and vulnerable in the bath. Not only are we made conscious by this framing of our own voyeurism, but our presence adds to the bodies already in the room and the virtual heat and pressure upon the uncomfortable virgin as, her arms upraised, her hair is plucked and her body rubbed and anointed. The correlation between our presence (the present Arab women conflated with potential Western audiences) and the silent bride's reaction is intended: as the camera/Palestinian film-maker/audience penetrates the crowd, the bride is overcome and drops forward in the bath in a dead faint. In another room, another bath, the groom enjoys a homosocial gathering: Adel laughs and sings as the young, similarly bare-chested men surrounding him rub him with oil and spray him with liquid. He shows no desire to escape. Although undergoing similar ritual events, bride and groom have dichotomous experiences: the groom appears to be fêted by friends, the bride to be painfully prepared by experts. The camera both exposes and offers the Arab woman for consumption by strangers, effectively displaying her luscious nakedness, inability to protect herself, and helpless succumbing to the gaze; the faint betrays a precious Victorian gesture of the appropriate feminine erotic. With this and other encryptions of Arab behaviour, Khleifi portrays an Arabic sensibility willing to prostitute the female bodies it supposedly venerates, and capable of playing back (writing back) the Orientalism we now strive so stringently to deny.

Eating Arabs

The coarsest representation of the colonizers occurs at the wedding in the throes of the celebratory feast. The rapaciousness of the Israelis exceeds their covenant to watch over the Arabs. Their plates are piled high, their mouths disgustingly full. The behaviour of the Israelis is a dramatic contrast to that of the Arabs, who eat sparingly and almost delicately. Immediately upon returning from rescuing the mare, the older Israeli officer asks jokingly if the others have saved him any food, then plunges back into the feast.

As Samaya encounters the young male soldier outside the women's house in search of Tali, the Arab woman within is sensuously massaging Tali's chest and mouth, undressing her, and in general presenting the ambiguous image of Arabic sexuality and provocation that has come to signify the Arab world for Westerners. It is unclear whether the gesture is representative and mimetic, or self-conscious in recognition of Western voyeurism. Samaya plays graphically on Israelis' fear of Arabs, telling the Israeli soldier, 'We're going to eat her alive after the ritual.' The choice of words is deliberate – 'eating' connotes digestive but also sexual consumption – the mention of an unnamed 'ritual' intentionally mysterious and titillating. In case the soldier cannot understand Samaya (she does not know that he speaks her language), she mimes eating her own forearm.

Filmic cuts to the Arab woman's hands on Tali's breasts leave no doubt as to this alternate meaning. Samaya mocks the soldier's concern ('She's your girlfriend?') with seductive laughter. When he disclaims the connotation, Samaya invites him to dance with the women – if he takes off his uniform. The costume of the aggressor is exchangeable for that of the oppressed; one has only to remove it to restore the body of original experience and move closer to the Other. The Israeli soldier cannot remove his uniform without making himself naked, Everyman. But the scene suggests that such a transference – the external accoutrements of Western militarism for the spiritual pleasures of Islamic sexuality – occurs as a seduction, indeed as a betrayal: out of uniform, the Jew in the Arab camp is almost at as great a risk as the Arab woman found in his bed. Both would be subject to death.

But Tali is consumed in and by a world for which she suddenly has no reference: not the world of Arabs but the world of women. In a frame so fleeting that multiple rewindings have failed to reveal it fully, Tali seems at one point to drink from the cupped hands of a woman bending over her. And why are there repeated frames and syncretic noises of perfume bowls, bracelet bowls and glass bottles, first being used then standing silently, if not to suggest that the Arab women are not there at all, that they exist only in Tali's (or the viewer's) overheated imagination, and are therefore our manifest desires? Tali has been transparently transplanted to an Arab 'harem'; the Israeli soldier (who an hour earlier thought only of Arab danger – and his belly) now struggles ardently to reach her.

Tali's conversion to Arab wife is external, the desire of the Israeli woman to experience the Other, a bridge she is more likely to build than her male counterpart whose loaded submachine gun psychologically prohibits the intimate contact it filmically signifies. She can, however, be a bride. Like the Arab bride Samia, her hair is unbound and anointed, her body entirely naked (Samaya is shown partially nude); the uniform falls away and her feet step from the trousers as if from a pool of water (the bride Samia's bath). The nakedness and smallness of the feet are made more sensuous by the camera's attentive focus upon them as Tali dresses. The door opens to show her belted in white and holding two candles, a replication of Samia's wedding dance among the women. Only the candles are unlit, indicating that the act has not (or cannot) be completed, halted at the threshold of sanctity.

And after all the most significant act of the wedding has not, cannot, be consummated: under the conditions of curfew, conspiracy, attempted murder, Israeli rescue and female consumption, the Arab groom collapses, seems childlike and helpless. Adel's impotence is apparent not only to his people but to the Israeli soldiers at the feast: the military governor has sworn that he will wait until the sheet has been bloodied. The people outside, the expectant audience, have become an impenetrable shroud wrapping the bride, who rhetorically encourages her husband, 'If virginity is a woman's honour, where do you find the honour of a man?' Eventually Samia demonstrates the sexuality necessary to seduce a man and even a community: forcing herself on to her own fingers, she pierces her own hymen and bloodies the white sheet for display to the village. With this painful act, she proves herself a virgin and a courageous, self-sacrificing woman, but only she and her new husband will ever know what has occurred. Heroism is a domestic duty.

Participating in Western binaries, *Urs bil Kalil* produces a world governed by Arab women and Israeli men – in reality at furthest poles – tacitly respecting each other's boundaries because the dangers of transgressing are understood by both sides to be fatal. The world of the Israelis, encoded as triply masculine – male, soldier, Israeli – is one which swallows its neighbours. In contrast, the Arab men's impotence weights them at every level: rape, murder and finally loving fulfilment escape them. Only a beautiful and speechless animal can hope to run between the borders. After the wedding, the soldiers will go home, but for the Arab women there is no way out. Samaya, who wears the Israeli's modern garments, speaks of being stifled, but the movie never indicates that she considers leaving. Likely she is a traitor – to the conspiracy to kill the military governor. Her Uncle Khamis, Abu Adel's dissident brother, enters moments before the attack, and the assassination, like every other male plan, falls flat. Ironically, Khamis is not against the attack, but only opposed to this plan, which will cost Arab lives.

Stereotypes, including those in circulation about Arab sensuality and aestheticism, contain a portion of the truth, but the movie traffics in signs and symbols which, in the hands of an Israeli film-maker, would be found reprehensible, proofs of an Orientalizing mentality. The Arab world is womblike, dreamlike and welcoming; its women are sensuous, mysterious and experienced in seduction. During the film's most compelling cinematography, when music and images become liquid, we might be convinced it is all fantasy and we shall soon find ourselves sitting merrily at the banquet, eating Arabs. The final scene belies this possibility, when Tali is led from the harem by the young soldier, who must now unquestionably become her lover. Still wearing the Arab garments, she follows in an unprotesting stupor. The fabric of transformation is too newly woven; given more time, real comprehension might come about. But there is no time. As the Israelis walk through the village en route to the military vehicles, the Arabs at last show their hostility by flinging trash and personal items before the Israelis' feet. Nothing has been achieved – not the death of the tyrant, not relaxation of the curfew's chokehold, not even a real wedding with promise of new life. *Urs bil Kalil* would not represent quite so disturbing a picture were it not that it depicts an incontrovertible fact. Years after the surprise Oslo signing (summer 1993), the image of waste abides; Palestinian Muslims and Jewish Israelis represent opposing economies of gender and culture. We all still sit at the table. We have nowhere else to go.

Notes

1 For a better understanding of Jewish/Muslim politics, see especially Stone and Zenner (1994); Shipler (1986); and Weingrod (1985).

2 The ambivalence of some (leftist) Israelis is well expressed in 'Ora Yarden's' interview on life as an Israeli woman activist and lesbian: 'My feelings about the Old City stemmed from 1967. I viewed the Territories as Palestinian [...] If Israelis were to start claiming Hebron, the Old City, the West Bank, then the Palestinians had the right to settle in their old territories – Jaffa, Haifa and Akko. I believe we have no rights in the Occupied Territories, just the power.'

3 Arab Christian culture carries its own negating practices and edicts.

4 In Arabic, 'West' and 'foreign' come from the same root letters, gh.r.b., hence Maghreb.

5 Christians recognize the Jewish legacy in the Middle East, especially in Israel.

6 Ziad was previously incarcerated and tortured in an Israeli prison.

7 Although Arab women's stories are now finding publication, biographical work by (or told by) Palestinian women is relatively rare. Of these, see Gorkin and Othman (1996); Najjar with Warnock (1992) and Shaaban (1988).

8 For an account of the problems of indigenous anthropologists, see Altorki and Fawzi El-Solh (eds) (1988).

9 See Westermarck 1914: 136 and elsewhere. The bride is compared to a (cultivated) field, splattered with water instead of milk if it is a dry year and rain is wanted (p. 180).

10 In his explication of Moroccan customs, Westermarck notes that the mother of the bride walks behind the horse the bride rides, holding its tail so that someone cannot push a finger into its vulva or anus, 'deflowering' it as if it were the bride (ibid., pp. 172–3, 179, 185, 205).

11 The murder of raped women – rather than their rapists – is usually handled by the victims' fathers, brothers or uncles. This is by no means an obsolete custom, as recent Israeli newspapers and radio reports corroborate.

References

Abdul-Rauf, M. (1972) *Marriage in Islam, a Manual*. New York: Exposition Press.

Abu-Lughod, I. (ed.) (1982) *Palestinian Rights: Affirmation and Denial*. Wilmette, IL: Medina Press.

Altorki, S. and C. Fawzi El-Solh (eds) (1988) *Arab Women in the Field: Studying Your Own Society*. New York: Syracuse University Press.

Bhabha, H. (1983) 'The Other Question – The Stereotype and Colonial Discourse', *Screen* 24 (6): 21–32.

Boone, J. A. (1995) 'Rubbing Aladdin's Lamp', in M. Dorenkamp and R. Henke (eds), *Negotiating Lesbian and Gay Subjects*. New York: Routledge, pp. 148–77.

El Messiri, Abd Al Wahhab M. (1982) *The Palestinian Wedding: A Bilingual Anthology of Contemporary Palestinian Resistance Poetry*, trans. A. M. El Messiri. Washington, DC: Three Continents Press.

Gabriel, T. H. (1989) 'Towards a Critical theory of Third World Films', in J. Pines and P. Willemen (eds), *Questions of Third Cinema*. London: British Film Institute, pp. 30–52.

Ginat, J. (1987) *Blood Disputes Among Bedouin and Rural Arabs in Israel: Revenge, Mediation, Outcasting and Family Honour*. Pittsburgh, PA: University of Pittsburgh Press.

Gorkin, M. and R. Othman (1996) *Three Mothers, Three Daughters: Palestinian Women's Stories*. Berkeley: University of California Press.

Holy, L. (1989) *Kinship, Honour and Solidarity: Cousin Marriage in the Middle East*. New York: Manchester University Press.

Khleifi, M. (1987) *Urs Bil Kalil* [Wedding in Galilee] Videorecording, Marissa Films [Arabic with Hebrew subtitles].

Mernissi, F. (1991) *Women and Islam: An Historical and Theological Enquiry*, trans. M. J. Lakeland. London: Basil Blackwell.

Mohanty, C. T., A. Russo and L. Torres (eds) (1991) *Third World Women and the Politics of Feminism*. Bloomington: Indiana University Press.

Najjar, O. A. with K. Warnock (1992) *Portraits of Palestinian Women*. Salt Lake City: University of Utah Press.

Said, E. W. (1978) *Orientalism*, 1st edn. New York: Pantheon Books.

— (1994) *The Politics of Dispossession: The Struggle for Palestinian Self-Determination, 1986–1994*. New York: Pantheon.

Shabaan, B. (1988) *Both Right and Left Handed: Arab Women Talk About Their Lives*. Bloomington: Indiana University Press.

Shipler, D. K. (1986) *Arab and Jew: Wounded Spirits in a Promised Land*. London: Penguin Books.

Shohat, E. (1994) *Israeli Cinema: East/West and the Politics of Representation*. Austin: University of Texas Press.

Shokeid, M. (1993) 'Ethnic Identity and the Position of Women Among Arabs in an Israeli Town', in Y. Azmon and D. N. Izraeli (eds), *Women in Israel*. *Studies of Israeli Society*, vol. VI. New York: Transaction, pp. 423–64.

Stone, R. A. and W. P. Zenner (1994) 'The Arab–Israeli Conflict and the Victory of Otherness', in R. A. Stone and W. P. Zenner (eds), *Critical Essays on Israeli Social Issues and Scholarship*, Books on Israel, Vol. III. Albany: State University of New York Press.

Weingrod, A. (1985) (ed.) *Studies in Israeli Ethnicity: After the Ingathering*. New York: Gordon and Breach.

Westermarck, E. (1914) *Marriage Ceremonies in Morocco*. London: Curzon Press.

7 | Stranger masculinities: gender and politics in a Palestinian–Israeli 'third space'

DANIEL MONTERESCU

A divided soul, which was divided once more. The negation of negation, very similar to Jews who have negated the negation of the Diaspora, the negation of every synthesis [...] Only the exile is home. Identifies with the Intifada but not with its songs and symbols, and not with the culture, which it ostensibly produced. Loathed by the symbols and loves the symbolized [...] Not on the suturing point between the two, but simply not here nor here. (Bishara 1992: 8)

'I envy you,' said Hisham, a Jaffan Palestinian friend, in a moment of sincerity; 'you have two citizenships – Israeli and French – while I have only half a citizenship, but too many identities, the only bad thing to have too much of!' 'We are Banadiq,' added his wife; 'I am a hybrid, a bastard.' This statement epitomizes one of the central dilemmas in the hyphenated existence of the Palestinian citizens of Israel, the dilemma this chapter relates to patterns of gender and masculinity in the Palestinian–Israeli mixed town of Jaffa.[1] The analysis situates practices and conceptions of Arab masculinity within the wider network of institutions and ideologies, arguing that masculinity (*Rujula*), as a central code of behaviour and a dominant category in Arab-Palestinian culture, provides a perspective from which one can examine the politics and poetics of identity in an urban, politically and culturally laden context. By outlining the forces which constitute the Palestinian *Rujula* and by drawing on a postcolonial interpretation of Simmel's concept of 'strangeness' (1971), this chapter unravels Palestinian men's strategies of negotiating, through discursive and non-discursive practices, the tension between conflicting cultural and political alternatives.[2]

The deep sense of estrangement and entrapment that emerges from the epigraph, from my informants' statement, and from additional gender and political identity narratives of Palestinian men in Jaffa, is not without precedent in the cultural history of the Middle East. In 1952, Frantz Fanon was probably the first to address the relations between colonialism and masculinity in his call for the decolonization of both black and white men's minds by means of a process of 'disalienation'. The predicament of the Palestinian citizens of Israel – a trapped minority in a Jewish state – results in a similar strangeness, both as a position of estrangement from and towards the Israeli state and as a mental state of individual and collective 'depersonalization'. Such similarities between the Palestinian and the Algerian cases suggest a colonial common ground for analysis.[3] In this vein, this chapter attempts to write both through and against Fanon: while accepting his main insights, I argue that the mixed context of Jaffa further complicates a colonial space no longer 'a world cut in two' (Fanon 1990), but precisely the spatial dismantlement of such dichotomy. The Palestinian citizens of Israel in general and Jaffa's specific sociological mixed context cannot be reduced to a social world simply divided between the colonizers and the 'wretched of the earth'. By posing a theoretical problem for such a polarized understanding whereby 'the dividing line, the frontiers are shown by barracks and police stations' (ibid., p. 29), the Palestinian–Israeli context calls for a refinement of the analytical tools. The embedded existence of incongruent fissures and contradictions is precisely what constitutes the mixed Jaffa case as a postcolonial site.

This chapter therefore explores the under-studied interface between postcoloniality and masculinity studies (for a path-breaking articulation of this interface, see Ouzgane and Coleman 1998). Combining a theoretical revision of Simmel's conceptualization of 'strangeness' with a postcolonial paradigm, I portray Jaffa as a 'third space' (Soja 1996; Bhabha 1990) betwixt and between social boundaries and dichotomies – a space of constant reformulation of subject positions whose continuing fissures and paradoxes will be the objects of elaboration.[4] In the realm of gender, this space has given rise in Jaffa to a new postcolonial 'multi-essentialist' situational model of masculinity, which embraces but at the same time undermines the main cultural alternatives, namely the Islamic and the liberal–secular essentialist models of masculinity.

The following discussion is three-phased. The first phase surveys the historical and cultural background of the Palestinian minority in Israel during the last fifty years and its influence on patterns of gender and on the patriarchal order. In the second phase, building on ethnographic materials collected in Jaffa and drawing on the Simmelian concept of 'strangeness', I suggest a sociological conceptualization of the encounter between the Palestinian residents and the Jewish 'other'. Finally, following the theoretical lead of Connell's model of hierarchical masculinities (1995), the third phase locates the hegemonic category of Arab masculinity within the context of 'strangeness'. Throughout, the chapter shows how questions of masculinity broaden our understanding of the political embeddedness of gender. These questions offer both the Palestinian men and the cultural analyst a strategy for respectively coping with and making sense out of a paradoxical reality that confronts two sets of discursive opposites: the glory and promise of the past vs. the frailty, fracturing and failure of the present; male hedonism vs. normative responsibility; that which is constructed as 'traditional' vs. that which is conceived as 'modern'; 'Orient' vs. 'Occident'; colonized vs. colonizers. All the above, of course, is not limited to Jaffa, but reflects deep structures in the Arab society in Israel at large. The Jaffa context, however, brings to the surface the conflicts embodied in the asymmetric interface between a dominant and a subaltern culture.

Identity conflicts and dilemmas of the Palestinian citizens of Israel

In his article 'On the Palestinian Minority in Israel', 'Azmi Bishara (1993) criticizes two biased directions in the sociological research on Arabs in Israel. The first is 'the lack of a discussion of the sociological uniqueness of the Arabs in Israel from a Palestinian point of view', and the second is the tendency in research 'to deal only with the political perspective, and more precisely with the "political behaviour" expressed before and after the elections to the Knesset and to local municipalities'. The problem of identity, concludes Bishara, is thus connected only to political behaviour, and vice versa.

As a result, the socio-historical research on the Palestinian citizens of Israel may be divided into two interpretive paradigms (Ghanem 1998). The first – the 'normal development' – may be summarized in its consensual argument that the Palestinian minority has been developing 'normally'. The researchers belonging to this paradigm (Smooha 2002; Rekhess 1998) claim that the Arabs in Israel had recovered from the 1948 trauma, and since then they have undergone a process of national crystallization and are establishing leadership and autonomic political frames of their own. Gradually, the sub-groups of the Arab minority – the Christians, the Muslims, the Druse and the Bedouins in the Negev and the Galilee – are renouncing their separate local clan and religion-based identities and sub-identities, and are adopting one identity, which is national-Palestinian, and parallel to it another identity, which is civil-Israeli. This approach claims that the Palestinian citizens of Israel can now be unproblematically both Palestinians (nationally) and Israelis (civically). In contrast to this normative paradigm, I follow Ghanem in arguing for the 'crisis development' paradigm. This approach rejects, on the one hand, the argument – embraced for opposite reasons by both Zionist normativists and Palestinian nationalists – for one national-Palestinian identity within Israel, and, on the other, the claim that Arabs in Israel had succeeded in establishing an effective unified political leadership and active institutions on the national level. Alternatively, I argue, there is no such continuous and linear line of development along which occurs the alleged undisturbed double process of national 'Palestinianization' and civil 'Israelization' (Smooha 2002: 41). On the contrary, as a result of the state's 'divide and rule' policy, the Palestinian minority in Israel, almost a fifth of the total population, exhibits an intensified process of fragmentation and splitting to local, religious and regional–factional sub-identities. In other words, Palestinians in Israel cannot, under the present structural constraints, adopt a full Israeli civil identity, but neither can they embrace a national Palestinian one. At most, they can hold fragments of identity from the different spheres in which they participate. And indeed, in journalistic interviews, public debates and private conversations with Palestinians in Israel, the following phrases are constantly recurring: multiple identities, dual identity, split identity, paradoxical identities, schizophrenia, strangeness, masks.[5] These expressions reflect the liminal position of the Palestinian citizens of Israel – a 'trapped minority' (Rabinowitz 1996) between nation and state and between conflicting frames of identity.

The mixed context in Jaffa: otherness, strangeness and stereotypes

Jaffa presents a case of a national and cultural minority quartered within an urban environment densely populated by Jewish neighbourhoods (Falah 1996). Fifty years of occupation, land expropriation, exclusion and intentional negligence have made Jaffa a site of volatile and unstable social and cultural boundaries. The 1948 cessation in the urbanization process, the lack of an intellectual elite and of social leadership, and the deep sense of cultural anomie have contributed to the fraying of this social fabric, a severe drug problem and a high crime rate (Mazawi and Khoury-Machool 1991; Shaqr 1996).

This state of a 'suicidal society', as one local resident put it, has caused the breakdown of the system of social norms and has had a significant impact on the patterns of Arab patriarchy, family, and on perceptions of gender and sexuality. Men, traditionally conceived of as guardians of the normative and ethical system (Sutra), stand in the front-line of this confrontation.

During the first years of Israeli statehood, Jaffa was transformed from an Arab into a Jewish city. It lost the autonomous municipal status in effect until 1948 and, following a short period of Israeli military administration, was annexed to Tel-Aviv (Mazawi and Ichilov 1996: 69). The former Arab metropolis, the 'Bride of Palestine', underwent radical demographic changes. The majority of its Palestinian-Arab population – including most of the local elite – were forced to leave during the hostilities of 1948. Only 3,500 (5 per cent) remained of an Arab population estimated to have numbered previously 70,000.[6] At the same time, Jewish mass immigration from Europe and the Middle East poured into Israel and settled in the emptied city. Jaffa, an important seaport and international trade centre during the Ottoman and British rules, became a dilapidated suburb of Tel-Aviv (Avitsur 1972). The 1948 war with its ensuing events precluded any further natural urbanization of Palestinian cities, thus sealing Jaffa's fate.

The social history of Jaffa, as told by my male informants, is a chronicle of moral decay and disintegration of norms and practices that constituted a framework for the old social order. The co-existence imposed upon Jaffa since 1948, claim many Jaffans, is part of a government plot to do away with the spatial differentiation between Jaffa and Tel-Aviv, and thus to 'Judaize' Jaffa and subject it to economic dependence on Tel-Aviv. Following the implementation of this plan, the number of Jewish residents in Jaffa increased. The new reality, influenced by the cultural presence of the Tel-Aviv metropolis, defied predominant codes and eroded the Arab man's authority.[7]

Viewed by residents of Jaffa, the 1948 defeat (*al-nakba*, translated as 'the catastrophe') with the ensuing occupation is a key structuring event for deciphering the bleak historical process taking place in the city. In the socio-cultural sphere, in addition to the experience of national humiliation and deracination from a once flourishing city, an alarming pattern of surreptitious moral disintegration has been creeping in. This process is related essentially to images and practices of Arab masculinity.

The events of 1948 had disrupted the communal and family life of Christians and Muslims alike in Jaffa. The strain was due not only to the dispersion of kin and the relative isolation of the nuclear family, but also to the new type of social environment in which the Arabs were now living, which meant Jewish next-door neighbours and Jewish fellow students, clients and employers (Shokeid 1982: 34).

Postcolonial 'strangeness': ambivalence as an existential state The principle of common belonging, which organizes the symbolic codes of the imagined community, determines who is the 'other' existing outside it and who is the 'stranger' located on its boundaries (Hazan 1997: 161). This middle entity, which I will call (following Simmel, Bauman and Beck) 'strangeness', is located on the boundary between the group and what lies outside it. Consequently, it constitutes a cursor against and through which cultural identity is modelled, but also a threatening object that must be dealt with.

Life in Jaffa embodies a similar inherent tension, a mixture of dense daily co-existence between Arabs and Jews, interwoven with deep cultural distance: from minute daily practices – shopping, dressing, discourse and table manners – to national identity. The combined effect of the actual co-existence, for over fifty years, along with the fact that the next-door neighbour, the employer, or the employee is Jew, blurs the clean-cut dichotomous distinctions between 'us' and 'them' – distinctions which are cognitive and moral. This condition creates a hybrid dialectic between closeness and remoteness, 'here' and 'there', 'otherness' and 'familiarity', locals and foreigners, friends and enemies. It undermines the spatial ordering of the world – the sought-after co-ordination between moral and topographical closeness, the civilized 'here' of friends and the barbaric 'there' of enemies. It creates, in Bauman's terms, a city of 'strangeness': 'There are friends and enemies. And there are strangers. The stranger disturbs the resonance between physical and psychical distance: he is physically close while remaining spiritually remote. He represents an incongruous and hence resented synthesis of nearness and remoteness' (Bauman 1995: 60).

In this vein, 'strangeness' can be understood as a conceptual borderland between communities, categories and cultures; and Jaffa – as a space that produces and inhabits instances of 'strangeness'.[8] This state constitutes Jaffa as a 'third space' which corresponds to Bhabha's conceptualization (1990: 21): 'The importance of hybridity is not to be able to trace two original moments from which a third emerges; rather hybridity is the "third space" which enables other possibilities to emerge [...] The process of cultural hybridity gives rise to something different, something new and unrecognizable, a new area of negotiation of meaning and representation' (Soja 1996: 139).

Jaffa's 'third space' is unique in that its hybridity is not temporary or individual, but permanent, collective and embedded in the social structure. The sliding of the 'other' into the domains of the 'familiar' is present throughout daily interaction. Adopting 'strangeness' as an analytical tool, therefore, results from the desire to avoid reducing the social world of men in Jaffa to 'traditional culture' and to examine it in its spatial–urban and its political–historical contexts. Conceiving the Jaffa case as a colonial product of a modern (Zionist) project, 'strangeness' (and later masculinity) serves as a prism through which the encounter between discourses of 'tradition' and 'modernity' as well as colonial and postcolonial expressions of fragmentariness may be examined.

To modernity and back:[9] three competing models of masculinity

Being a 'stranger' is a structural state embedded within a historical process. For men in Jaffa, it creates an incongruity between the 'real' world of inferior socio-economic and political status and the 'ideal' world of proud

Arabness and patriarchal manhood. Life in the Israeli reality, under the threat of the crumbling of the patriarchal order, paved with asymmetrical interactions with the state and the Jewish local 'stranger', results in an ongoing, intensive confrontation with bureaucratic, spatial and cultural boundaries. One of the expressions of that, for Arab men in Jaffa, is a ceaseless preoccupation with sexual boundaries in general and those of proper masculinity in particular.

Elsewhere I have analysed the relational dynamics of Arab masculinity, whose central mechanism operates through a differential definition of the hegemonic model by its negation (Monterescu 1998): the negation of femininity (Bourdieu 1990), of homosexuality (El-Maniac in Arabic, see Tapinc 1995; Lancaster 1988) and of other types of failed masculinities (Connell 1995), namely, the Western (or the Jew as its private case), the Muqaren (the Cuckold), the Tartur, controlled by his wife, and the Da'if (the weak), who has not sufficiently internalized the codes of manhood, has 'stumbled' and thus manifested one of the traits forbidden to men. As a constitutive category, therefore, masculinity stands at the centre of an imagined polygon and communicates dialectically with each of the vertices. These categories serve as symbolic referential axes from and to which one measures the appropriate cultural distance which marks the inferior alternatives to the hegemonic Arab masculinity.[10]

Although an accurate description of the basic power dynamics of masculinity, this relational polygonal map gives the erroneous impression that hegemonic masculinity is homogenous and coherent (Connell 1995).[11] In Jaffa, the encounter of this polygonal masculinity map with the centrifugal forces of 'strangeness' splits and deconstructs the stable appearance of the hegemonic model.

Just as 'strangeness' deconstructs the 'other' and splits it apart (the 'Jew' conceived as inferior and superior simultaneously), it deconstructs hegemonic masculinity as one category of identity. This cultural struggle takes place in Jaffa between and within different hegemonic masculinities. In the structure of conflict within which Arab society struggles for its identity, different social actors create different forms of essentialist hegemonic masculinities. Thus, in Jaffa, three central models compete over the image of society, man and masculinity: the Islamic, the liberal-secular and the situational.

Strategic essentialism I: Islamic masculinity

Be damned those who resemble the women among the men, and who resemble the men among the women. (Sheikh Bassam, the Imam of Jaffa, quoting a hadith)

129

A city of strangers, Jaffa is an arena of conflict between opposite tend-encies. Against the backdrop of the cultural and political anomie of the town, this confrontation gives rise to strategic essentialisms which mobilize public opinion around the idea and ideology of authenticity: the 'Islamic Movement', continually strengthening in Jaffa – around universalistic, all-inclusive Islamic principles, and the secular intellectuals; around the particularism of the nationalist idea. These two strategies are also an answer to a part of the masculine patriarchal crisis.

THE POLITICAL ESSENCE: ANTI-IMPERIALISM The Islamic movement in Jaffa is a social agent that carries an all-encompassing ideology – the main principles of which are threefold: the return to the sources of Islam, the turning away from Western culture, and the fight against imperialism through pragmatic activism combined with a strengthening of the Islamic educational infrastructure (Meyer 1989; Israeli 1993).[12] These principles are articulated in the words of Sheikh 'Abd-Allah Nimr Darwish, the head of the movement: 'We adhered to the west, we aped its culture, and in this process we lost our personality. Imperialism drew its armies from the Arab countries, but western ideas and life-styles still prevail there. Now, the Arab nation understands that before even being defeated in the battlefield, it was defeated in the realm of principles and ideology' (Hassan, 1989: 36).

The abandonment of Islam is conceived, then, as the primary source of evil for the Arab world, and modernization as the main reason for its failure and weakness. Thus, only the return to religion and the rejection of Western culture, the restoration of religious education, and the establish-ment of Islamic regimes founded on the principles of the Shari'a can heal the disease of the Islamic world.

Today, the Islamic Movement attracts increasing numbers of women and men of all ages, turning to religion for meaning and a cure against crime, corruption and nihilism. 'Islam is the Solution' – the slogan of the Islamic Movement – denotes a sociological truth that clarifies the circumstances of its success. It offers a total yet pragmatic solution for the problems of society and a mythical yet concrete prescription for every personal and societal pain.

THE GENDER ESSENCE: 'COVERED' WOMEN AND PIOUS MEN The Islamic 'solution' dictates also specific perceptions and practices of gen-der.[13] From the image of society explicit in the Islamic Movement's ideology, we can extract its implicit image of masculinity. The model is constructed, on the one hand, against the backdrop of the Western anti-thesis, conceived as materialistic and corrupting, but also against conventional customary

'Arab' norms (opposed to 'Islamic' ones). The cultural struggle with the 'West' (including in Jaffan eyes, Israeli state institutions and hegemonic culture) and the rejection of its values is a central motif in gender perceptions and sex roles among the members of the Islamic Movement. Sheikh Bassam wrote a satirical essay on the occasion of Women's International Day, to which he objects as 'demeaning' for women, because he believes women ought to be respected all year long, and not for just one day. He writes in *Al-Mitahq*, the official journal of the Islamic Movement (March 1998):

> They want to celebrate child's day, and human rights' day and women's international day. But, God knows that they don't respect the innocence of the child, nor the human rights, or the purity and honour of the woman. They want to free the woman from male domination and give her equal rights? Is she a prisoner in her home that she needs to be freed? They free her from morality and purity. They make her into a cheap merchandise, she goes to parties as if she was a model, but not to show her clothes but rather to expose as much as possible of her body to the eyes of the human wolves who might not control themselves and might trap her in their sly nets and pollute her purity and add her to the list of the traitors to the Holy marriage.[14]

The grammar brought by the Imam of Jaffa marks a central cultural tendency which characterizes the Islamic model of masculinity. This model anchors the symbolic capital in an ordered worldview, in religious practices and in codes, which define the division of labour, the nature of conjugal relations and the space of permitted behaviours. In contrast with the concepts of 'openness', 'progress' and 'modernization' in the 'secular' discourse, this model preaches to 'modesty', 'shyness', and 'purity' and presents an institutional position of 'authentic' masculinity.

Strategic essentialism II: liberal-'secular' masculinity

> At our place, to tell you the truth, it's not clear who is the boss. The religious man is allowed according to the Shari'a to beat his wife a bit. But when someone educated is beating – it's not appropriate. (Rafiq, social worker)

The main cultural alternative to the Islamic model in Jaffa is a secular one opposing the categorical rejection of the modern West (Chatterjee 1993). Indeed, in the political-cultural discourse in Jaffa, the concepts of 'modernity' and 'secularism' are used extensively as a token of liberal enlightenment and as a rhetorical device in the polemics with the Islamic

131

Movement. This cultural preoccupation with the concepts of the 'West', 'modernity' and 'progress' links the discourse on Arab-Palestinian nationalism with the discourse on masculinity, gender and family.

THE POLITICAL ESSENCE: LIBERAL PALESTINIANNESS The programme of the Islamic Movement presents an ordered and efficient agenda for the re-formation of Muslim individual and community striving for the Utopia of the Islamic Shari'a society. In contrast, the secular-nationalist position represented by the Rabita, the local association 'for the promotion of the Jaffan Arabs' interests', focuses mainly on community organizing and political protest at the municipal level to mobilize the Palestinian inhabitants in terms of a united national Arab identity. One of the association's brochures reads: 'The Rabita unites a large number of the highly educated and politically conscious in the community. It is based on a national basis rather than on a religious-factional basis.' The escalating tension between the nationalist-secular and the Islamic discourses includes all social realms, except for one discursive meeting point: the political struggle against imperialism embodied in the image of the USA and Israel. Otherwise, on the cultural level, the ideological gap is unbridgeable and does not allow for institutional co-operation or conceptual compromises. In spite of the Rabita's declared political alienation from 'the state' and 'the imperial West', its self-identification as a 'modern' and 'pluralistic' nationalist movement equates it with ideas and values constructed as 'Western' (including conceptions of gender roles). In addition, whereas the members of the Islamic Movement do not have a socio-economic common denominator, most of the supporters of the Rabita belong to the educated middle class in Jaffa. This sociological correspondence between cultural 'Western' or 'modern' principles and a certain class position renders the conflict between the two social actors even more fraught. In the eyes of the pious Muslims, seculars are conceived as responsible for the current return to the Jahilyya (the pre-Islamic era of ignorance), which characterizes times of crisis. On their part, the supporters of the Rabita accuse the religious Muslims of extremism, and of responsibility for the current political state of divisiveness. The Islamic Movement and its factional isolationist course of action, the Rabita supporters complain, harm the whole Arab community.

In opposition to the Islamic discourse, which revolves around the construction of a religious 'authentic' essentialism, the secular-nationalist ideology is forged as national essentialist representation of authenticity. Its central symbols are the language and the place: to purge Arabic of Hebrew influences, intellectuals in Jaffa treat Arabic as an icon of cultural authenticity, while constructing a national nostalgia to pre-1948 Mandatory Jaffa – the 'Bride of the Sea' or the 'Bride of Palestine' – the mythical place which is to return to its glory.

THE GENDER ESSENCE: 'LIBERAL' AND 'EGALITARIAN' MASCULINITY
The secular discourse of modernization and progress in Jaffa is articulated as a discourse of a society in transition between 'tradition' and 'modernity' (*bein eltaqlidi walhadith*, the title of an article in the local magazine '*Arus Elbahr*, June 1998: 16). The gender facet of this liberal discourse focuses on the welcome enfeeblement of the patriarchal power structure, the changing roles of motherhood in the family, and women's struggle for equality – in short, the restructuring of the division of sexual labour and the sexual division of labour. At the basis of this discourse stands the demand to bind women's liberation with the liberation of Arab society as a whole from the chains of colonialism, but also from those of religion. This liberal-secular discourse, because of its identification with attitudes considered 'Western' and because of its harsh criticism of the 'backwardness' of Arab society, is trapped between constructions of East and West and maintains ambivalent relations with perceptions of 'tradition' and 'Islam'. Here is Rafiq, a social worker, describing the dilemma of Arab men:

> Men don't have a choice today. On the one hand, they try to climb the ladder of modernization and openness and, on the other, they want to keep their authority as men. They are in a bind – to be a modern man who gives the woman her rights, he must be an open-minded man, and there are very few like that in Jaffa.

The liberal-secular gender perception tries to walk the line between egalitarianism and patriarchy and between permissiveness and conservatism.

In spite of the struggle between the Islamic and the secular-liberal models of masculinity, they rest on the same cultural logic. They are constituted through essentialist value systems based on 'big' places (mythical pre-'48 Jaffa in the nationalist imagination or Jerusalem, the capital of the Islamic state) and mythical time ('the days of the Arabs', referring both the national glory of the pre-1948 days and the golden age of the Islamic conquest in the seventh century).[15] Challenging these two, in the 'small' place of everyday life, is a third strategy whose power stems from the absence of an ordered ideology framed in terms of big place and mythical time.

Multi-essentialism: situational masculinity The two models described above represent only a small group of the Palestinian population in Jaffa. According to a rough estimation, the Islamic and the liberal-secular models

133

represent no more than 20 per cent, whereas the silent and disorganized majority constitutes more than 80 per cent of the Arab population. Opposed to these two identities anchored in an ordered ideology of 'big' place and time, the majority adopts a pragmatic stance.

The masculinity product of this majority maintains ambivalent relations with the Islamic and the liberal poles on the ideological continuum, relations that change according to situational interactions. In Jaffa, men come to terms with their tertiary, trapped position according to the general principles, albeit vague and ambiguous, of Arab 'tradition' (*el-usul*). However, unlike its essentializing static sociological stereotype that has become predominant in the socio-anthropological literature (Herzfeld 1987), this popular loose and dynamic discourse about 'tradition' seems at times to renounce essence altogether, thus constituting a 'non-essentialist' masculinity. However, its uniqueness is that it moves between several essences, manoeuvres between them and manipulates them to serve its needs. At other instances, situational masculinity praises the code of 'tradition' and seems to subscribe to it, but de facto it expresses a playful stance towards it and towards its own position. This masculinity is colourful and performative, a masculinity of leisure, of mistresses (Arab or Jewish, married or single), a masculinity of declared avoidance of any direct cultural confrontation with Islam or nationalism. Situational masculinity pays lip-service to all essences in the cultural force field.

THE 'NINJAS': THE ISLAMIC MODEL IN THE EYES OF THE SITUATIONAL MODEL Says Kifah, a mechanic, aged thirty:

> The situation is bad, all the customs and the traditions are eroded – the rules of behaviour are falling apart. Today's generation is the worst (*el-jil halaq awsakh jil*); they respect no one. The situation is crucial – the father sniffs, doesn't have time for his children, and the mother 'goes down to the street'. Even the 'sheiks' [*el-mashyekh*, the common nickname for the members of the Islamic Movement] don't do anything. These 'Ninjas' [a term comparing the women's veil to a ninja uniform], the penitents – they are crazy. Take Maha, my sister; she didn't come to my daughter's wedding because we had whiskey there, but when she went for a trip to Egypt, everyone danced in a nightclub; 'Once every couple of years it's OK,' she says, 'why, how many times does a man get married?' And Khaled [her son, an active member in the Islamic Movement], you think he didn't know about it? And the educated – they are disconnected from the people.

Kifah's ambivalence towards the Islamic ideology and praxis, common to most men in Jaffa, combines reservation and appreciation. On the one hand, the Islamic Movement is conceived as the last resort to save the honour of Arab masculinity and society;[16] on the other, Kifah condemns the hypocrisy of its members and their extremism.

THE 'EDUCATED': LIBERAL MASCULINITY IN THE EYES OF SITUATIONAL MASCULINITY Situational masculinity's conception of the liberalness of the 'educated' is twofold: on the one hand, liberal men are closer to men such as Kifah than the Islamists because of some similarity in lifestyle, but on the other they are separated by both education and class. As Kifah put it: 'Normally, an educated guy will sit with you in a wedding, will drink with you, will talk with you, but there is a difference in style. He has other things on his mind.' Once the liberal and the Islamic options are rejected, men in Jaffa choose a third solution. This choice relies on the loose discourse of the 'Arab tradition' which is different from the Islamic Sunna and cosmology, but also removed from the Western alternative. This discourse enables them to keep certain conventional elements of the stereotype of Arab masculinity, but, simultaneously, also to adopt situational solutions borrowed from the Islamic or the liberal discourses, turning them on and off when needed (Waters 1990). This situational solution stems from the anomic and paradoxical context of 'strangeness' in Jaffa, which prevents many men from adopting a coherent position or identity. In particular instances, it allows fathers to transmit double messages to their young daughters: on the one hand, the father does not want his daughter to initiate any relations with young men; however, because of the scarcity of adequate potential husbands, and the abundance of drug addicts and dealers in Jaffa, he feels compelled to encourage her to be more active to ameliorate her chances. These men can be seen preaching for the purification of Jaffa from moral decay while at the same time maintaining several married mistresses. Such paradoxical practices reflect the gender crisis in Jaffa, the loss of a hegemonic meta-narrative capable of organizing social life around one coherent cultural essence.

Between the Islamic pious masculinity and the 'modern' liberal model, men practise a masculinity which defines itself as first and foremost Arab. Thus when I asked Dahood, a man in his late forties, why he forbids his daughter from studying away in Jerusalem, he answered, 'Because we're Arabs', and did not resort to the Islamic code, even though it would have backed up his argument more strongly. This masculinity model attempts to symbolize a return to 'traditional' patriarchal values, although it allows locally for liberal practices, which clearly contradict the 'tradition' discourse. Thus, for instance, while his teenage daughters were spending their vacation in Sinai after they convinced him to let them go without his supervision, Sami complained, noticing a permissively dressed woman walking in the street, about the weakness of men who 'do not guard their women', and asserted his commitment to the manly Arab tradition: 'When there are men, there is hukume, there is authority and control. We need more men with balls (*m'a bedat*). If my daughter dresses like that, I will cut her legs.' These men are not nationalists, they are not religious, nor are they secular. Their life is an ongoing escape from 'boredom' and emptiness while holding to the idiom of Arab masculinity as a source of meaning. Their identity is a contradictory mix of discourses, essences and practices not anchored in an ordered ideology. This mixing – nihilistic at times – complicates the contradictions of their social and cultural predicament, both as members of the Palestinian minority in Israel and as 'ex-patriarchal' men. Examples of this situational and fluid position may be observed every Ramadan. After the month of fasting, during which the mosques are full of worshippers attempting to observe all commandments, many men celebrate 'Id el-fitr with parties watered with alcohol. At these parties a belly dancer and a band of players are invited, and people drink till they drop. To my question, Sami answered with a famous religious phrase adapted to the time and the place: '*fih fard wafih sunna*' (there is a commandment to fast, and there are customs common at the time of the Prophet, which are not compelling). 'I've fasted thirty days,' continued Sami; 'now I sin'.

SITUATIONAL MASCULINITY AS AN 'IDENTITY PLAY' The ethnographic data call for a conceptualization of 'situational masculinity' in terms of 'play'. Based on an understanding of playfulness as a mediating mechanism between political and gender identities (Handelman 1977, 1990), masculinity can be described as a playful movement between essences. This play mediates between the players' religiosity and their secularity, between their Palestinian and their Israeli identities, between the public and the private and between declaration and action. Play not only enables the existence of multivalent worlds, but also enables the players to locate themselves on the boundary between these worlds, to cross them at will, to commit to one of them, or to stay at a middle-liminal position without exposure and without taking any clear position (Steinberg 1995).

From this perspective we can understand play as an organizing principle of practices and meanings, as a mode of communication anchored in its conflicting social context. The wandering of men between one world of meaning to another, and their ability – through the loose discourse on Arab 'tradition' – to be both 'Muslims', 'liberal' and mainly 'real men', present a paradoxical strategy which reflects the crisis of their liminal position. The double messages transmitted by the play are solutions to the

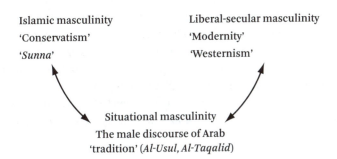

Islamic masculinity   Liberal-secular masculinity
'Conservatism'   'Modernity'
'Sunna'   'Westernism'

Situational masculinity
The male discourse of Arab
'tradition' (*Al-Usul, Al-Taqalid*)

FIGURE 7.1 Hegemonic masculinity – 'strangeness' as a floating
point between identity poles

identity paradox of Palestinian men in Jaffa trapped between the poles of
'strangeness'. One can illustrate the dynamics of Arab masculinity in Jaffa
as a constant motion between essentialist poles of identity.

Stranger masculinities as postcolonial products

Postcolonial criticism calls for location. It calls for cultural critics to look
for more than liberal 'diversity'; they must attend to the ways in which the
various forms of diversity (in the present case, among different kinds of
masculinity) are products of specific cultural, political, geographical and
economic locations and their accompanying psychological determinants
(Soja 1996; Ouzgane and Coleman 1998). Products of the ambivalent Israeli
postcolonial predicament, the three masculinity types reviewed maintain
complex relations with colonial representations of the 'West' and the
'state' as well as with the cultural presence of the 'stranger' (Westerner/
Jew/modern). Thus, Islamic masculinity views the colonial 'West' as an
emblem of decay and a threat to the values of family and society, while
declaring itself the embodiment of the 'authentic' return to the values of
Islam. Conversely, secular-liberal masculinity conceives itself as close, yet
remote, from cultural representations of the 'West', and in a hesitant position in relation to it: on the one hand, the cultural package of the 'West'
is conceived as a source of welcome 'progress', and on the other, one has
to be careful not to draw too near it. In the midst, situational masculinity
chooses not to commit itself, enabling dynamism and a movement between
'Islamic' and 'secular' identity components. It renounces any clear ideological decision, and remains in the realm of everyday life.

These strategies demonstrate the fundamental dilemma of living in a
postcolonial city of 'strangers'. The cultural choices stem from the fluid
position of men trapped in a 'floating point' between contradictory identity

137

frames. This third position enables them to choose between two essentialist options or a multi-essentialist identity play vacillating between essentialist discourses. As a coping strategy, they move to and fro – to the Tel-Aviv metropolis and into the Jaffa enclave, to religion and away from it, to modernity and back. In sum, multi-essentialist play constitutes a central strategy for coping with postcolonial 'strangeness'. As a cultural condition, 'strangeness' becomes for most men in Jaffa also a source of identity.

Notes

1 This chapter is based on fieldwork I conducted between 1996 and 1998 in Jaffa, south of Tel-Aviv, among a group of Muslim men and their families. Actors in the field are specific men in sites of male sociability, situations of work and moments of expressiveness. However, although remaining anchored in this ethnographic context, the discussion dialectically moves between these specific 'men' and the abstract categories of 'masculinity' which constitute their cultural universe.

2 'Israeli' and 'Palestinian' refer to Jews who are citizens of Israel and to the Palestinians, also Israeli citizens, and usually referred to in Israeli research and media as 'Israeli Arabs' (Rabinowitz 1993). Arabs who remained in Israel following the establishment of the state had come to constitute a minority of 13 per cent of the total Israeli population, and at present form about 17 per cent of the entire Israeli population.

3 For a comparative discussion of Israel as a colonial settler-state, see Yiftachel 1988: 37; Stasiulis and Yuval-Davis 1995; Vanneste 1996.

4 'Strangeness' appears first in Simmel's essay 'Der Fremde' (1908) where it describes an individual 'social type' which exhibits a 'distinctive blend of closeness and remoteness, inside and outside' (Simmel 1971: 149). Later, with sociologists Zygmunt Bauman (1995) and Ulrich Beck (1996), the concept was generalized to theorize a collective cultural condition symptomatic of 'high', 'post' or 'reflexive' modernity. I employ this theoretical apparatus to decipher – in the realm of gender – the contradictions of a specific colonial case. For an analysis of the relations between 'strangeness' and the modern nation-state, see Alund (1996).

5 Multiple identities (lectures organized by the Islamic Movement, Ben-Gurion University, 19 May 1998), divided identity (Amara and Kabha 1996), schizophrenia (Makram Khoury, in Horowitz 1993), masks (Bishara 1992), strangeness (Bishara 1993), alienation (Nakara-Haddad, in Horowitz 1993).

6 In Jaffa there are 16,000 Arab inhabitants – 70 per cent of them Muslims, 30 per cent Christians – making up 24 per cent of the total mixed population (according to the official municipality statistics).

7 Elsewhere (Monterescu 1998) I describe the influence of the legal, demographic and socio-economic changes on the patriarchal status of Arab men in Jaffa. Here I only mention that these changes have brought about the formation of a dialectical process, moving between the hardening of some patriarchal practices and codes and the loosening of others.

8 'The borderlands are physically present wherever two or more cultures edge each other, where people of different races occupy the same territory, where under, lower, middle and upper classes touch, where the space between two individuals shrinks with intimacy [...] Living on borders and in margins, keeping intact one's shifting and multiple identity and integrity, is like trying to swim in a new element, an "alien" element that has become familiar' (Anzaldua 1987).

9 By using the terms 'modernity', 'tradition', 'seculars', 'Islamists,' or 'masculinity', I do not intend to ascribe to them any reified existence or meaning detached from their expression in discourse and practice. The concept 'tradition', for instance, takes and strips form and content, and is charged by different meanings in the mouth of different actors. In what follows, I show how the discourse about 'tradition' constitutes a means of coping with and reconciling the two essentialist poles in the cultural force field – 'Islam' and 'secular liberalism'.

10 The mediating relations between the above categories are bi-directional since hegemonic masculinity constitutes each anti-thesis but is also constituted by it, and by the action of constituting. Masculinity is understood as a cultural idiom which does not 'exist' in any concrete place; it is built dialectically from its expressions in discourse and practice.

11 Connell's model of hierarchical masculinities provides a useful apparatus for analysing the kinds of interstitial, hybrid postcolonial subjectivities theorized throughout the essays of Homi Bhabha. See *Jouvert*'s special issue *Postcolonial Masculinities* (Ouzgane and Coleman 1998).

12 The contemporary Islamic Movement began to operate in Israel in the 1970s under the leadership of Sheikh 'Abd-Allah Nimr Darwish (Abu-Ahmad) from Kafr Qassem (Meyer 1989). Inspired by Hassan al-Banna, the founder of the 'Muslim Brotherhood', Darwish combines preaching with the distribution of manifestos, religious statements and political publications. The Islamic Movement's intensive activity is focused mainly on the local social domain, but since the elections of 1996, also on the national level and in the Knesset.

13 This chapter touches mainly on the ideological level; the practice dimension, fascinating and full of tensions and paradoxes, remains beyond the range of this chapter.

14 The article continues: 'They called to free the woman from the ruthless rule of men. And now, their base laws send anyone who dared to hit his wife to the prison, even if she rebelled against her husband. These laws are so horrible that when a husband desires his wife and wants to sleep with her, he may be imprisoned with the accusation of "rape". Another liberty allows women to go to work, without any social or financial need, only to accumulate money and to buy jewelry and expensive clothes. And now, women neglect their noble duties in educating their children and cooking for their husbands [...] And with time, the man develops a mental complex, falls into a state of laziness and decides to quit his job and to settle for his wife's earnings. In the end, this unnatural state causes quarrels and sometimes ends with divorce [...] The man sits unemployed in coffee houses, the woman works and accumulates money and the children run around in the streets and learn the bad ways of crime.'

15 The coupling of 'the big place' and 'the small place' (Gurevitch and Aran 1991) denotes different symbolical planes. A 'big place' is one of values, ideas, aspirations and images; a 'small place' is a physical, daily, earthy place. Jerusalem, for example, is a superimposition of 'big' and 'small' places: it bears myth and eschatology combined with a reality and activity of the daily. Jaffa, because of its historical significance and present political position, is often construed as a 'big place' in local discourses. The "big place" is more than a specific site and even more than all sites – it is the idea itself' (ibid., p. 11).

16 When rumours say that a woman was unfaithful to her husband, one often hears, 'Where are the religious?' They should 'fix her and her husband'. Religion, therefore, offers men a sanctioned, much esteemed, patriarchally acclaimed and dignified social 'masculine' role.

References

Alund, A. (1996) 'The Stranger: Ethnicity, Identity and Belonging', in S. Gustavsson and L. Lewin (eds), *The Future of the Nation-State*. London: Routledge.

Amara, M. and S. Kabha (1996) *Divided Identity: A Study of Political Division and Social Reflections in a Split Village* (in Hebrew). Givat Haviva: Jewish–Arab Center for Peace.

Anzaldua, G. (1987) *Borderlands/La Frontra: The New Mestiza*. San Francisco, CA: Spinsters/Aun Lute.

Avitsur, S. (1972) *The Port of Jaffa in Its Height and in Its Decline: 1865–1965*. Tel-Aviv: Avshalom Institute, Malo Press.

Bauman, Z. (1995) *Modernity and Ambivalence*. Cambridge: Polity Press.

Beck, U. (1996) 'How Neighbours Become Jews: The Political Construction of the Stranger in an Age of Reflexive Modernity', *Constellations: An International Journal of Critical and Democratic Theory*, 2 (3): 402–20.

Bhabha, H. K. (1990) 'The Third Space: Interview with Homi Bhabha', in J. Rutherford (ed.), *Identity: Community and Culture Difference*. London: Lawrence and Wishart, pp. 207–21.

— (1994) 'The Other Question: Difference, Discrimination and the Discourse of Colonialism', in *The Location of Culture*. London: Routledge.

Bishara, 'A. (1992) 'Between Space and Place', *Studio*, 37: 6–10.

— (1993) 'On the Palestinian Minority in Israel', *Theory and Criticism*, 3.

Bourdieu P. (1990) 'La Domination Masculine', *Actes de la Recherche en Sciences Sociales*, 84: 4–31.

Chatterjee, P. (1993) *The Nation and Its Fragments: Colonial and Postcolonial Histories*. Princeton, NJ: Princeton University Press.

Connell, R. (1995), *Masculinities*. Cambridge: Polity Press.

Dyer, R. (1995) *The Matter of Images: Essays on Representation*. London: Routledge.

Falah, G. (1996) 'Living Together Apart: Residential Segregation in Mixed Arab–Jewish Cities in Israel', *Urban Studies*, 33 (6): 823–57.

Fanon, F. (1967) *Towards the African Revolution*. London: Penguin.

— (1991) *Black Skin, White Masks*. London: Pluto.

— (1990) *The Wretched of the Earth*. London: Penguin.

Ghanem, A. (1998) 'Margins in a Marginal Society: The Bedouin Uniqueness', in E. Reckhes (ed.), *The Arabs in Israel: Dilemmas of Identity*. Tel-Aviv: Moshe Dayan Center, Tel-Aviv University.

Gurevitz, Z. and G. Aran (1991) 'On the Place: Israeli Anthropology', *Alpayim*, 4: 9–44.

Handelman, D. (1990) *Models and Mirros: Towards an Anthropology of Public Events*. Cambridge: Cambridge University Press, p. 187.

Hassan, A. (1989) 'We are the Strongest', *Politics*, 21: 36–8.

Hazan, H. (1997) 'On Cultural Effacement: The Body Politic and Collective Memory in Communication Texts', in D. Kaspi (ed.), *Communication and Democracy in Israel*.

Herzfeld, M. (1987) *Anthropology Through the Looking Glass: Critical Ethnography in the Margins of Europe*. Cambridge: Cambridge University Press.

— (1997) *Cultural Intimacy: Social Poetics in the Nation-State*. New York: Routledge.

Horowitz, D. (1993) *Like a Stuck Bridge* (in Hebrew). Beit-Berl: Center for the Research of Arab Society.

Israeli, R. (1993) *Muslim Fundamentalism in Israel*. London: Brassey's.

Kimmerling, B. (1993) 'State–Society Relations in Israel', in U. Ram (ed.), *The Israeli Society: Critical Aspects*. Tel-Aviv: Mehirot Publishing House.

Lancaster, R. (1988) 'Subject of Honour, Object of Shame: The Construction of Male Homosexuality and Stigma in Nicaragua', *Ethnology*, 27 (2): 111–25.

Mazawi, A. and O. Ichilov (1996) *Between State and Church: Life History of a French-Catholic School in Jaffa*. Frankfurt: Peter Lang.

Mazawi, A. and M. Khoury-Machool (1991) 'Spatial Policy in Jaffa: 1948–1990' (in Hebrew), in H. Luski (ed.), *City and Utopia*. Tel-Aviv: Israel Publishing Co.

Meyer, T. (1989) 'The "Young Muslims" in Israel', *The New East*, 32: 10–21.

Monterescu, D. (1998) *The Cultural Construction of Arab Masculinity in a Palestinian–Israeli Mixed Town (Jaffa)*, Unpublished MA Thesis.

Ouzgane, L., and D. Coleman (1998) 'Postcolonial Masculinities: Introduction', *Jouvert*, 2 (1).

Prakash, G. (ed.) (1995) *After Colonialism*. Princeton, NJ: Princeton University Press.

Rabinowitz, D. (1993) 'Oriental Nostalgia: The Transformation of the Palestinians into "Israeli Arabs"', *Theory and Criticism*, 4.

— (1996) *Overlooking Nazareth: The Ethnography of Exclusion in Galilee*. Cambridge: Cambridge University Press.

Rekhess, E. (1998) 'Introduction', in E. Rekhess and T. Yegnes (eds), *Arab Politics in Israel at a Crossroad* (in Hebrew). Tel Aviv: Moshe Dayan Center, Tel-Aviv University.

Said, E. (1978) *Orientalism*. London: Penguin.

Schutz, A. (1964) 'The Stranger: An Essay in Social Psychology', in *Collected Papers*, vol. II. The Hague: Martinus Nijhoff.

Shaqr, N. (1996) *The Jaffan Community on an Existential Crossroad* (in Hebrew). Tel-Aviv: Tel-Aviv Municipality.

Shokeid, M. (1982) 'Ethnicity and the Cultural Code among Arabs in a Mixed Town: Women's Modesty and Men's Honour at Stake', in S. Deshen and M. Shokeid, *Distant Relations*. New York: Praeger Special Studies.

Simmel, G. (1971) 'The Stranger' [1908], in *On Individuality and Social Forms*. Chicago, IL: University of Chicago Press.

Smooha, S. (2002) 'The Model of Ethnic Democracy: Israel as a Jewish and Democratic State', *Nations and Nationalism*, 8 (4) (October): 475–503.

Soja, E. (1996) *Thirdspace*. Oxford: Blackwell.

Stasiulis, D. and N. Yuval-Davis (eds) (1995) *Unsettling Settler Societies*. London: Sage.

Steinberg, P. (1995) *Identity Play*, MA Thesis, Department of Sociology and Anthropology, Tel-Aviv University.

Tapinc, H. (1995) 'Masculinity, Femininity, and Turkish Male Homosexuality', in E. Plummer (ed.), *Modern Homosexualities*. New York: Routledge.

Turner, V. (1969) *The Ritual Process: Structure and Anti-structure*. London: Routledge and Kegan Paul.

Vanneste, D. (ed.) (1996) *Space and Place: Mirrors of Social and Cultural Identities?* Leuven: Geography Institute, Catholic University of Leuven.

Walby, S. (1991) *Theorizing Patriarchy*. Oxford: Blackwell.

Waters, M. (1990) *Ethnic Options: Choosing Identities in America*. Berkeley: University of California Press.

Yiftachel, O. (1998) 'Nation-Building and the Division of Space: Ashkenazi Domination in the Israeli "Ethnocracy"', *Nationalism and Ethnic Politics*, 4 (3): 33–58.

THREE | **Masculinities and social practice**

8 | Gender, power and social change in Morocco

DON CONWAY-LONG

Of central importance to understanding Moroccan men is their perception of the relations between men and women in their society. I found, in fieldwork in Rabat, Méknès and Casablanca in the early 1990s, that men knew that change in the society, the economy and the family surrounded them, and that men and women were, by necessity, undergoing transformations accordingly. This would imply an awareness that the relations between the sexes are being modified somehow. I delved into this awareness in a series of questions on the relations between the sexes. In the process, I discovered the ways in which men perceived ongoing shifts in gendered power, the appropriateness of traditional divisions of labour, the impact of the world economy on their own position, and, ultimately, the ways they experienced and interpreted the process of social change in the sex/gender order.

Of forty-eight men in three cities, I asked: 'What kind of power does a man have in society? What kind of power does a woman have? How is society changing right now in ways that influence the behaviour of men and women in Morocco? Are these positive or negative changes, as far as you are concerned?' Several themes emerged in their answers. A man's power was seen as centring in work, in his word or his intellect, in his personal control over decision-making, and in political power and leadership. Women's power, when they were perceived as having any at all, was placed in the realms of sexuality and the body (including reproductive power), in magic and sorcery, and over children and food preparation. But such a simple summary cannot do justice to the complexity and range of these men's opinions on this key concept of power.

> Morocco's constitution gives men more power than to women, which is closely related to Islamic principles. The clearest power is that the man has the right to divorce the woman, to rule over her in the family. Woman has no power, but has certain rights [...] Power is important. It has to be used against the woman so as to stop her because women abuse their freedom; they are not aware enough of the importance of freedom. They don't deserve equality because they are not sufficiently aware. The Moroccan woman is unfaithful, treacherous, which I believe from my own experience.
> – Jaouad[1]

Jaouad appeared to believe that men's power, given by religion and political reality, and expressed in their role as head of family, had to be used to keep women in check, because they could not know how far they abused their freedom, or what was truly correct, what was best for their nation. It was men, to Jaouad, who lived the rational, intellectual life of wisdom. It is as if men's power was not only political and social, but sex-linked; women, after all, were different. Another man carried this idea in a different direction:

> Men [have] intellectual and physical power; women – from their body as a desired object. Deep in our consciousness, people think women have always been marginalized, repressed. So we try to sympathize with them; we tell ourselves we should free them. Hassan II has emphasized the freedom of women in a recent speech, pointing out that many rules are changing. These things are becoming a power which women are trying to use as much as possible. – Rachid

Current social reality has given support to women's claims for change, from sources as influential as the news from abroad or the late King himself. Women's rights have become part of the discourse. Some, however, see this process as having progressed so far as to have displaced men's traditional sources of power.

> Men used to have the power of provision in the family, money. Now, though, man has lost his personality and with it, his power. Man used to have the power of divorce (associated with being the provider of money), so now it is less of a threat to the woman since she can make money. The concept of relations [al-irtibaat] is changing now. It is now a relationship of benefit and mutuality, since women can also bring in money. Women have no power in society but at home they have power over children and the household. She has the right to run the household the way she wants, e.g., the power of a woman inside the home is like a man's. When children are disobedient, she threatens them: 'Just wait till your father gets home,' appropriating her husband's power. – Nabil

To this twenty-seven-year-old technical worker, men are not only losing their position as providers, but the system in the home is making it possible for the woman/wife to 'appropriate' the home-based power of the man/husband/father as disciplinarian. The domestic realm more and more belongs to women, even as they are making regular inroads into the public realm once uniquely male. Mernissi's argument (1987) that Moroccan men fear women's power in the home is given credence by the words and attitudes of many men I interviewed. Even for those no longer living in the extended family, in which most women are at home while the men are out at work or in the café, the feeling that the home is a woman's place remains. For example, a forty-year-old academic, living in a nuclear family in an apartment, said this about the power of women:

> The power of women is real. She has a strong relationship with her children; the power of biological reproduction is impressive. The power of the preparation of food (and the threat not to prepare it). These things are a kind of oppression that women exert over men. Some women use sexuality as an oppression over their husbands. This is contrary to the Islamic roots: a woman cannot withhold sex, the man should satisfy her – yet the man can withhold sex as punishment (even the Prophet Mohammed did this). Yet a woman can ask for divorce if she is not satisfied by her husband. The women can remind the man of all the services they provide at home, saying 'your public success is dependent upon me'. This is a 'reminding power' – especially in popular classes [the working class, uneducated people]. This makes men feel inferior. – Abdellah

Several important points illustrate his point of view as an 'oppressed' family man. First, he identified 'womb envy', an awe for women's biological role in pregnancy and birth; then, the service of provision of food in the home, and the threat of its refusal. He next noted the overturning of the Islamic rule that women are forbidden to withhold sex from their husbands, followed by the newer secular law that permits women to seek divorce in Morocco. This man and others like him recognize that they are dependent upon women for many services: food, cleaning, sexuality, and the entire realm of domestic daily reproduction of the 'working man'. At the same time, his power to control his home was being subtly eroded; case in point: he was no longer the only one to control the divorce proceedings. This issue alone is a paradigm shift of great importance. Leila Abouzeid's novella *Year of the Elephant* (1989) tells the depressing and realistic tale of a woman, who had been active in the war of resistance against France, who was divorced by her husband just after independence and sent packing with the required hundred days of sustenance. But the times have rapidly changed, and men know it. They can now be the ones sent packing.

The question of the felt oppression of men must be addressed. When privilege is called into question, any shift in the make-up of socially accepted power relations seems to be experienced as a reversal of institutional power to the detriment of the prior beneficiary of an unequal system. As the means by which a member of a dominant social group maintains the daily experience of power become challenged, no longer acceptable as mechanisms of absolute control, he often experiences the shift in social reality as 'oppression'. Hence, since men are supposed to be, by definition, powerful, experiencing a loss in power becomes a situation in which the 'other', the female, must be punished for her natural ability to disrupt a man's sense of control. This kind of experience was reiterated to me a number of times in Morocco. Yielding such power to disrupt to women was perceived as certainly not in the best interests of the continued institutional power of males as a dominant group. It thereby became grist for the cultural mill, leading, in the Moroccan case, to numerous tales of women's sexual allure and power, simultaneously with the seemingly deliberate attempt to keep women in a dependent position relative to men. The same may be true, I suppose, anywhere that patriarchy is perceived as threatened by a changing balance of power between the sexes.

The irony of the position is that it is women who are far more likely to be physically endangered by men's behaviour, not the other way around. Men who see women as such a threat as to necessitate fantasy or real actions of vengeance are, in some sense, the vanguard of patriarchal privilege. Their interpretation of male–female interaction is derived from perception, not fact; from ideology, not statistical reality. But the experience of the power inversion is a reality for those who feel it. Whether we are talking about racism, sexism, heterosexism, ethnic hatreds or other structures of inequality as seen through the lens of reverse oppression, it becomes the job of an ethnographer to identify clearly the revisionist, reversed perspective, while simultaneously placing it in a wider social context that clarifies the difference between an individual's social experience and the institutional system of power that continues to benefit that individual in many (perhaps unseen) ways. It is decidedly not the job of an ethnographer to dismiss such perspectives as unworthy of attention. Men's perception of oppression by women can be as integral a part of a system that benefits men in general as their failure to perceive the ways they continue personally to perpetuate a system of inequality in which women and children lose out. Systems of power cannot be portrayed as one-dimensional structures in which all Y are powerful, and all X are powerless (see Lipman-Blumen 1984 for an explication of the complexities of power relations). Theories that present a sex/gender order in the simple, static terms of male-dominant/female-subordinate are inadequate to the task of portraying the real felt experience of human social reality. It is the same in Morocco or in the West, where, as Carrigan, Connell and Lee (1985: 580) note, in their criticism of sex-role analysis: 'The notion of the overall social subordination of women, institutionalized in the marital division of labor, but consistent with a fluctuating and occasionally reversed power situation in particular relationships, is not a conception that can be formulated in the language of role theory.'

What these scholars are discussing is the problem of concentrating on abstract differentiation between two static constructs of masculine and feminine as opposed to the concrete, and sometimes variable relations between the sexes. The point of any proper analysis of power dynamics is to seek to uncover the forms of daily negotiation and struggle, the sites of resistance and rebellion, and to clarify the institutional abstractions which ossify an ideological system in the minds of its participants. No structure is permanent, no power is unresisted, no ruling class always rules efficiently and effectively. The expectation of contradiction and paradox should be explicit in any cultural investigation of power, dominance and subordination.

And that is what we find in Morocco, particularly in the minds of men. Their perceptions of the social order of the sex/gender system seem often to focus on the ways in which women have been gaining on men, and not on the ways in which men still have a great deal of institutional power. They often do recall, though, the golden age when they once had a great deal more power than they do now. As one twenty-eight-year-old man put it:

Men – the constitution gives special treatment to the power of men, which is contradictory to the concept that men themselves have in their own mind. For example, a man beats his wife because he thinks he has power over her, but the rules forbid him from doing so. He refuses this, but in the eyes of the constitution, men and women are on an equal footing, and this cripples the power of men. Women – before independence they suffered from ignorance, deprivation, and backwardness which prevailed then. The woman was marginalized and everything was in the hands of men. After independence, and because of the openness of Morocco to other cultures, other ideas entered, and the woman acquired not only power, but different kinds of it. Going out to work is one, and working in any job is another, as is formal education. Her contribution to literary, artistic and cultural worlds is a kind of power. Legally speaking, she has the right to bring up children – even before men [meaning prior to or superior to men's right to do so]. The opportunities for work are more open for her than for men. Nowadays, the idea of engagement, of divorce is legally discussed. So the power of woman is growing over time. – Hicham

And the implication is that the power of men must be reducing over time in response. The idea of the zero-sum game, that is, what one gains another must lose, is a preoccupation in much gender ideology. In the voices speaking to this transformation we can viscerally feel this perceived flow of power between the genders. And when men perceive that they are losing something once seen as fundamental to masculine identity, frequently there are found the beginnings of the desire to take it back again. A twenty-seven-year-old says:

> The man is weak. And he is becoming weaker with women's resistance.[2] Nowadays men are just having a kind of quasi-power – it is not real, because family matters are directed according to women's views, not men's. A woman, though, has the power to educate her children, to study and work, to assert herself in different fields, political and economic fields, also the power to be employed. Women are not too demanding, in terms of salary – they'll work for less. – Hassan

Women's standing up makes men weak, he says. They seize men's power in the public realm, while keeping it, even building on it in the private realm of the family. He ends by implying an explanation for how women take away men's jobs – a point made by others, perhaps as a way to assuage the embarrassment of high unemployment for men in the face of increased employment for women. (The actual percentage of women in paid employment remains low; Moghadam [1993] estimated it as less than 25 per cent in the 1980s.) If those women accept less money, well, it is obvious how they get the job. A man who insists on more loses out. Through this perspective, women are made the economic scapegoat for the losses to men in the age of Third World industrialization. There is little evident awareness of the overall transformations in the neo-liberal global economy, the shifts in the nature of employment, the relation of population growth to job availability, or the inequities of class society. Instead, the simple answer is that women are stealing men's jobs. This is quite serviceable as ideology, since it matches the discomforts of concurrent transformations within the home and within personal relationships.[3]

Women are perceived as having advantages in love and relationships. One advantage is their use of magic or sorcery. 'Women know how to make a man more submissive, in terms of finding another woman, spending his money or obeying his wishes' (Mustapha). I was told by college-educated men that 'even college-educated women' use the apothecary shops to buy herbs and amulets to control men.[4] 'When women have power over men, it is either his weak personality or the use of magic or sorcery' (Mohammed). Men do not do this kind of apothecary magic, even though many of the apothecaries are male.[5]

And, as has often been the case in other cultures, magic, sexuality, glamour and love are somehow conflated in a powerful mixture that lies behind the so-called 'feminine wiles'.

Women have no power at all. Though, they do have the power of witchcraft and love. When a man falls in love, and she becomes conscious of it, she knows she can do what she wants with him. They may have their body as power for the attraction and manipulation of men. – Mokhtar

Both witchcraft and love, in men's experience, can rule them. Other men identified feeling enraptured, ensorcelled by the glamour of women. 'For women, they have a physical power; their body is a power to reach their ends' – (Abdelkader); 'Women have the power of fascination' (Abdelfettah). As 'glamour' originally meant in English a magic spell or an enchantment, so in the Moroccan world today the same feeling is expressed by many men as they talk of their resentment of the power of women's sexual allure. Eva Rosander, in her study of Northern Morocco, links these sources of power to one more that men have already been quoted as resenting: 'men do not dare to eat the food or drink the tea or coffee prepared by women they do not trust. For food, drink and sex – three of the most essential physical needs of a human being – men are dependent on women and at the mercy of their magical potential' (1991: 250). This fear is so extensive and men's dependence on women so great in exactly these three areas that some say, 'Women are relatives to Shaitan [Satan],' as Mohammed, an illiterate labourer, put it.

This fear of magical control by women, of course, is not a new idea in Morocco. Stories of women and their manipulation and sorcery skills are abundantly in evidence in proverbs and folk tales. 'The cunning of women is strong, the cunning of the devil is weak,' says one (Westermarck 1930: 66). This reference is to one wonderfully revealing tale of a pair of clever women manipulating Shaitan himself into serving them in perpetuity. In a related tale, Edward Westermarck noted the following in his 1926 work on *Ritual and Belief in Morocco*:

> other kinds of shör [suhur] are in particular practiced by women. When Shamhâruš, the sultan of the jnun, died, he left behind a daughter who is still alive and assists her own sex in doing evil; hence women are even better versed in witchcraft than [male] scribes. While the charm written by a scribe easily loses its efficacy before long, a woman's enchantment has generally a more enduring effect. Women can do wonderful things by sorcery [...] The sorcery of women is specially rife at certain seasons – cura, New Year's Tide, and Midsummer – but it's frequent enough at all times. It is said that married women commence victimizing their husbands at the wedding, and continue to do so for as long as the marriage lasts. (V.I, 571)

There is a common belief that the longer a man and woman live, the more they reverse their relative positions on morality. One proverb puts it this way: a boy is born with 100 jnun, a girl with 100 angels. Each year a jinn passes to the woman and an angel to the man. By age 100, the man has 100 angels, the woman 100 devils (Westermarck 1930: 68). Mernissi quotes others in the same vein: 'A man who reaches eighty becomes a saint, a woman who reaches sixty is on the threshold of hell,' and, 'What takes Satan a year to do is done by the old hag within the hour' (1987: 124). Such sex antagonism, if we follow the arguments of Karen Horney (1967) and other post-Freudians, is likely to be firmly founded in fear. I know of no cultures in which similar fear of the female is not paralleled with outright fear of women's power to disrupt the masculine order of things.[6] It is the same in Morocco. The virgin, pure and unknowing about sexual matters, is unthreatening; the older a woman gets, the more threatening she becomes, especially after she has been 'opened' to sexual intercourse. Then, the crone, the post-menopausal woman, becomes even more threatening; *fitna* (chaos) is the concept for the disorder brought on by women's wiles. The most curious aspect of this is that these ideas co-exist with an ideology argued to be strongly respectful of women's sexual power and desire, as long as it is kept within the marriage bond. Controlled female sexuality is just fine; it is the uncontrolled, the out of control, that threatens the social order so distinctly. The cultural contradictions inherent in this complex of ideas are quite immense. On one hand, the woman begins life far more pure than the male does; it is boy children who are disruptive. But once a woman is introduced to sexuality, something viewed as her right within marriage, something she has strong social support for claiming, then she becomes explicitly dangerous to all men (though not as much to her husband) thereafter. But she is also wily enough to control her husband through manipulations and herbs; stories are plentiful that discuss the herbal concoctions that can make a husband impotent with any woman but his wife if he merely steps over the bag so that his genitals are momentarily exposed to them. In addition, a woman's beauty must be shielded by a *hijab*, a 'curtain', because a man is unable to control himself if he sees such beauty uncloaked. The concept of curtain is extended to physical space dividing the safety of the female-centred home from the public, male-oriented marketplace. It is the disruption of this system that leads to the most frequent complaints about the *fitna*, the disorder of the 'modern' world of Morocco. The great irony of the system is that the entire structure seems designed to protect men from the wiles of women.[7] It is my contention that such ideological systems of male dominance are inherently responses to the fear and dread of women's potential power, power that would be released, set free to chain men, were it not for the limitations, ideological, spatial, physical, placed upon women. It is from this point of view that any attempt to measure the relations between the sexes must begin.

Ultimately, what one finds in this examination of sex/gender ideologies is the continued preference for the existence of a (safely separated, ideologically constructed and falsely conceived) dual system, perceived most simply as:[8]

Sex space	Realm	Concept	Power over
Men public/world	work	light/day	other men, women, children
versus			
Women private/home	sex	night/dark	children (men?)

This is, of course, the way it's 'supposed' to be, with the exception of the non-sanctioned power women gain over men through their use of sexuality and sorcery.[9] Yet, in the words of the men themselves, we can see clearly that it is often not this way at all. Violations are often dealt with deliberately, immediately. Consider the possibly apocryphal anecdote told to me by a visiting Palestinian Fulbright scholar: he recalled a story of an independent 'modern' Moroccan woman who decided to reclaim the public space of a particular all-male Rabat café, and walked in one day and ordered. Every man in the place simply got up and left – no struggle, no argument, but with powerfully articulate kinesics.

How then do men perceive the process by which the system got 'out of balance'? To find out what they believed about this, I asked them how they felt about the evident social changes taking place, and what was good and bad about such transformations. As a segue to that issue, I present one last quote, this one from a fifty-one-year-old, well-educated and well-travelled man who noted the complexities of sex/gender power, and placed it into a historical perspective:

Men have financial and economic power; they are civil servants, they have ministerial, administrative, bureaucratic power – it is all men at the top. Women have it all behind the scenes. My mother used to have all the power at home. Like an English woman now, she is responsible for everything. Her husband brings money, he thinks he has the power but he works for her, she has the power at home, sexual power; he says before other people, 'I am the master' but between them [the man and woman], the woman is the master. Now the woman has great manipulative power to get what she wants from the man; she even has the power to make him do wrong for her. Her control is not public, but it is there. Yet sometimes she, if she is more

educated or makes more money, even shows herself the master in public.
– Abdellatif

Here we find an illuminating description of the change in the relations between the sexes over the years. Abdellatif depicted the power fantasies of men, the difference between inside and outside the home in the presentation of that relationship; he described the slow but irresistible force that was women's growing social power. He was not alone in his perception.

Social changes

'From the 70s to today there is a dangerous change, because we've lived in twenty years a period that we were supposed to live in 100 years' (Kamane). So spoke a twenty-four-year-old master's candidate. He managed, in this pithy phrase, to summarize the complexities of the impact of the Western world on the transitional economy and society of a Third World nation. Urban Moroccans are extremely aware of change; it is evident all around them. No one can walk through any part of a city in Morocco without seeing the co-existence of several lifestyles and life patterns, even several distinct time periods, or so it might seem. The Western romanticization of the Orient is at least partially built upon such a perception of timelessness alongside the modern, as when we see hooded herders carrying staffs alongside bankers in business suits with briefcases, or modestly dressed women walking and chatting with a woman in make-up and a shorter skirt. The speed of the transformation is apparent to all with eyes to see. As another man put it, 'Everything has changed' ['*Kul shi tghiir*'] (Driss).

Once again we find the repeating pattern of some men pleased and supportive of the changes, some ambivalent, some angry and rejecting of their experience of the changes. As might be implied by Kamane, there exists a great awareness among Moroccans of the social transformations in their economy. In fact, this may be the primary realm in which Moroccans perceive or experience the changes in the social order. It is possible that economic forces may open the door for social and familial shifts. As Fluehr-Lobban argues, there have been tremendous strides forward in access to economic resources by women in the last decade alone (1994: 82). One must recognize that the economy has powerful transformative effects upon many other seemingly non-economic realms of society. Abdellatif, quoted at the end of the previous section, noted the change in terms of the shift from protectorate to independent nation, seeing clearly how that change affected his social world:

The economic relationship is changing, no question about it. As women got more education, more access to jobs after independence, [which was] a quick process, actually everything changed. Everyone then began working for the state and the competition changed. The departure of the French led to a great vacuum – both men and women stepped in to fill the jobs. It was a political change that led to a great economic transformation. You know, I miss the stability of the old order; socially now things are in too much uproar. My son who has grown up in this new form of economic equality will see it differently than I do. The later generation will grow accustomed to it all. – Abdellatif

The interconnection between the departure of the French and the growth of availability of jobs and other opportunities for women was made explicit by many in Morocco. There is a certain irony that the exit of the colonial dominator laid the socio-economic foundation for the appearance of a new type of struggle for men – against the women of Morocco in their new roles as educated and employed people. Many men perceived this change for women as something that undermined men's control, and, in doing so, they clearly made a link between economic power and a generalized social and familial power, as if loss in the former area produced a loss in the latter.

'taghiir bzaf' – many changes. Good and bad: the positive – gives more opportunity to women; the negative – opportunity for work for men becomes less and less and women feel they have the power to confront men and are no longer afraid to do so. – Mohammed

Others were more ambivalent about the transformations. Some saw the equality of human rights under the law as good, yet still held on to some more customary ideas about the necessity or correctness of men's primary economic position, and felt that the degeneration of that position was leading to social, and moral, collapse.

We are going from conservatism to liberalism on all levels. But it is a kind of hidden liberalism. Man as the head of the family is changing, since women have this position too (with or without a man in the house). Education enables women to become chiefs. These changes have positive and negative aspects: positive – men and women enjoy the same rights. This kind of equality leads to the development of the country in different fields. Negative – women get jobs men should have. Men have no jobs; it means they have no money to get married, and this leads to debauchery. This leads to 'respectful prostitution', that is, dating or sexuality without marriage with 'good' girls. – Mokhtar

And, as has accompanied some people's perceptions of social trans-

155

formations in many other places, the changes were seen to be bringing about a breakdown in moral inhibitions, primarily but not exclusively in women. The economic changes include the commodification of sexuality, a consumerist trend towards Westernized clothing and make-up, as well as other goods, and a perception of the rise of selfishness reminiscent also of Western values of individualism. The result, as viewed by some, is an intensification of the gender war between women and men.

> There are changes, e.g., now men and women can meet before marriage. There is consciousness on the part of men and women. There is family planning. These changes are positive in people's consciousness and because our life is becoming easier because of technological development. But there are also negative changes because we are more and more incorporated into Western ways of thinking, Western traditions, e.g., clothing. If women wear revealing clothes, this makes men weak with sexual desire, and thus their masculinity is shaken. – Babaya

Here, the West is allied with women, especially in the ways it is affecting patterns of dress. It is a shift in the symbolism as used by other men, who linked women's allure to their traditional use of herbs and sorcery, while men's power was linked to the West. The arbitrariness of how the West is read as a symbol is evident.

Another man put the struggle between women and men into the classic 'money versus sex' dichotomy, repeated by several of the respondents in my interviews. One woman told me that 'Women here are forced into a mercenary attitude; the man is [seen as] a source of stuff'. And some men see the situation similarly.

> On change – the woman has become one of the luxuries men are trying to have, [in their search for] as much pleasure as possible. By the same token, men have become a goal for women to realize their dreams. Each is trying to make the best of a situation – men have money, women have sex. Hence, we have the emergence of women and the disappearance of men. – Hicham

Sex beats money? Or does he mean that commodification (particularly of sexuality) is a force that reduces men's patriarchal power? This emergence of women into an equal relationship in struggle with men over social resources definitely angers a faction of those religious Muslims who interpret the Qur'an and Islamic tradition as more in support of male dominance than some others do. This is one of the strains of 'fundamentalist' theological interpretation found today in many parts of the Islamic world.

There are two kinds of men: those who are influenced and those not and who reject the intrusion of the woman in general. Equality of the sexes means the destruction of religion. These changes are negative! They are against the doctrines of Islam. If the woman wants to work outside, society should provide her with suitable jobs and specific jobs such as teaching – only of women, and nursing – only of women. I want discrimination between women and men. And women reduce men's opportunities in getting work because they ask for less than men. – Mustapha

While Morocco has not been one of the more obvious sources of such Islamist reaction, there was a frequent underlying motif that identified a basic dichotomy between Islamic morality and Western consumerist hedonism. That such a dualism is falsely conceived should be self-evident; no such powerful social forces are ever so clearly distinguishable as that.

There is a quick change going on, with two viewpoints: (1) Islamic – we have a new faction of Muslims whose purpose is to spread the true Islamic concepts about persons and their role in life, but they are small in number; (2) materialist – most people live to fulfil material goals, such as owning a house, a car, luxuries, travelling, pleasure. Here the impact of the West is clear because most people are following this Machiavellian pattern. – Hicham

This dichotomy, steeped in the anger of postcolonial experience and class inequalities, and in the frustration of seeing cherished forms of familial organization dissolving, points towards a simple explanation for the complex disruptions of the contemporary world, disruptions as familiar in New York as they are in Rabat. Some of my informants, though, framed their experience in terms of the alienation of capitalist modernity in general.

There are changes in the relationship between husband and wife, father and mother, and their children. The ties are not as strong as before. Individualism grows and has influence on relationships between friends. [It] leads to thinking in terms of individual profit. There is a negative effect on the psychology of the individual whose happiness is endangered because of a decline in human ties. – Ahmed

More men were ambivalent (23 of 48) about the social changes than were either opposed to them (16) or supportive of them (9), which stands to reason, since it is difficult to separate the benefits of these changes from the problems effected. But in their answers, anti-West and pro-Islam statements stood out as a measure of how the individuals related to the changes they saw around them. Far more of those under thirty expressed some sort of anger at Western pressures, Western styles, Western consumption

157

patterns (9 out of 33) than those over thirty (1 out of 9).[10] As to education, the only thing that stood out was that college-educated men were deeply ambivalent, which may speak to the complexity of gaining a Western-style education in a land where the privileges of such knowledge are uncertain. Income did have a clear effect: none of those with the highest incomes (above 8,000 dirham per month) was either opposed to the social changes taking place, or expressed anger at the West in general. That stands to reason as well, since their income guarantees more of the benefits of change, and is likely to bring them into more contact with Europe and the United States.

This question about the perceptions of social changes illuminates many of the central themes that I found repeated among the men I interviewed. Family roles and organization, economic roles and opportunities, and the global politics of a (post)modern world were the most salient issues about social change for many men. I will end by placing in contradistinction two seemingly paradoxical answers to this question, which display the co-existence of hope and uncertainty, a societal cognitive dissonance that is more and more the standard condition for the human being in trans-formation.

We are at a crossroads; we are living in an amalgam, i.e., no one knows the results of the present situation. Our situation is leading us to a gloomy future. We're heading towards a state where we'll be neither Moroccans nor Westerners [...] We can't tell what the influence is or will be; we are still waiting for the result. – Youniss

We are moving toward equality. There are fewer differences. We are more and more cultivated or learned. Women are more and more conscious of their rights and responsibilities. And they are struggling to get both legal and material equality. Men are accepting the change, despite religion. This is positive. – Lhouari

Notes

1 All names have been changed.

2 *Muqaawama* – a lovely image in Arabic referring to standing up, as for one's rights.

3 It will be interesting to see whether the new *maquiladora*-type com-ponent assembly factories moving into Morocco continue the pattern estab-lished for the rest of the Third World: high percentages of females, especially young, dextrous and obedient, make up the workforce. That will certainly fuel this vision of women benefiting where men lose out, as it has elsewhere.

4 This was corroborated by one well-educated woman I interviewed, though about other women.

5 Deborah Kapchan quotes an apothecary druggist as saying: 'That which women do here! The wonders of God! They have that way [...] just women do that. They do it to a man so he'll want them. He finds that something's been done to him; he's sick or something. Or else she wants him not to love his mother anymore. She does something to him. And then it ruins him' (1996: 241). Her study, *Gender on the Market*, of Beni Mellal of Northern Morocco is useful in its nuanced presentation of women's use of sorcery and magic as 'counter-hegemonic discourse'. This idea is also corroborated by Eva Rosander, in *Women in a Borderland*, in which she calls talk of sorcery and evil a female 'rhetorical genre' (1991: 228), a clear form of female power in an unbalanced sex/gender system.

6 For example, see Herdt's extensive work on the Sambia (1981, 1982) or Thomas Gregor (1985) on the Mehinaku.

7 Note the following quotation from Davis and Davis (1995) who write from their research in the small semi-rural Moroccan town of Zawiya: 'The emphasis on female sexuality as the force that drives erotic relations for both partners in heterosexual encounters accords well with our reading of the role of magic and possession in love affairs. The male is anxious about his powerful longings for physical intimacy and the loss of autonomy it implies, and he projects desire onto the female, casting her as the agent of unrestrainable lust' (1995: 223).

8 The chart has some similarities to the left hand/right hand charts of Pierre Bourdieu in his work on honour in Kabyle society (1965: 222).

9 Kapchan puts it this way: 'The sorceress is involved in a power struggle. The disorder she represents is specifically the breaking down of the patriarchal value system, which gains its identity in part through the control it asserts over women. But unlike the social manipulation of women, manipulation of men via magical practices is not socially sanctioned' (1996: 254).

10 The number of informants is forty-two; five of those interviewed did not speak of this problem of West and East at all.

References

Abouzeid, L. (1989) *Year of the Elephant: A Moroccan Woman's Journey Toward Independence*, trans. Barbara Parmenter. Austin: University of Texas Press.

Bourdieu, P. (1965) 'The Sentiment of Honour in Kabyle Society', in J. G. Peristiany (ed.), *Honour and Shame: The Values of Mediterranean Society*. London: Weidenfeld and Nicolson, pp. 191–241.

Carrigan, T., B. Connell and J. Lee (1985) 'Toward a New Sociology of Masculinity', *Theory and Society*, 14: 551–604.

Davis, S. S. and D. A. Davis (1995) 'Possessed by Love: Gender and Romance in Morocco', in W. Jankowiak (ed.), *Romantic Passion: A Universal Experience?* New York: Columbia University Press, pp. 219–38.

Fluehr-Lobban, C. (1994) *Islamic Society in Practice*. Gainesville: University Press of Florida.

Gregor, T. (1985) *Anxious Pleasures: The Sexual Lives of an Amazonian People*. Chicago, IL: University of Chicago Press.

Gender, power and social change

Herdt, G. (ed.) (1982) *Rituals of Manhood: Male Initiation in Papua New Guinea*. Berkeley: University of California Press.

— (1981) *Guardians of the Flutes: Idioms of Masculinity*. New York: McGraw-Hill.

Horney, K. (1967) 'The Dread of Women', in H. Kelman (ed.), *Feminine Psychology*. New York: W. W. Norton, pp. 133–46.

Kapchan, D. (1996) *Gender on the Market: Moroccan Women and the Revoicing of Tradition*. Philadelphia: University of Pennsylvania Press.

Lipman-Blumen, J. (1984) *Gender Roles and Power*. Englewood Cliffs, NJ: Prentice-Hall.

Mernissi, F. (1987) *Beyond the Veil: Male Female Dynamics in a Muslim Society* [1975], rev. edn. Bloomington: Indiana University Press.

Moghadam, V. M. (1993) *Modernizing Women: Gender and Social Change in the Middle East*. Boulder, CO: Lynne Rienner.

Rosander, E. E. (1991) *Women in a Borderland: Managing Muslim Identity Where Morocco Meets Spain*. Stockholm: Stockholm Studies in Social Anthropology.

Westermarck, E. (1926) *Ritual and Belief in Morocco*, 2 vols. London: Macmillan.

— (1930) *Wit and Wisdom in Morocco: A Study of Native Proverbs*, with S. 'Abd-Es-Salam El-Baqqali. London: Routledge.

9 | Masculinity and gender violence in Yemen

MOHAMMED BAOBAID

Gender identities emerge from specific processes of socialization that imbue men and women with different social characteristics and power. In a report by UNIFEM (2002: 4), the author writes: 'Masculinity is often associated with characteristics such as aggressiveness, competitiveness, dominance, strength, courage and control. These characteristics result from a combination of biological, cultural and social influences, and relate to our understanding of power in society as a whole.'

Children learn about and develop gender identities from an early age and gradually begin to avoid behaviour they believe inappropriate for their sex. Boys often identify with a concept of masculinity associated with power and control. In many countries, ideologically and culturally constructed roles are socially consolidated and reinforced by legislation enacted to define and perpetuate the control of women by men. Specific cultural understandings and traditions in societies influence how power is exercised and realized by men and women. Since most societies have patriarchal traditions, power is generally associated with masculinity, and violence against women is a means by which men express their power and masculinity. The production and content of gender ideologies reflect the interests of the powerful, and work to sustain inequalities between men and women. Since patriarchy affords men greater social power, the articulation of gender norms reflects the male-biased interests of society. Thus, gender differences are created and reinforced through the manipulation of cultural and religious beliefs officially codified at the national level through political and legal texts.

In countries, for example Yemen, which are more conservatively patriarchal, men have the responsibility of protecting female members and the family as a whole. Women, on the other hand, are defined by their role as keepers of the family honour. Yet, while women represent the family's honour publicly, men exercise control over the content and definition of honour. Thus, the male role of family protector is enacted in a manner that gives him authority over the behaviour of women to defend family honour. This means that male violence against women in Yemen is understood in terms of male obligation to protect family honour. The combination of traditional beliefs and socio-cultural norms creates an unhealthy situation in which a woman's safety in Yemen is dependent upon her submission to her husband. These norms of gender inequality are further strengthened in legal codes that limit an independent legal identity for women, and that legislate women's social dependence upon their husbands.

Concepts of masculinity and gender relations are key to understanding the phenomenon of violence against women. The few reports on men's violence against women in Yemen, most of which were conducted in the last five years, show that women are subjected to the same types of violence found in countries around the world. Research I have conducted over the years has documented the common occurrence of beating, torture and attempted murder. Other violent acts such as hostage-taking, forced marriage, early marriage and polygamy have also been documented. Women in Yemen who experience violence in their lives most often suffer at the hands of their husbands. The psychological pain that Yemeni women in an abusive marriage experience is of great concern since women have no one to turn to for emotional support.

While the forms of violence are consistent with those found elsewhere, the consequences may be graver for women in Yemen. A woman in an abusive marriage is unlikely to return to her family of origin. Many families cannot afford to feed and meet the financial costs of supporting a returning daughter and her children. At the same time, women can expect little protection from the police. Cultural constraints prevent women from seeking help from government institutions. In Yemen, the husband and male relatives make decisions on what women may or may not do, and on what is deemed proper or improper. For example, a woman is often told whether or when she may leave the house. The lack of personal control over their own social movements means that women are unable to report violence and, thus, the problem remains largely hidden. The silence surrounding this abuse is exacerbated by the fact that violence against women in marriage is perceived as 'normal' by large portions of Yemeni society.

The conservative patriarchal culture of Yemen and durable practices of gender inequality make it difficult to confront the issue of abuse. Violence against women, especially domestic violence, constitutes a form of abuse entrenched in the familial, social, political and legal culture, and is born out of a concept of masculinity that relies upon the manipulation of patriarchal cultural and religious beliefs to secure men's dominance. This gender oppression is reinforced in Yemen through legal codes that deny women equal rights with men, and that ensure women remain dependent on men. It is important to recognize how challenging it is for women to speak out about violence in the home, to seek out help and to find support in society when both traditional practices and legal norms contend that a woman's safety is best ensured by husband and male relatives.

Methodology

This chapter relies on results obtained from studies I conducted between 1998 and 2000 on the issues of violence against women and women in conflict with the law in Yemen. Both qualitative and quantitative methods were used to gauge not only the extent of the violence, but also to understand how women felt about their status in society. Another aspect of these studies concerned learning about how Yemeni society and the legal system respond to women's rights.

I examined all police records that dealt with various types of abuse against women. Official records from both the Central Police Department within the Ministry of the Interior and the Central Department on Crime were gathered for all of Yemen for 1996 and 1997. In addition, extensive qualitative research was carried out to hear directly from women. An initial pilot study was carried out that consisted of lengthy in-depth interviews and focus group discussions with female participants recruited through friends and acquaintances. This foundational information was analysed to support an extensive exploratory study on the forms and levels of violence against women in Yemen.

A stratified sample of 120 women living in Sana'a was drawn that consisted of women from upper, middle and lower economic classes. Six trained students from the Department of Psychology and the Centre for Women's Study at the University of Sana'a interviewed 120 female participants in their homes in an informal fashion. A modular questionnaire was used that relied upon both open- and closed-ended questions oriented towards discussing various incidents of violence that the participant may have experienced and towards understanding how the participant coped with violence in her life. Despite the difficult questions, most women were eager to talk.

Understanding gender violence within the family

Violence against women is specific. All over the world, women are believed to be victims of several kinds of physical and psychological violence. Women are vulnerable to violence particularly because of their unequal social status, their generally weaker socio-economic positions, and legal and cultural constraints. They are the victims of public violence like robbery, assault, rape and discrimination, but by and large women are abused in the home.

Although growing research has addressed violence against women, relatively little remains known about the particular situation of women in developing countries. Generally, studies show that women are more afraid of victimization than men. It is also known that women are disproportionate victims of violence, much of which is experienced within the home. The International Crime Victimization Survey estimates that women's chances of being assaulted in their own homes are twice as high as those of men (Alvazzi del Frate 1998: 70). Surveys in the United States estimate that women are five or six times more likely to be the victims of violence by persons with whom they have intimate relations (Craven 1997; Bachman and Saltzman 1995). In the United States, 93 per cent of violent assaults are committed by male individuals aged eighteen and over; and 76 per cent of women physically assaulted or raped since age eighteen suffered at the hands of a husband or partner (Tjaden and Thoennes 1998).

Studies in other countries reveal the same pattern. A study in Egypt (Abd el-Wahab 1994), which used newspaper items and court files as data, showed that the majority of female victims were married. Ammar (2000) reports on a study in Egypt which estimates that 35 per cent of women are physically abused by their husbands at least once. In spite of under-reporting, the results of studies from various countries – developed and developing – also show that the majority of murdered women are killed by their partners (Heise et al. 1994). All in all, much of the violence experienced by females throughout the world is suffered within the confines of the home.

Assaults by intimates are less likely to be reported to the police than assaults by strangers (Alvazzi del Frate 1998). Tadros (1998) found that women living in an informal settlement in Cairo did not report incidents of domestic violence as they deem it inappropriate to report the 'father of one's children'. Hammoud (2001) reports on a survey in Egypt that estimated that 93 per cent of abused women did not report to the police. This same study showed that even if a violent crime by a close relation is reported, police have been known to view the matter as a private affair. And crimes of domestic violence that are reported frequently do not result in prosecution, since most victims are psychologically and economically involved with the offender, and more likely to dismiss the case (Gowdy et al. 1998). Prosecutors have historically been disinclined to pursue convictions in domestic violence cases because of problems in finding evidence and because of the belief that families have a right to privacy. In Yemen, 94 per cent of the interviewed policemen showed empathy for men who used violence against a female relative (Baobaid 2000). A small study carried out by Abd el-Wahab (1994) in Egypt that looked at murder and attempted murder revealed that only ten out of twenty court cases ordered reparation to the victim's family through a fine. In many countries, women are often punished for trying to escape an abusive situation as court decisions often deliver the children into the custody of the husband guilty of violent behaviour because he owns the home and has an income.

Afkhami et al. (1998), while stressing the diversity of Arab society, see male dominance as the underlying cause for violence against women. The authors argue that women in the Arab world are caught in a vicious circle of suffering and isolation because they have been systematically deprived of the knowledge of their rights. They also argue that Muslim fundamentalist doctrine singles out women's rights as the supreme test regarding cultural authenticity. In many Muslim societies, family laws have not adjusted to modern conditions of human rights and gender equality and, thus, continue to form the basis for unequal power relations between women and men. In the Abd el-Wahab study (1994), arguments over the confiscation of women's property, disagreements over income, unhappiness over living with in-laws, problems regarding the 'moral' behaviour of women, the husband's wish to marry another wife or the woman's desire for a divorce constitute areas of conflict that often trigger violence. Hammoud (2001) focuses on the concept of 'societal violence' to discuss domestic violence in Arab countries. He argues that acceptance of domestic abuse as 'normal' within marriage in Arab societies constitutes a form of collective 'societal violence'.

The status of women in Islamic countries

The status of women and their relationships with men, the family and society remains controversial in the lives of Muslims. This status is conditioned by interpretations and traditions of Islamic teachings and cultural practices. In most Muslim countries, the teachings of Islam have been mixed with inherited cultural traditions. Both Islam and culture have been practised in a manner biased in favour of men. Islam's position towards women's status in society is actually more progressive than many people think. In many respects, the Qur'an was revolutionary in the rights it afforded women. However, Islam has been adopted in different regions of the world in a manner consistent with existing cultural practices and traditions. Inherited cultural practices have particularly influenced how Islam is applied to gender roles and relationships by encouraging a continuation of practices and beliefs that allow men power and control over women.

While Islam clearly articulates equality between men and women, the Qur'an has been interpreted in a manner supportive of male dominance and patriarchy. One example that illustrates the equality between men and women as proscribed in Islam is the time the Prophet Muhammad said, pointing to his wife Aisha, 'Take half of the teachings of your religion from her.' The Prophet emphasized that women have the right to interpret the Qur'an for themselves and others. Today this right along with many others is often ignored or downplayed by many Muslims, especially the male religious and political establishment. In most Muslim societies, the rights of women are not understood independently, but are linked to the interests of the family. Both Islamic and cultural understandings of family dynamics give husbands rights over their wives. Thus, we see that in some Muslim countries women are not able to exercise mobility independently; they must be accompanied by a male family member. In Saudi Arabia, for instance, women are not permitted to drive. While the rights and freedoms of women across the Muslim world vary, men have been able to manipulate religion and culture to sustain and reinforce gender inequalities.

To appreciate the progressive quality of Islam, we need to examine the status of women before the advent of Islam, about 1,400 years ago, when the Arabian peninsula was occupied mainly by nomads. Their lifestyle involved raising cattle, engaging in trade and battling with other tribes over land and resources. Men were responsible for much of the tribal welfare, while women's role was essentially limited to procreating and raising children. The Arabian peninsula became famous for the degrading manner in which women were treated like property and had to endure such practices as polygamy; captured women were forced into marriages and the inheritance of wives went to the eldest son upon a husband's death, with the wives deemed part of the inheritance. In some tribes, tradition allowed husbands to offer or lend their wives to guests or friends. While Islam brought progressive practices, more freedom and better protections for women, some of the tribal traditions from the Arabian peninsula were integrated to become part of Islamic heritage.

With the spread of Islam to other cultures and regions, the Qur'an was interpreted through local traditions, norms and beliefs. For example, during the Ottoman Empire, inherited Turkish cultures and traditions were integrated as though they reflected and represented Islamic teachings. During the time of the Ottoman Empire, women were segregated from men, a practice which emerged out of cultural traditions in the region but was enforced as though it were part of Islam. In addition, the history of Islam is not one of continuous progression and development. While scientific and artistic contributions are part of Islamic heritage, Islamic culture also suffered from periods of stagnation. During this period of the 'Dark Ages', scientific and intellectual interpretations of the Qur'an were actively suppressed. During such times, the rights of women were often denied, and oppressive notions regarding the role of women in society emerged and became lodged as part of Islamic teachings.

This review shows how different traditions were incorporated within the body of Islamic religious teachings. Once patriarchal interpretations of Islam were integrated, they became entrenched as part of Islamic culture through two primary processes still with us today. The first process by which male bias is reinforced concerns the manner by which young boys and girls are socialized to learn about each other and themselves. In many Muslim societies, boys are given greater social recognition and rewards than girls. Thus, women learn to live with gender discrimination and male privilege from an early age. The second process involves the manner by which notions of gender inequality and practices of discrimination become firmly rooted in society through legislation. In many Muslim countries, legislation has been enacted that limits the freedom of women and restricts their roles in society and the family. In many legal articles governing personal status laws in many Arab countries, the rights of women are ignored. Examples include depriving a married woman of the right to a divorce and essentially making the husband her legal guardian. Muslim clerics still differ on many issues regarding Islam and the roles and rights of women; the issue regarding the need for wives to obey their husbands is particularly controversial. Some clerics believe that wives are obligated to concede to their husbands' wishes and that disobedience should result in some form of coercive or financial punishment. Others feel that marriage constitutes a partnership based on mutual respect, and thus reject ideas of obedience and punishment. The liberal clerics and scholars recognize the rights to women given by the Qur'an and support the idea of equality between men and women.

Mohammed Fathi Nagib (2001) discusses how the inherited cultural traditions of Muslim societies have negatively influenced the formulation of legal and social codes in Arab countries. This is partly because conservative clerical and social forces have been able to manipulate those tenets in Islam open to interpretation to their own benefit. Nagib (2001) writes that the Qur'an outlines religious tenets that are either negotiable or non-negotiable. Non-negotiable practices include such obligations as fasting during the holy month of Ramadan and praying five times a day. Many other beliefs and practices are open to some interpretation, although it is generally accepted that interpretations should reflect the central spirit and message of the Qur'an. An area of great religious negotiation concerns those passages and texts that relate to the status of women within Islam. While the Qur'an unequivocally states that men and women are equal with respect to one another, other passages and sayings have been interpreted in ways that limit the rights of women and deny equality. One area of negotiated interpretation concerns the content and application of Shari'a[1] in society and its role in shaping legislation related to the family and women in Arab countries, and since all of the interpretative work has been and is carried out by men, the overall tone of such legislation is biased towards men to the disadvantage of women.

One of the main political objectives for activists working on the issue of violence against women in the Muslim world today is to try to undo the patriarchal legacy of inherited cultural traditions and manipulated religious interpretations, and to advocate for a return to more liberal and equitable interpretations of Shari'a and the Qur'an with regard to the status of women. It is necessary to remind Muslim societies that Islam does not condone the abuse of women and grants both husbands and wives equal rights and responsibilities. The Qur'an provides the foundation for beliefs, practices and norms that can challenge ideas currently dominating social and legal systems in Muslim countries. In order to ensure the empowerment and personal safety of women in the region, it is necessary to question and do away with manipulated readings of Islam and patriarchal cultural traditions that have resulted in social ideologies and legislation that serve to subordinate women by unjustly restricting their rights and freedoms.

Yemen society

Yemen is situated on the southern tip of the Arabian peninsula. Until 1990, Yemen consisted of two countries: North and South Yemen. North Yemen was highly traditional, governed until 1962 by an Imam not inclined to maintain any relations with outsiders. The South, on the other had, was Marxist and maintained close links with Eastern European communist countries. South Yemen practised a more liberal attitude with regard to the role of women; women in the South experienced a higher literacy rate and generally enjoyed a more favourable status. After the collapse of communism in Eastern Europe and the disintegration of the Soviet Union, South Yemen could no longer rely upon its communist allies for economic and financial support. At the same time, North Yemen was suffering both economic and social turmoil as the result of the Gulf War in the region that saw many migrant workers from the Gulf states sent back. This had a marked effect on the North since it no longer benefited from remittances by overseas workers that kept the economy afloat.

In 1990 the North and South merged and, in the ten years since, the effects of political and economic upheavals have taken their toll. Many families in Yemen live in poverty, the cost of living has more than doubled, healthcare services are scarce and insufficient, maternal and infant death is among the highest in the world, and male literacy sits at 67 per cent while female literacy is at 24 per cent. As in many other developing nations, a large portion of the population is young; at least 49 per cent of the population is under the age of fifteen. Much of the population in Yemen lives in rural areas where access to schooling facilities has declined in the past years and illiteracy rates remain high. While larger urban areas fare better than rural ones, institutions and facilities are strained. Yemen ranks among the lowest thirty countries on the United Nations' human development index, a measure of human development calculated using such information as life expectancy, healthcare, education and standards of living (UNDP 2001).

Yemeni society places great emphasis on family and tribal loyalties and can, therefore, be thought of as traditional. Gender segregation is practised and women are subject to confining codes of proper conduct that limit their roles outside the family. Notions of family honour force women to face a number of restrictions on their behaviour. In many of the smaller towns, women exercise limited public mobility, and when they do step outside the home, they veil completely in a black cloak and headdress that covers the entire body. Tribal and traditional structures that govern much of Yemeni social and familial interactions make it difficult for women to act independently in their own interests because men are given the right to govern over the lives and identities of women.

Violence against women in Yemen

Women in Yemen are exposed to various forms of violence and repression. Yemeni culture teaches men to control female family members to ensure that women do not behave in ways that undermine enforced gender values and jeopardize family honour. How women behave and with whom they interact in public are matters of serious concern. If a woman is caught, or even suspected of, conducting an 'illicit' relationship with a man, male relatives may agree to kill her to restore family honour. Male relatives who carry out such honour killings are generally not punished. This extreme example illustrates the level of violence against women in Yemen and the extent to which they must fear for their physical safety in a society that lives by patriarchal values of family honour. Women in Yemen are subject to a range of gender acts of violence that reinforce the privileged and powerful position of men and that remind women of their lesser and dependent status.

Societal violence Societal violence refers to practices, norms and beliefs that limit women from exercising fully their social and personal rights. Societal violence includes the large range of repressive and abusive actions and practices women suffer and endure in their lives. The existence of societal violence strongly affects the status of women by supporting norms that limit women's access to education, employment and political participation. Hammoud (2001) argues that pervasive and accepted negative societal attitudes towards women in Arab societies constitute an integral factor in the existence of domestic violence. She suggests that we look at acts of domestic violence not in isolation, but rather that we should understand the existence of and tolerance of acts of domestic abuse through an understanding of the larger social culture towards women. Thus, the blame for violence against women rests not only with the actual perpetrators, but also with general social and cultural attitudes that discriminate against and oppress women, and that treat them as property.

In such patriarchal societies as Yemen, for example, early marriage constitutes a typical example of societal violence against women, since it reinforces the position that women should not experience independence in their lives and must be treated as property to be passed along from fathers on to husbands.[2] The average age of marriage in Yemen is sixteen years (Baobaid and Balquis 2001). Marriages are arranged by family elders and are treated as a social and economic agreement between two families or tribes. Women themselves have little or no voice in the making of decisions about their own lives and do not have the freedom to pursue their own wishes. Another common example of societal violence against women involves unilaterally male-initiated divorce. Many women in Yemen are faced with the fact that their husbands can divorce them without their consent. This constitutes a form of abuse both because once again decisions impacting on the lives of women are made without their participation, and because life for divorced women is very difficult in Yemen. Many divorced women live in poverty and are socially isolated because they become stigmatized. The fact that life is miserable for divorced women also has the implication that women in abusive marriages are unlikely to seek out a divorce, and are, therefore, effectively trapped within an unhealthy marriage.

These examples indicate how social ideologies and practices that uphold a conservative structure of patriarchy constrain women from exercising independent control over their lives and, thus, generate and support conditions that trap women in abusive ways. The traditional culture of masculinity that structures Yemeni society fosters a culture of violence against women by ensuring that women remain isolated and vulnerable. By treating women as less valuable than men, Yemeni social norms produce social structures and practices of inequality that support a generalized atmosphere of abuse. An analysis of the interviews conducted with 120 women in Sana'a revealed that women understood that society was structured such that their oppression is not only produced, but also treated as though it were natural (Baobaid and Bijleveld 2002). One woman articulated the experience of societal violence best: 'Women have no rights. They have to suffer; society does with us as they please. We are second-class citizens. Nobody listens, nobody cares, people think this is normal but it is not normal.' Indeed, several of the participants in the study ranked early marriage[3] and polygamy as important practices of societal violence. One woman said: 'This society always favours men. Nobody thinks of us. We suffer many injustices, even ones that no one thinks about such as polygamy and early marriage.' Respondents indicated these two practices led to deteriorating family relations and created a family climate conducive to violence. The women also mentioned acrimonious divorce processes, the customary confiscation of women's inheritances, and the manner in which male dominance over women permeated all levels of society. An older woman spoke of how her husband unilaterally decided to divorce her, and of how she now suffers from social stigmatization:

After twenty years of marriage and six children, he divorced me. He sent me to my family house. It was a big shock for me and for my whole family. People tried to mediate between us, but no success. I am now living with my family in a very small house. Everybody blames me and is looking at me with mean eyes. Nobody welcomes me here. The members of the family often tell me that this divorce is my fault. Many times I have thought of killing myself, but I am afraid of Allah, and I think of my children. I always pray that I will get justice.

The women also talked about how ignored they felt in society and said they had little confidence in the idea that society took their plights seriously. The following statement reflects the sentiments of one woman on the issue of male bias and privilege in Yemeni society:

I don't believe what I hear from the media about equality between men and women in our society. Our society is men's society. Men decide what is right and what is wrong, not only in the family but also in the whole society. They interpret the holy Qur'an in harmony with their interest. We know that our religion guarantees many rights for women, but men accept only what is good for them and don't accept what is not good for them. For example in some parts of Yemen the community doesn't accept women's inheritance: this is against Islamic law! This is because they don't accept a woman as a person.

A number of women interviewed also stated that even their own relatives seemed to show little concern for their physical and psychological safety. Women stated that family members, and society at large, told them that they should act only to please their husbands. They were also told that acting contrary to their husbands' wishes constituted justified grounds for their husbands to beat them. One woman touched upon the isolation that women experience: 'When people have to choose between the word of a man and the word of a woman, they will believe the man. Even my close relatives believe my husband. So I have no one; I simply have to solve this problem myself.'

Physical violence Physical violence refers to 'any use of the physical aspects of men that is intended, or has the result of gaining power over partner or children' (Changing Ways 2001: 75). The consequences of physical violence not only involve physical injury or death, but also damaging emotional psychological effects. Battered women often talk about the pain that results from the emotional pain of physical violence more than the pain of physical injuries. A survey conducted by the author in 1999 showed that the number of incidents involving physical violence against women in Yemen increased from 348 in 1996 to 460 in 1997. Also, incidents of assault against women also increased in the period from 1996 to 1997 from thirty-six to 142. These numbers show that women abuse in Yemen does exist and is becoming a growing problem, even though Yemeni society does not consider violence against women to be a serious problem. The interviews conducted with 120 women in Sana'a, none of whom reported violence to the police, also clearly indicate that violence against women within the home is widespread and serious in nature. Of the women interviewed, more than 50 per cent reported experiencing physical violence. Their experiences with violence included: rape, attempted rape, assault and torture. Women also revealed that most of the offenders were close family relatives: 61.8 per cent of the respondents reported that they suffered abuse at the hands of their husbands; 28.2 per cent of the women implicated their father and brothers; 5.6 per cent of women were abused by their sons; 11.8 per cent faced violence from their mothers; 7.3 per cent suffered abuse by a paternal uncle; while 5.5 per cent named a maternal uncle; and 31.8 per cent named another individual.[4] In total 69.1 per cent of all respondents reported being subject to acts of violence by someone close to them, and 16.4 per cent of participants spoke of being abused or assaulted by a stranger. These figures indicate that women are 4.5 times more likely to be the victim of violence by someone they know than by a stranger. Thus, analysing the data gathered through the interviews in Sana'a, it is clear that women face greater risk of physical and emotional harm by someone close to them.

Some of the women our interviewers spoke to suffered severe physical injuries as a result of the violence they were subjected to. One woman lost her eyesight, and another was handicapped for life. Some women talked of having cigarettes extinguished on their bodies, and others were stoned. Several women reported having been locked inside their houses, and one woman talked of having been confined to a cellar for days on end. All of these abuses caused not only great physical harm, but emotional harm as well. Some of the more painful moments for many women involve the lack of sympathy and support from family members when they reported suffering abuse by their husbands. It is therefore fair to say that women in Yemen frequently suffer abuse twice over. Abuse is both experienced as the actual physical and emotional violence directed at them and in the lack of support or concern they receive from family members once they confide in them about the initial violence directed at them. The fact that women are forced to suffer in silence and told that it must be their fault their husbands are abusing them constitutes a form of violence directed at women as well. It is an example of the societal violence that encircles women; it is an example that illustrates the extent to which women are vulnerable, isolated and trapped. The emotional and physical pain of abused women in Yemen is greatly exacerbated by social norms and beliefs that do not take women's suffering seriously and that tend to blame women for the violent actions of others. These uncaring and unconcerned attitudes often lead women to accept their own abuse. A number of the women interviewed viewed the violence they endured within their homes as 'normal' and, therefore, felt that it was not important to take any form of action to stop the abuse or to seek out support from outsiders. Data in Yemen reveal that only 3.4 per cent of women report abuse to police, more do confide in parents, relatives or friends, but a large segment (27.6 per cent) say or do nothing. These figures reinforce the point that social attitudes in Yemen that devalue women create a climate in which women facing violence suffer alone and with little help and empathy.

The legalization of gender violence

Male violence against women is not only tolerated by Yemeni traditional beliefs and customs; it is has also been perpetuated through official institutional practices such as the law. It can be argued that violence against women in Yemen has undergone legalization. In particular, some of the articles of Yemen's Personal Status Law and Yemen's criminal and penal law are structured such that they deny women independence and, in fact, produce their dependence on their fathers, husbands or sons. By denying women legal identities and rights of their own, the legal system sustains and reinforces societal violence against women. The content and application of the law mimic patriarchal cultural beliefs and practices that give men a far greater status than women and force women under the control of men. Legal articles and rulings that deny women equality with men as independent individuals serve to institutionalize cultural customs of male privilege that establish women's subordination to men.

For example, Article (16) of the 1992 Personal Status Law deprives women of the right of choosing a husband and instead confers this right on a guardian or next of kin, such as a father or elder son. This article, therefore, reproduces cultural traditions and serves to reinforce male control over the lives of women. Other sections of the Personal Status Law, such as Articles (6) and (40), clarify in law a wife's marital obligations towards her husband; these sections reinforce beliefs that devalue women and imply that women exist to serve men. Another area of social practice that has been legally encoded and functions to reduce the status of women concerns the practices of *diya* (blood money) and *arsh* (wound money). *Diya* and *arsh* are traditional practices of compensation or social insurance and manifest attitudes of discrimination against women. Both are governed by a system of rules that is similar to the manner in which inheritance functions. Rules of inheritance posit that a woman should be compensated at half the rate of a man (Colburn 2000). This cultural practice is entrenched in Yemen and is based upon the belief that a woman is of lesser value than a man; however, the unequal distribution of inheritance between daughters and sons is not to be found within the Qur'an. Rather, valuing a woman's worth as half that of a man is a socio-legal practice established by manipulated interpretations of Shari'a by the clergy in Yemen. *Diya*, too, is applied differently in cases where the victim is a female. Usually the injured party can expect some form of financial compensation for their loss and pain from the individual or family that has committed the crime. However, in cases of honour killings, a murder that involves a male family member killing a female member of the family for some alleged moral transgression, *diya* is forfeited. Criminal and penal law do not require males to pay a fine for killing a female member of the family if the accusations against the woman involve claims of adultery. Legal codes, therefore, institutionalize and legalize patriarchal social practices that deny a women equal status with men. The fact that honour killings are legally exempt from punishment shows the extent to which a woman's life in Yemen is deemed worthless and the extreme extent to which men are able to oppress and violate women without social and criminal punishment and moral censure. Furthermore, the manner in which crimes such as adultery are viewed and dealt with demonstrate the force of male privilege and bias in Yemen's social and legal culture. Only women are held morally and criminally responsible for adultery, men who commit adultery are often not punished. Thus, the institutionalization and legalization of cultural beliefs and practices of gender inequality in Yemen produce and reinforce the power and freedoms of men while ensuring that women remain vulnerable and subordinate to men.

Another area of concern involves the treatment of women by the justice system. While women are subjected to the same law as men for criminal offences, the implementation or application of the law is much harsher on women than on men. Women are not afforded the same legal treatment as men and must often endure personal and legal violations. Women accused of crimes face great disrespect and antipathy. Many workers in the justice system feel that the women they encounter merit no empathy, and believe that they deserve to be treated harshly for bringing shame upon their families and society. Women are frequently pre-judged and treated as guilty and in need of punishment before any ruling on the case has been made. Thus, the justice system is implemented in a biased fashion against women and frequently punishes women more severely. For instance, 80 per cent of all women imprisoned in Yemen[5] are guilty of moral offences such as adultery or for being in the company of an unrelated man. Often, a woman is sent to prison even though there is no evidence of her having engaged in a sexual relationship. Mothers must keep their children with them in prison, and children born in the prison often remain there until they reach the age of twelve. In addition, women may find themselves in prison for much longer than their sentence because release is dependent upon the approval of a male family member.

The response of society towards gender violence

How Yemeni society responds to violence against women differs according to social class and geographical location. In rural and tribal areas the conservative patriarchal culture produces attitudes that are more tolerant of violence against women than those found along the coastal areas. It is important to note that more than 70 per cent of the population in Yemen lives in rural areas, meaning that the majority of women in Yemen live in a social setting that produces and supports cultural attitudes and practices of male privilege and superiority. Indeed, it would be fair to say that most Yemenis regard the concept of violence against women as something unfamiliar to Yemeni society, and a product of Western societies imported to damage long-standing Islamic cultural and tribal traditions that regulate family life. In Yemen the issue of domestic abuse is not understood as a form of human and criminal violation against women; it is not believed that women have a right to live in a marriage free from violence. Rather, much of Yemeni society sees the use of physical and emotional violence against women as a right owned by men to ensure the integrity of family life and family honour is maintained. Since the status of men in Yemen is greatly defined by the honour of the family or, to be more precise, by the reputation and behaviour of women, men regard using violence against women to discipline and control their actions as their right and responsibility. Notions of family honour establish the idea that men are superior to and more valuable socially than women, which then allows for practices of male power and control over women. This belief in male privilege and superiority results in a culture of masculinity and patriarchy that structures every aspect and level of society. As seen above, notions of family honour are protected and institutionalized in law to allow for honour killings. It is important to understand just to what extent tribal and religious leaders have been able to use family honour and its structure of male domination within the home to inform the configurations and work-ings of society and the justice system. The structure of male privilege and patriarchy that emerged out of tribal religious and cultural practices has been manipulated and reinforced by those men in power to influence the social and institutional character of Yemen such that women are treated as lesser individuals than men.

The majority of Yemeni men understand women's rights as a tool used by women to challenge traditional social orders of society and dominance of men. Violence against women is not viewed as the fault of men, but rather women themselves are blamed for the violent actions of men (Baobaid 2000). Cultural norms dictate that women are responsible for the abusive actions of men because it is assumed that it must have been their 'bad' behaviour that led to male violence. In this equation the abusive actions of men are completely justified and legitimate. This attitude affects how police officers and judges treat reports of violence made by women. Since it is popularly believed that violence against women constitutes legitimate domestic behaviour on the part of men, women in Yemen face an uphill struggle in getting abuse recognized as criminal behaviour.[6]

Even though general public opinion in Yemen is that violence against women is not widespread, the issue has gained more attention over the last five years. Some newspapers have openly begun to discuss the issue by printing stories of domestic violence, despite the fact that heavy restrictions are placed upon the freedom of the press. Also, university professors have started to conduct research on the topic and have been able to publicize their findings. Yemeni society is slowly becoming more aware of the exist-ence of violence against women, and has even begun to view this as an important social problem. However, political activism and awareness on the issue of gender violence is challenged by powerful traditional forces in the country. Conservative political, tribal and religious leaders view any challenges to the male power structure as a threat to their own position in society and, therefore, react strongly to any social activism on this issue.

In 1999, for example, the Centre of Women's Study at the University of Sana'a, established in 1996, was shut down after extremist religious and cultural groups launched a campaign of violence and intimidation. These groups attacked the work of the centre and charged the professors and researchers with corrupting culture and Islam. The work on gender was regarded as immoral and extremist groups used the media and the mosques to attack the centre on the grounds that it was promoting homosexuality and, therefore, constituted a threat to Yemeni cultural and Islamic values. Following a commission of inquiry set up by Parliament, the centre was disbanded in December 1999. The public outrage of extremist groups was meant to ensure that changes to the status of women would not be realized. By attacking the work of the centre as that of Western cultural imperialism, and succeeding in shutting it down, extremist groups were able to reinforce beliefs that violence against women does not exist in Yemen. From this example it is clear that civil society organizations working on behalf of women's rights face serious challenges and dangers. Those who benefit from the current patriarchal structure are unlikely to tolerate activism that seeks to improve the status of women, viewing such challenges as threats to their power. While it is encouraging to see that small steps have been taken in Yemen to acknowledge the issue of violence against women, there still remains much work to be done to improve women's situation. In order to carry forward their work, civil society organizations in Yemen would benefit greatly from the support of the international community.

Conclusion

One of this chapter's main intentions was to make the link between violence against women inside the home and the widespread existence of social practices of gender inequality and subordination sustained and accepted as part of Yemeni culture. This chapter employed the concept of societal violence to understand how violence against women within the home is a symptom of the culture of violence and oppression born out of patriarchal ideologies and practices that dominate and define Yemeni society. The central point that must be understood is that in a socially conservative male-structured country like Yemen, domestic abuse constitutes one form of violence among many. The dominating culture of masculinity that shapes and organizes Yemeni society essentially creates a cultural climate where women face repression in practically every sphere of social interaction, and where widespread abusive actions towards women are tolerated. Violence against women in the home, therefore, represents a specific form of violence linked to and supported by other forms of abuse and oppression directed at women throughout society. Thus, domestic abuse is not an isolated practice of violence that women suffer, but must be understood as embedded in a larger culture of violence that defines the social fabric of Yemen. It is very important that a political link is made between the existence and tolerance of violence in the home and the existence of a governing patriarchal culture that subordinates women and dismisses their rights. This produces a reality for women in Yemen where abuse and oppression are deeply entrenched in the daily and overall social and cultural structure of the country.

Women in Yemen suffer some form of violence in almost every area of their lives because they lack rights that are respected and observed. Women have little or no power to influence choices regarding education or employment, marriage and mobility, and have weakened access to legal rights and justice. The embedded tolerance for the subordination of women that permeates every level of and relationship in society creates a situation that normalizes violence directed at women. It also creates a climate of denial of female abuse because beliefs and practices of gender inequality are regarded as ordinary and acceptable customs.

The subordination of women in Yemen is secured in the structure of society not only by ideologies that support the dominance of a culture of masculinity and male privilege, but also through social and institutional practices that reinforce the dominant position of men over women. One important area, discussed in this chapter, where such gender discrimination and subordination are realized, is through the legal system and notions of legal rights. Although the Yemeni constitution guarantees gender equality, in practice this is not realized in either the legal system or the society. There is a significant discrepancy between what is to be found written in the constitution and the content of laws (especially with reference to family law) and their application. Over the years, laws have been passed and applied in a manner that undermines the guarantee of equality between men and women. Women rarely see their rights protected or enforced in Yemen because the manner in which laws are interpreted and justice is practised reflects patriarchal culture and interests. Thus, we can argue that violence against women has, in essence, been legalized. The legal system in Yemen functions in a manner that reflects and reproduces the same beliefs and norms of male dominance and privilege practised within families and throughout society.

The normalization of inequalities and abuse towards women in Yemen requires that work to combat violence against women is pushed forward on many fronts. One of the main areas of activism involves challenging the ideology of masculinity that has informed social practices towards women. In order to encourage beliefs, norms and practices that encourage a positive change in the treatment of women, it is necessary to disseminate values of human rights and gender equality. An important area in which to begin work is within the school system. If young boys and girls can learn to create an alternative cultural framework that is founded upon notions of gender equality, equal rights, shared freedoms and mutual respect, then perhaps the patriarchal framework that dominates Yemeni society at present can begin to be displaced.

To replace the current patriarchal structure and culture of masculinity and male privilege so deeply embedded in Yemeni social relations today with a construction of gender relations that is equitable and reflects human rights, not solely male rights, it is necessary to engage in effective strategies of public education. One strategy involves raising the level of public awareness on the issue of violence against women in society, and on focusing on the serious consequences such abuse and oppression have not only on the health of women, but on that of families and society as a whole.

It is important to talk to women and to listen to their experiences and needs, and to provide women with psychological, social and legal supports. Outreach and public education, however, should not be restricted to women. In order to realize a culture of gender equality it is necessary to work with and through political, religious and tribal leaders in order to effect significant and long-lasting changes. To address seriously the issue of violence against women in society and the home, practices and beliefs that shape the current negative attitudes towards women must be challenged. It is important for civil society organizations to try to dismantle those cultural and institutional barriers that treat women as though they are worthless and without rights.

I also strongly feel that it is important to work with men not only to educate them on the issue of violence against women, but also to encourage men to adopt a restructured definition of masculinity. Since many people in Yemeni society view the issue of woman abuse as a concept forced upon them by Western societies, it is important to approach the issue carefully. Rather than alienate men, and particularly those men in a position of authority, it is necessary to work with them. To realize a true displacement of the culture of male privilege and domination, both men and women must learn to value gender equality.

In addition to working with ordinary men and women in Yemen to challenge current structures of male domination and privilege, and the

179

generalized climate of societal violence directed against women, it is equally important to change the content and application of the legal and justice systems. Western donor agencies should make an effort to support not only the work of civil society organizations, but also government institutions. By helping the government of Yemen restructure its legal system, much can be done to improve not only women's safety, but also their ability to exercise their rights in a just and respected manner.

Appendix

Case Study 1 A lady in her thirties sat in a crowded room of Alhudaida women's prison surrounded by her three daughters. When I came to speak with her she could not speak for crying. She told me that she had just moved from Taiz to Alhudaida with her three children after she got divorced. She wants to be independent from her extended family and her village people. She thinks she did a good job, because she started to make bread for restaurants and do other house work that she could sell to make money. She continued saying that she had started to forget her divorce tragedy and had hopes for a new life. It was the first time in her life that she was able to enjoy freedom and independence. She told me her story in these words: 'I met a guy called Saleh who was working in a restaurant and was helping me delivering my bread to the restaurant. He was very nice to me and very respectful. I never let him come in to my house. I only met with him in a public place in front of people. He is a shy person. He told me once that he wants me to marry him. I answered that I am not ready for that now. I had a bad experience in my previous marriage. I needed time to be prepared for another intimate relationship. It seems that he understood my situation. During that time I was harassed by a powerful man in our neighbourhood. I was very angry with him and resisted his harassment. One day Saleh came to me as usual. While I was talking with him outside my door, a police car came and stopped in close to us and pushed us into the car. They didn't have any consideration for my crying and the cries of my daughters who came out when they heard me crying. When I mentioned about my children, they said your children will come with you. Since that day until now I am here for no reason.' At that time she had been there for about one month. The director of the prison showed some sympathy for her and tried to take some action to help her. She gave us the name of her cousin who works in the same city. I contacted this man and explained her situation. He promised to come and help her with the authorities. After two days the director told me that her cousin apologized but could not come, because that would adversely affect his job. My discussion with the attorney in the prison was without success.

The director of the prison released the three daughters. Unfortunately, he did not do anything further. He told me later on that the prison attorneys considered this case a sexual crime. Any chance of helping her is very limited. They have to stay in prison until her case gets to court.

Case Study 2 Noora was eighteen years old when she went from her city, Lahj, to Alhudaida. She visited her mother's relative, and spent some time there. She met a boy called Ahmed. He invited her for a walk at the beach. She was very happy and hopeful. They took a walk several times, expressed their feelings and spoke about future plans. Ahmed told her he wanted to speak with her mother's relative about his intention to marry her. She was very excited and happy to hear that news. She cried from happiness. At that time he came close to her and wiped her tears with his hand. Suddenly everything changed dramatically. They were surrounded by policemen, and forced into a police car. The beautiful moment was killed. The beautiful hope was destroyed. When I talked to this girl at the women's prison in Alhudaida she was very depressed and hopeless. She said, 'Everything has gone. Nobody wanted to believe me that nothing wrong happened between Ahmed and me. My mother was told by her relative about my situation. She is very disappointed with me because of what happened. I am very sad about that.'

Notes

1 Shari'a law concerns Islamic jurisprudence based upon religious principles in the Qur'an and has for centuries been used to govern Islamic societies.

2 Lamis Nasser, 'Violence Against Women and Children in Arab Countries' at <http://www.amanjordan.org/studies/lamis/htm> (2001).

3 A Yemeni saying claims that girls are ready to be married by the age of eight.

4 Note that the percentages need not add up to 100 as women may have been victimized more than once by different perpetrators or the same violent act may have been carried out by more than one individual.

5 In 1998 there were at least 1,000 women imprisoned. This is a high rate for a country with a population of only 17.5 million. Also, the prisons fall below the most basic international standards. Access to healthcare is limited and pregnant women are not provided with adequate medical or dietary support.

6 When domestic violence is talked about in Yemen, if at all, most people believe that it is a problem experienced mainly by those of the lowest class and primarily by foreigners or Yemeni migrants who have returned from other countries, especially from East Africa.

References

Abd el-Wahab, L. (1994) *Al Unf al Usari fi Masr* [Domestic Violence in Egypt]. Beirut: Dar al Mada Lil Thaqafa wa Al Nashr.

Afkhami, M., G. Hofman Nemiroff and H. Vaziri (1998) *Safe and Secure: Eliminating Violence Against Women and Girls in Muslim Societies*. Bethesda, MD: SIGI Institute.

Alvazzi del Frate, A. (1998) *Victims of Crime in the Developing World*. Rome: UNICRI.

Alvazzi del Frate, A., and A. Patrignani (1999) *Women's Victimisation in Developing Countries*. Rome: UNICRI.

Ammar, N. (2000) 'In the Shadow of the Pyramids: Domestic Violence in Egypt', *International Review of Victimology*, 7: 29–46.

Bachman, R. and L. E. Saltzman (1995) *Violence Against Women: Estimated from the Redesigned Survey*. Bureau of Justice Statistics Special Report. Washington, DC: US Department of Justice.

Baobaid, M. (2000) 'Attitude of the Yemeni Police Toward Violence Against Women', *Journal for Faculty of Arts*, Sana'a University.

— (2002) *Women and the Yemeni Criminal Justice System*, Paper presented to the Ontario Community Justice Association Conference, London, Ontario, Canada.

Baobaid, M. and A. Balquis (2001) *Gender and Partnership in the Yemeni Family*, Survey presented to ESCWA.

Baobaid, M. and C. C. J. H. Bijleveld (2002) 'Violence Against Women in Yemen', *International Review of Victimology*, 9 (3): 299–348.

Bijleveld, C. C. J. H. (1998) 'Methodological Issues in the Study of Domestic Victimization Prevalence', *European Journal on Criminal Policy and Research*, 6: 316–43.

Changing Ways client manual, collective authors, 2001.

Colburn, M. (2000) *A Situation Analysis of Gender and Development in Yemen*. Yemen: Oxfam.

Council for Scientific Affairs (1992) 'Violence Against Women. Relevance for Medical Practitioners', *Journal of the American Medical Association*, 267: 31–84.

Craven, D. (1997) *Sex Differences in Violent Victimizations, 1994*, Bureau of Justice Statistics Special Report. Washington, DC: US Department of Justice.

Gowdy, V. C., T. Cain, H. Corrothers et al. (1998) *Women in Criminal Justice: A Twenty-year Update*. Washington, DC: US Department of Justice.

Hammoud, R. S. (2001) *Violence Against Women in the Arab Region*, Paper presented at the Arab Conference for Women's Development, University of South el Wadi, 4–6 February 2001.

Heise, L. L., A. Germaine and J. Pitanguy (1994) *Violence Against Women. The Hidden Health Burden*. Washington, DC: World Bank.

Heise, L. L., A. Raikes, C. H. Watts and A. B. Zwi (1994) 'Violence Against Women: A Neglected Public Health Issue in Less Developed Countries', *Social Science and Medicine*, 39: 1165–79.

Kornblit, A. L. (1994) 'Domestic Violence – an Emerging Health Issue', *Social Science and Medicine*, 39: 1181–8.

Levinson, D. (1989) *Violence in Cross-Cultural Perspective*. Newbury Park, CA: Sage.

Moone, J. (1994) *Juvenile Victimization: 1987 to 1992. Fact Sheet*. Washington, DC: Office of Juvenile Justice and Delinquency Prevention.

Nagib, M. F. (2001) 'The effects of the marriage contract on the Arab legislation regarding to the personal status', at <http://www.amanjordan.org/womenandlaw>.

Shalhoub-Kevorkian, N. (2000) 'The Efficacy of Israeli Law in Preventing Violence within Palestinian Families Living in Israel', *International Review of Victimology*, 7: 47–66.

Tadros, M. (1998) *Rightless Women, Heartless Men: Egyptian Women and Domestic Violence. A Report on Violence in Manshiet Nasser, an Informal Settlement in Cairo*. Cairo: Legal Research and Resource Centre for Human Rights.

Tjaden, P. and N. Thoennes (1998) *Prevalence, Incidence and Consequences of Violence Against Women: Findings from the National Violence Against Women Survey*. Washington, DC: National Institute of Justice, Centers for Disease Control and Prevention.

UNDP (2001) <http://www.undp.org/hdr2001/indicator/cty_f_YEM.html>

UNIFEM (2002) 'Masculinity and Gender Violence' in *Gender Issues Fact Sheet No 5* <www.unifem-esasia.org/Gendiss/Gendiss5>.

10 | Opportunities for masculinity and love: cultural production in Ba'thist Iraq during the 1980s

ACHIM ROHDE

When the Ba'th regime assumed power in 1968, it turned the question of gender relations into an issue related to its project of building a modern Iraqi nation, and it undertook various measures likely to improve the situation of Iraqi women (Mokhif 1991). Women were given access to education on a broad scale. The regime introduced new labour laws aimed at encouraging women to enter the wage labour force, particularly sectors like teaching, health-related professions and the civil service; the state provided kindergartens and paid maternity leave.[1] The amendments to the Personal Status Law of 1959, promulgated in 1978, were its single most important reform project, addressing the issue of gender relations also in the spheres of conjugal and family life. They improved the status of women in the family in some respects, motivated mainly by the regime's aim of increasing the number of women in the labour force, but left women in an inferior position in many other respects (Efrati 1995: 44–51). Much of the research published in Western academia on gender in Iraq addresses this legislative reform. It has been termed 'a radical change to the legal position of women within the family' (al-Sharqi 1982: 84), including 'a number of daring innovations' (al-Hayani 1993: 177) such as women's right to obtain a divorce under certain circumstances. The more sceptical Amal Rassam, too, has noted a number of significant, if limited, improvements in the status of women in Iraq, particularly in education and work, but also within the family (Rassam 1982, 1992). Suad Joseph examined the whole range of reforms the Ba'th regime had introduced regarding women during the 1970s and argues that the Ba'th's main aim was to turn women's allegiance away from traditional foci of loyalty such as the extended family, the tribe or the ethnic group to fully mobilize their labour potential, which according to data disclosed by the semi-official General Federation of Iraqi Women (GFIW), had reached 26.3 per cent of the total workforce by 1987 (Joseph 1991). Focusing on the authoritarian character of Ba'thist Iraq, Samir al-Khalil and others denounce the gender policies as another exercise in consolidating the power of the party and the leader (al-Khalil 1989: 88–93; Farouk-Sluglett 1993; Ismael and Ismael 2000). Researchers with a focus on women in state-building processes, such as Deniz Kandiyoti, interpret the Ba'thist legislation on women as part of an overall attempt to exert social control over the potentially subversive 'private realm', emptying women's relative gain in status within the family of all emancipatory dimensions. She compares Ba'thist Iraq to other examples of dirigiste states, such as Turkey under Ataturk or Nasserist Egypt, and maintains that integration into capitalist markets rather than legislative reforms was the most decisive factor in changing traditional gender relations in Middle Eastern societies (Kandiyoti 1993). Kandiyoti has introduced the concept of a 'patriarchal bargain' to Middle Eastern Gender Studies, indicating the existence of a limited, male-dominated discursive space – power relations, laws, traditions, cultural images – which all social actors within a given society share, whether willingly or through coercion. Within this given discursive space, gender relations are constantly being negotiated, contested and redefined. Such a concept takes into account the possible existence of conflicting interest groups within a given society and the historical mutability of gender regimes. The Ba'thist policies in this field thus reflect the balance of power within society, the outcome of the 'patriarchal bargain' at specific moments in history.

In February 1975 a Conference of the Arab Working Woman, held in Baghdad and attended by delegations from all over the Arab world, achieved considerable coverage in the Iraqi press. A caricature published in the daily newspaper *al-Thawra* (11 February 1975) showed a woman with open hair and dressed in blue collar holding a wrench in her right and an automatic rifle in her left hand. The regime at this stage officially promoted a small nuclear family with two working parents, including some symbolic transgressions of established gender roles: a threefold caricature published around International Women's Day (9 March 1975) showed a happy father feeding a baby while his wife is out, a father and two children offering flowers to the wife, and a woman on her way to work, holding a baby in her right hand and a trowel in her left hand. This modernist atmosphere changed some time after the outbreak of the Iran–Iraq War in 1980. By the late 1980s, a notable swing occurred in the regime's rhetoric regarding women, away from education and work towards procreation and motherhood. During the early years of the war, the regime had encouraged women to enter the labour force and fill the vacancies caused by men's military recruitment. By 1986 the regime encouraged women to give up paid employment in other than health-related and engineering professions and to devote themselves to childcare and procreation. In 1987 the regime initiated a broad national campaign to increase women's fertility rate.

Various researchers have addressed the ambivalence discernible in the regime's policies regarding women. Amal Rassam sees the question of

185

women's status in society as locked up between the Ba'th's two conflicting agendas of modernization and development on the one hand and 'cultural authenticity' on the other (1982: 98). She is echoed by Sana al-Khayat, who sees a system of male dominance based upon normative Islamic values and traditional Bedouin culture well installed in contemporary Iraqi society, despite the 'Westernizing' influences of the Ba'thist modernization and development policies. According to al-Khayat (1990), Iraqi women are hostages of an 'ideology of honour and shame', which ascribes to them the function of being the symbolic markers of moral and cultural purity. While the existence of more or less influential honour codes in Iraqi and other Middle Eastern societies and their oppressive potential vis-à-vis women needs no further discussion, Rassam and al-Khayat imply the existence of an ultimate cultural core that links all Iraqis together, temporal, spatial and social stratification notwithstanding: the eternal Iraqi Masculine. Such an approach has been criticized for being empirically problematic, homogenizing and ahistorical (Mohanty 1988). Referring to Kandiyoti's concept of a 'patriarchal bargain', Noga Efrati (1999) argues that the regime's ambivalent gender policies during the Iran–Iraq War resulted from conflicting pragmatic demands such as the need to replace male workers and employees sent to the front on the one hand, and the need to compete with Iran's numerical superiority and the regime's wish to provide employment opportunities for discharged soldiers on the other.

Nationalism and gender

In the past decade, the phenomenon of nations and nationalism has attracted a great deal of attention in numerous disciplines. Nevertheless, systematic attempts in Middle Eastern Studies to apply the various contemporary theoretical concepts of nationalism to Arab countries have so far been rare (Jankowski and Gershoni 1997; Gocek 2002). Many works on nationalism in the Middle East reflect the idealist assumptions of nationalist ideologues themselves and tend to view nations as culturally homogeneous entities, the borders of which should be congruent with the administrative borders of a given nation-state. Distinctions between natural and artificial nations derived from this set of criteria usually rest on the inherent assumption of the exemplary nature of European nations. Nations here are mostly defined as self-generating homogeneous cultural entities following the supposedly iron rules of European modernity (Tibi 1997). But recent scholarship on European nationalisms has reached a broad consensus around the invented nature of any nationalism and any national history; it stresses the changes nationalist discourses underwent over time and points to the heterogeneity of European societies. The concept of a nation as an ethnically, culturally and politically homogeneous entity has been criticized by various researchers. Homi K. Bhabha (1994) has formulated a critique of the homogenizing tendencies apparent in this idea. Nations, in his view, are caught permanently between two poles: they are the objects of a nationalist pedagogy, formulated by a country's ruling elite or by the leaders of a nationalist movement, and at the same time they are the subjects of the performative process of their daily self-construction. Nations are historical practices through which social and cultural differences are both invented and performed; they are a site of permanent struggle between the various social actors in a given society. From this perspective, nations no longer symbolize a modernity that seeks to dissolve cultural difference into a horizontal view of society, often implying totalitarian tendencies. Instead of trying to classify the 'organic' or 'artificial' character of one nation as compared to other nations according to a fixed set of criteria, Bhabha emphasizes the liminality, the tensions and ruptures within all those social conglomerates called nations.

Most of the influential works on nations and nationalism do not offer much insight concerning the gendered imagery of nationalist narratives. Benedict Anderson, for example, in his study on the origins of modern nations touches upon this issue only implicitly when he states that nations tend to be understood as a deep horizontal 'comradeship', as 'fraternities' (1983: 16). Bhabha's work contains no serious attempt to incorporate a gender perspective, despite his declared intention to develop a theory of nationalism informed by the perspectives of the marginalized, 'the colonized and women' (1994: 152). Indeed, despite nationalism's usual emphasis on the idea of popular unity, rarely ever in the history of nationalist movements have women's experiences been taken as a starting point for political organization. Rather, as Cynthia Enloe notes, 'nationalism has typically sprung up from masculinized memory, masculinized humiliation and masculinized hope' (1989: 44). Anne McClintock has explored the gendering of the national imaginaries of black and white South Africans. She shares most of Bhabha's theoretical assumptions, but criticizes the gender blindness evident in his work. McClintock (1995) does not subscribe to Anderson's Marxist view that the development of print capitalism was at the root of the popularity and mass currency of nationalist narratives. According to her, the appeal of nationalism is mainly an effect of the technique of performing the nation through ritual mass spectacles and various other forms of popular culture, and it is by looking at South African nationalisms from this angle that she renders visible their gendered character. This chapter applies McClintock's approach to the Iraqi context. It is based on a survey of the Iraqi daily *al-Thawra*.

Mass culture in Ba'thist Iraq

By the late 1980s, there were seven government-sponsored daily news-papers in Iraq, the largest being the Ba'th party's own *al-Thawra*, which prior to 1991 was published with a daily circulation of some 150,000 copies, and numerous magazines and periodicals on various subjects, the largest being *Alif Ba*, published by the Ministry of Information and addressing a range of issues of general interest (Hurrat and Leidig 1994). Ba'thist Iraq had until 1991 been an important market for contemporary Arab litera-ture; Iraqi writers and poets enjoy a high profile in public discourse, for instance in the mass media. The growing influence of modern means of mass communication during the 1970s and 1980s and the rapidly growing literacy rate in Iraqi society during this period changed traditional, oral and locally/regionally centred forms of popular culture.[2] At the same time, these factors made popular culture in Iraq more susceptible to modern means of mass propaganda (Ayalon 1995). True, the press and other media and literature in Iraq are subject to severe censorship; the regime regards them as tools to influence public opinion. But although the print media in Ba'thist Iraq are created not by but for the people, it would be erroneous to regard them as a mere imposition of elite values (Stauth and Zubaida 1987; Davis and Gavrielides 1991). The value of print media as a primary source differs from programmatic statements of the Ba'th regime, as newspapers, magazines and literature address a range of issues and include at least limited concessions to the changing tides of public opinion, cultural and intellectual developments, fashion, national and international events. Print media are intended for public consumption and thus inevitably invite the participation of their audience. For instance, during the Iran–Iraq War, the press published pieces of literature, poetry and drawings produced by Iraqi artists recruited to boost the war propaganda, but it also contained regular testimonies of Iraqi soldiers about their experiences at the front-line. It would be misleading to assume a simple dichotomy between a regime-sponsored mass culture and a (suppressed) authentic popular culture. A more or less dynamic interaction is taking place between the two.

Militarism, war and gender

One important aspect of Ba'th-inspired Iraqi nationalism was its inher-ent militarism. This aspect became most prominent during the eight years of the Iran–Iraq War, which dominated the second decade of Ba'thist rule in Iraq. During this war, Iraqi society was militarized to an unprecedented degree. The regime had already spent considerable sums on weapons and the modernization and expansion of Iraq's armed forces during the 1970s. During the war, however, Iraq turned into a veritable military machine:

between 1979 and 1988 the armed forces grew from 220,000 to 1 million soldiers. The percentage of people serving in the armed forces grew from 1.7 per cent in 1979/80 to 17 per cent of the total population in 1987/88 (Mofid 1990: 76–89). The available data suggest that almost 40 per cent of the Iraqi adult male population took part in the war (Taheri 1988: 198–9).

During a war soldiers sacrifice their private self and their individual self-interest for a public and national identity represented by the uniform. Soldiers become the executors of an alleged national will and as such enjoy high social prestige. In Iraq, as elsewhere in the world, military discipline and combat have been predominantly male experiences. Fighters and warriors are almost universally perceived as incarnations of masculinity. Femininity, on the other hand, is commonly associated with notions of warmth, care, beauty, physical weakness and passivity. Women are almost automatically perceived as non-fighters in need of protection by men, particularly in times of social turmoil and war. Constructions of masculinity in societies which place great emphasis on gender segregation between the sexes usually evolve around notions of autonomous male subjects carrying a heroic component that lies in their ability to stand up to countless challenges, to face enemies in a disciplined and self-confident way and to protect 'their' womenfolk (Gilmore 1990). In most contemporary societies, the formation of individual identities is influenced to a great extent by gender regimes, which enact binary notions of masculinity and femininity as two complementary sexual identities. The formation of these identities does not take place only on the individual psychological level. Nor can it be explained as merely an effect of genetic dispositions. It is a social and institutionalized process, forcibly inscribed upon the individual on a daily basis, the pedagogical in Bhabha's terminology. The same holds true for violent actions and warfare. War is not simply the effect of its participants' individual aggressive dispositions. Human aggressiveness, as other forms of human behaviour, is highly contextual and collectively structured (Connell 1987). Because of the predominantly male composition of most armies in the contemporary world, the military is an important institution in which the construction of masculinity and its inscription upon the individual can be localized (Ghoussoub and Sinclair-Webb 2000; Klein 2001). National armies are considered an important backbone of nation-building processes, an argument raised also concerning the Iraqi army (Salih 1996). A nation-state's gendered recruitment policies influence perceptions about gender relations. How powerful this influence can be depends, among other factors, on the numerical strength of its armed forces and upon the degree of social prestige allocated to the military in public discourse. During the Iran–Iraq War, the Iraqi armed forces both experienced a massive growth in numbers and enjoyed overwhelming prestige as 'defenders of the homeland'. Throughout the eight years of war, the Iraqi press frequently depicted the Iraqi nation in its fight against the Iranian forces through drawings, poems and short stories intended to boost war propaganda.

When the land is female, war is love and the nation is a family

A high degree of segregation between women and men and the strong influence of dualistic concepts of gender difference in Iraqi society were acknowledged in the Iraqi press throughout the period under scrutiny. But the press discourse on women and femininity during the 1970s was doubtlessly designed to weaken these perceptions by constantly depicting women in a growing variety of professions previously reserved for men. The regime's rhetoric up to 1980 referred to phrases like 'women's libera-tion'.[3] It was characterized by a distinctively anti-traditionalist stance, which sought to reform, not abolish, the cultural system of gender difference and male hegemony to fit the regime's need for an enlarged labour force. Nevertheless, the degree of gender difference promoted by the regime was an issue debated in the press and no fixed formula, particularly during the early 1970s.

At the start of the war, the regime was in need of mobilizing the popu-lation. During the early years, the press contained occasional displays of female militancy, reflecting the significant number of women who vol-unteered for the civil defence and the party militia (Rohde 1999: 75–95). The press pointed to the increased mobilization of women into the wage labour force, mirroring the regime's need to replace the economically active strata of men being recruited to the military on a massive scale. Beyond such news items, however, the press became rather obsessed by a trenchant militarism. The start of the Iran–Iraq War in September 1980 prompted a massive increase in displays of Iraqi military weight in the press, particularly during times when either of the warring sides took the offensive. Iraqi propaganda produced a never-ending flow of richly pictured articles commemorating the boldness and heroism of the ever victorious Iraqi men fighting at the front-line, including gruesome photos of slain Iranian soldiers scattered around on the killing fields. Saddam Hussein and high regime figures were depicted in war-related contexts, wearing military uniforms, meeting the troops, decorating soldiers for outstanding bravery, talking about the war. This obsession in itself indicates that a gendered hierarchy of social status was being reinforced in the press during this period, with men/soldiers at its top and women/civilians confined to auxiliary positions.

In the realm of cultural production, a whole new kind of war-literature was developed (Cooke 1996: 220–66), numerous examples of which were published in the press. Open letters, poems and short stories written by soldiers and artists alike were published, telling stories of heroism and martyrdom, and stories of love in times of war between soldiers at the front and waiting women at home. Such items were continuously published in all newspapers and magazines. Drawings of known artists were frequently published, depicting the nation at war. Children's literature was militarized, too. A special book series entitled 'Saddam's Qadissiya' was designed for children and consisted of sixteen volumes, each of which treated different aspects of the war, including the various weapons systems used by the Iraqi army and pictures of slain soldiers. A children's magazine called *Majallati* was fully dedicated to nationalist ideology, anti-Iranian propaganda and stories about heroic Iraqi men (Dhaouadi 1987: 82–3).

In the first half of 1982 a serialized novel by 'Adel 'Abd al-Jubar, entitled *Mountains of Fire, Mountains of Ice*, was published in twenty consecutive parts in *al-Thawra*, each covering a whole page.[4] It focuses almost exclusively on daily life at the front and on the boldness and heroism of Iraqi men. Women feature only rarely and as passive characters in this novel, as a 'symbol of beauty and femininity' in the eyes of a soldier who misses a girl from his neighbourhood at home, or as the secret girlfriend of a soldier thrilled by the prospect of 'a love affair with a beautiful girl [...] love in times of war [...] yes, something previously unheard of' (9 and 23 January 1982). In a poem by Ghazay Dara' al-Ta'i, the very notion of war contains eroticized allusions to love relationships bound to multiply the mobilizing effects of the poem. This is not the abstract nationalist love Michel Aflaq spoke of (1959: 29–30). If this imagery was at all inspired by the writings of the Ba'th party's founding father, the meaning of the term 'love' was altered and vulgarized to signify a plain romantic love between a woman and a man, with all the popular images associated with it:

> the homeland always comes first/ the dear homeland before the father/ and before the mother/ and before the wife, the brothers and the sisters/ [...] who said that love is haram?/ and that meeting the beloved under a palm tree is forbidden?/ and that speaking love and making love is forbidden?/ love is halal/ [...] my homeland/ O homeland of trembling love/ your loving hand, O soldier, is like a waterfall/ your loving hand, O people, is like a waterfall. (*al-Thawra*, 29 January 1982)

Patriotism in this poem is stronger than the man's relationships with his relatives (the homeland is more important than the wife, but what about the husband?); meetings with the beloved woman are allowed; the soldier's

Figure 1

loving hand is like a waterfall: national agency is clearly masculinized. The war becomes an act of love, carrying overt sexual connotations, between a male soldier and his beloved, the homeland. In the early years of the Iran–Iraq War, the equivalence of romantic and patriotic love was apparently applied in the Iraqi press as a tool to mobilize the male population. In the war's latter stages, when the regime increasingly used Islamic discourse to stabilize its rule, such items did not contain overt sexual connotations, and women were more frequently addressed as mothers. The equivalence of romantic and patriotic love is borne out most explicitly in an open letter written in 1982 by a soldier to his girlfriend, suggesting that such ideas might have been common also at the front, that writers and poets merely condensed the soldiers' feelings:

> During these days I and my comrades give concrete form to a love, which equals my love for you, and that is the love for the homeland. Oh my dear, this love, which is nothing but love [...] I will always be [committed] like you are committed to me. I will turn my memory of touching your tender fingertips into a firm embrace of my rifle, and the heat of my love for you into a fire in which I burn my enemy. (*al-Thawra*, 21 July 1982)[5]

This soldier turns his combat experiences into acts of love between himself, a firm and fiery soldier, and a feminized land, which carries the same characteristics he ascribes to his girlfriend: it is tender and committed, a foil for his fantasies with no agency of its own. The same motif was employed by the artist 'Ala Bashir in a charcoal drawing published by *al-Thawra* in 1986 (see Figure 1). It shows a massive masculine hand holding a rifle. The inner contours of the hand are marked by lines resembling the Euphrates and Tigris rivers, indicating that the hand represents Iraq. The imprint of feminine lips, situated in the midst of the hand, serves to feminize the land and illustrate what the soldier wrote to his girlfriend. The motif of a mighty virile hand rising into the air holding a weapon was later employed in the 'Victory Arch', a huge monument commemorating the Iran–Iraq War, reportedly conceived by Hussein himself and modelled on his own hands, opened to the public in August 1989 (al-Khalil 1991).

In early 1986, the poet Yusuf al-Sa'igh further developed the love metaphor in the context of war narratives in the most striking way. Shortly afterwards it was hailed by the literary critic Turad al-Kabisi as an outstanding example of Iraqi war poetry. According to him, a transcendental 'love' is the acting subject in this poem, expressing itself in various shapes and settings (al-Thawra, 10 April 1986). Al-Kabisi's interpretation mirrors the Ba'thist concept of nationhood, according to which the Arab national genius expresses itself in different shapes at various times.

In which sense is war similar to love/ an opportunity/ for masculinity and love/ O faithful mother/ my little bosom friend/ sleeping in the bed of her childhood/ allow me/ to call my machine gun after you/ and say to her: / O darling/ what is the similarity between love and war/ [...]/ don't let the Shatt sever what is between us/ the 'mother of the bullets'/ is an ornament for the fight/ for two nights a woman cried out for my sense of dignity/ she covers me/ when I lift her covers/ and go to fight/ in your name/[...] I faced death with your name on my lips/ I taught my machine gun/ to pronounce your names/ one by one/ I will teach her/ how to rejoice/ in the name of Iraq/ in the name of the palm tree/ in the name of the two rivers/ I taught her/ how to rejoice in your name/ O son of Hussein. (12 February 1986)[6]

To speak of this poem as expressing the Arab national genius in its war against Iran, one has to take a great distance from the text itself. As the poem says, the war provides men with an opportunity to enhance their masculinity, to reinforce the stability of this concept of self-identification in ways impossible under the 'constraints' of civilian life. Written from the perspective of a man/soldier, the poem mentions various female characters – 'Um Aufa', the faithful mother and wife, the soldier's daughter, his 'little bosom friend', and all the 'girls of our neighbourhood'. They all remain silent foils for the soldier's fantasy and are not even distinguishable from one another. They all seem to collapse into aspects of his machine gun, a dead and deadly feminized fetish, with which he all but seems to have an affair.

Similar imagery is discernible in a coal drawing by Ibrahim Rashid. It

Figure 2

is composed of overlapping layers and depicts soldiers in combat postures walking through a thicket-like environment dominated by the heads of two female figures, one of them resembling a Mesopotamian-style female mask (see Figure 2). Artists in Ba'thist Iraq frequently produced works that symbolize the Iraqi nation and project Iraq's national unity back into ancient Mesopotamia (Baram 1991). In Rashid's drawing, the figure of a mighty soldier is towering above in the upper part of the drawing and forms a triangle structure together with the two female head masks beneath. Women in this drawing come to symbolize both Iraq's alleged time-honoured national unity and the Iraqi homeland. Again, national agency in this drawing is masculinized; women become part of the natural landscape in which men act. Wisam Murqus employed a female figure symbolizing the enduring strength and fertility of the homeland in a drawing where two white horses emerge from the oversized womb of a woman whose body develops into a palm tree rooted in the earth (see Figure 3).

At the beginning of the war the party militia saw a massive and largely voluntary increase in membership, including some 40,000 women recruited to units that bore the names of ancient Arab women who had allegedly fought alongside men in the Prophet's wars and during the early Muslim conquests. A great ambivalence characterized the works of Iraqi artists who employed the image of women soldiers. In one of Mahmud Hamad's coal drawings published in 1987, a woman clad in a military uniform and carrying a rifle over her shoulder is seated amid stones protected by a pile of

Figure 3

sand sacks and nursing a baby. In another drawing a contemporary woman warrior and an ancient Assyrian warrior emanate from a tree; both stand ready for combat. A dove rests in this tree, symbolizing Iraq's wish for peace. The two figures symbolize Iraq's alleged time-honoured national unity and the organic connection of the Iraqi nation to the territory ascribed to it. A third such drawing depicts an armed woman clad in a military uniform situated inside the courtyard of a house; a rocket emerges from the plait of her hair (see Figure 4). Female militancy in these drawings is always broken by non-combative elements: although the woman soldier in the first drawing is situated in a front-line setting, she does not actually fight but nurses a baby, thereby assigning a military value to procreation. The woman warrior in the second drawing is depicted together with an ancient Assyrian warrior, a metaphorical figure just like herself. Both stand ready for battle but do not actually fight. The woman soldier in the third drawing is engaging in combat metaphorically. Moreover, she is placed in a domestic setting. Never did I encounter drawings that depicted a woman soldier engaging in combat in a front-line setting. Never did I encounter drawings that showed a woman soldier together with a contemporary male Iraqi soldier.

By 1986 Iraqi artists and writers addressed women almost exclusively in the context of family life, most prominently as mothers. Moreover, by 1986 the high social prestige ascribed to soldiers from the outset of the war was translated into an overt social hierarchy, with soldiers at its top and

Figure 4

women/civilians as deficient supporters: the whole nation was represented as a family of a higher order. On 3 May 1986, the writer and journalist Daisy al-Amir acknowledges these developments in an article published in *al-Thawra*: 'In the big solid family its members do not account for the gifts, and no one judges the other. We as writers are part of this big loving family whose name is the homeland [...] I thought about the equivalence of what we as writers do and what the heroes out there at the front offer. I felt ashamed by the comparison.'

Her article proved a prelude to a spectacular and highly publicized meeting between President Hussein and the GFIW, where he officially distanced himself from its modestly reformist agenda and called upon all women to give highest priority to family life and procreation.[7] Women

Figure 5

candidates lost ground in the elections to the National Assembly in April 1989; their number in the new parliament decreased from thirty-three to twenty-seven out of 250 MPs. The regime had previously amended the Assembly Law to emphasize an active role in the war as the main source of legitimacy for candidates, whose election campaigns reportedly singled out their contributions to the war effort at the expense of any other issues (Bengio 1989: 379–80). The weak performance of women candidates at this election was later blamed on a low turnout among women and upon the failure to convince men of the importance of women MPs.[8] Wisam Murqus produced a drawing that sums up this trend. It depicts a nuclear family – a father, a mother and a girl – placed amid tank tracks and sea waves, which symbolize the front-line in the Shatt al-Arab. The mother holds a candlestick above her head; the little girl sits on her right arm and holds a toy in her hand, a rifle. The heavily armed father/soldier is situated at the centre of the drawing; he holds an Iraqi flag that contains the portraits of President Hussein, Salah al-Din and Nebuchadnezzar, symbolizing both Iraq's alleged time-honoured national unity and Hussein's megalomania. Numerous pierced hearts are lined up on the flag-staff like meat on a shashlik stick, symbolizing either slain enemies or the moral support of the Iraqi population for the soldiers at the front, maybe both: war is love and the nation is a family. All the parts of the drawing together form a Z-structure, underlining the alleged 'organic' connection between all members of the national collective and the land, with Hussein on top, the soldier at the centre and the Shatt al-Arab beneath (see Figure 5).

Conclusion

The regime's drive towards gender reforms, however limited and ambivalent it might have been from the outset, was partly reversed during the 1980s. Its gender policies during this period were located in a rigidly gendered setting of militarism and war: the reinforcement of binary concepts of masculinity and femininity, which became obvious by the late 1980s, had already been evident in the realm of cultural production since the early years of the war. The Ba'th's recruitment policies during the war and their gendered propaganda have reinforced images of male heroism and superiority, notions of gender difference, ideals of virility and practices of male bonding among the individuals affected by them and in Iraqi society in general, with obvious negative impacts on women. Pending a detailed investigation of state–society relations in Iraq during this period, it is safe to assert that the 'contradictory pragmatic demands' underlying the Ba'th's gender policies, as convincingly formulated by Efrati, included the exigencies of the war effort itself: for eight long years, the regime was in constant need to mobilize the (male) population into the war effort at the front and to rally the unconditional support of the civilian population for the combatants, including the acceptance of a superior social prestige awarded to soldiers. To foster a feeling of a closely-knit Iraqi national community united in its support of the fighters at the front, the regime was in need of war propaganda, which would contain the notion of a clearly defined distribution of tasks in society. To achieve this goal, the regime emphasized values such as family solidarity and readiness for sacrifice, and metaphorically referred to the institution of the patriarchal family in its discourse on the Iraqi nation, while distancing itself from its stated aim of gender reforms.

Notes

1 For a survey of the various laws and measures initiated by the regime concerning gender relations, see the Ba'th party's daily newspaper *al-Thawra* (henceforth: *Th*), 11 and 13 March 1987.

2 The term 'popular culture' carries various meanings depending on the context. For the purposes of this chapter, I use them in the widest possible sense as comprising aspects of 'folk culture' and of 'polite' or 'high' culture, both mediated through the modern means of mass communication technology and moulded into a state-sponsored 'mass culture'.

3 See President Hussein's speech to the GFIW Congress in 1980 (*Th*, 23 March 1980).

4 I had access to the parts 13–20 of this novel (*Th*, 5, 12 and 26 July; 2, 9, 16 and 23 August 1982).

5 Other soldiers dedicated the accounts of their life at the front-line to

their girlfriends without explicitly addressing them in this context (*Th*, 3 July 1982).

6 The poem ends by saluting 'the son of Hussein'. This term signifies Saddam Hussein himself, who claims to be a descendant of the Imam 'Ali, Hussein's father. This claim was made for example by 'Izzat Ibrahim, then deputy chairman of the Revolutionary Command Council (the highest body in Iraq's formal power structure), in a speech he gave in Najaf on the occasion of 'Ali's birthday (*Th*, 15 March 1987).

7 *Th*, 4 May 1986.

8 *Th*, 5 February 1996.

References

Aflaq, M. (1959) *Fi Sabil al-Ba'th*. Beirut: Dar al-Tali'a.

Anderson, B. (1983) *Imagined Communities: Reflections on the Origins and Spread of Nationalism*. London: Verso.

Ayalon, A. (1995) *The Press in the Middle East. A History*. New York: Oxford University Press.

Baram, A. (1991) *Culture, History and Ideology in the Formation of Ba'thist Iraq*. London: Macmillan.

Bengio, O. (1989) 'Iraq', *Middle East Contemporary Survey*, 13: 372–418.

Bhabha, H. K. (1994) *The Location of Culture*. London: Routledge.

Connell, R. W. (1987) *Gender and Power*. Stanford, CA: Stanford University Press.

Cooke, M. (1996) *Women and the War Story*. Berkeley: University of California Press.

Davis, E. and N. Gavrielides (eds) (1991) *Statecraft in the Middle East. Oil, Historical Memory, and Popular Culture*. Miami: Florida International University Press.

Dhaouadi, Z. (1987) 'Petrole, guerre et culture [...] de/pour l'etat irakien', *Peuples Mediterraneans*, 40 (July–September): 75–88.

Efrati, N. (1995) 'The Marriage Contract and Women's Roles in the Family'. Unpublished MA dissertation, University of Haifa.

— (1999) 'Productive or Reproductive? The Roles of Iraqi Women During the Iraq–Iran War', *Middle Eastern Studies*, 35 (2): 27–44.

Enloe, C. (1989) *Bananas, Beaches and Bases. Making Feminist Sense of International Politics*. Berkeley: University of California Press.

Farouk-Sluglett, M. (1993) 'Liberation or Repression? Pan-Arab Nationalism and the Women's Movement in Iraq', in Hopwood et al. (eds), *Iraq: Power and Society*. Reading: Ithaca Press, pp. 51–74.

Ghoussoub, M. and E. Sinclair-Webb (eds) (2000) *Imagined Masculinities. Male Identity and Culture in the Modern Middle East*. London: Saqi Books.

Gilmore, D. D. (1990) *Manhood in the Making*. London: Yale University Press.

Gocek, F. M. (ed.) (2002) *Social Constructions of Nationalism in the Middle East*. Albany: State University of New York Press.

Al-Hayani, F. A. (1993) 'Legal Modernism in Iraq: A Study of the Amendments to Family Law'. Ann Arbor, MI: UMI Dissertation Services.

Hurrat, K. S. and L. I. Leidig (1994) 'Iraq', in Y. R. Kamelipour and H. Mowlana (eds), *Mass Media in the Middle East. A Comprehensive Handbook*. Westport, CT: Greenwood Press, pp. 96–108.

Ismael, J. S. and S. T. Ismael (2000) 'Gender and State in Iraq', in S. Joseph (ed.), *Gender and Citizenship in the Middle East*. Syracuse: Syracuse University Press, pp. 185–211.

Jankowski, J. and I. Gershoni (eds) (1997) *Rethinking Nationalism in the Arab Middle East*. New York: Columbia University Press.

Joseph, S. (1991) 'Elite Strategies for State-Building: Women, Family, Religion and the State in Iraq and Lebanon', in D. Kandiyoti (ed.), *Women, Islam and the State*. London: Macmillan, pp. 176–200.

Kandiyoti, D. (1991) 'Islam and Patriarchy: A Comparative Perspective', in N. R. Keddie and B. Baron (eds), *Women in Middle Eastern History. Shifting Boundaries of Sex and Gender*. New Haven, CT: Yale University Press, pp. 23–42.

— (1993) 'Identity and Its Discontents: Women and the Nation', in P. Williams and L. Chrisman (eds), *Colonial Discourse and Post-Colonial Theory. A Reader*. Hertfordshire: Harvester Wheatsheaf, pp. 376–91.

Al-Khalil, S. (1989) *Republic of Fear. The Politics of Modern Iraq*. London: Hutchinson Radius.

— (1991) *The Monument: Art, Vulgarity and Responsibility in Iraq*. London: André Deutsch.

Al-Khayat, S. (1990) *Honour and Shame: Women in Modern Iraq*. London: Saqi Books.

Klein, U. (2001) *Militar und Geschlecht in Israel*. Frankfurt: Campus.

McClintock, A. (1995) 'No Longer in a Future Heaven: Nationalism, Gender and Race', in her *Imperial Leather. Race, Gender and Sexuality in the Imperial Contest*. New York: Routledge, pp. 353–89.

Mofid, K. (1990) *The Economic Consequences of the Gulf War*. London: Routledge.

Mohanty, C. T. (1988) 'Under Western Eyes: Feminist Scholarship and Colonial Discourses', *Feminist Review*, 30, pp. 65–88.

Mokhif, L. A. (1991) *Gender Inequality in Iraq, 1967–88*. Doctoral dissertation, University of Utah.

Rassam, A. (1982) 'Revolution within the Revolution? Women and the State in Iraq', in T. Niblock (ed.), *Iraq: The Contemporary State*. London: Croom Helm, pp. 88–99.

— (1992) 'Political Ideology and Women in Iraq: Legislation and Cultural Constraints', in J. G. Jabbara and N. W. Jabbara (eds), *Women and Development in the Middle East and North Africa*. Leiden: Brill, pp. 83–95.

Rohde, A. (1999) 'Gender and Nationalism: Discourses on Women and Femininity in the Iraqi Press, 1968–98'. Unpublished MA dissertation, Hamburg University.

Salih, K. (1996) *State-Making, Nation-Building and the Military: Iraq, 1941–1958*, Gøteborg Studies in Politics, 41.

Al-Sharqi, A. (1982) 'The Emancipation of Iraqi Women', in T. Niblock (ed.), *Iraq: The Contemporary State*. London: Croom Helm, pp. 74–87.

Stauth, G. and S. Zubaida (eds) (1987) *Mass Culture, Popular Culture, and Social Life in the Middle East*. Frankfurt and Boulder, CO: Campus and Westview.

Taheri, A. (1988) *The Cauldron: The Middle East Behind the Headlines*. London: Hutchinson.

Tibi, B. (1997) *Arab Nationalism. Between Islam and the Nation State*, 3rd edn. Basingstoke: Macmillan.

11 | On being homosexual and Muslim: conflicts and challenges

ASIFA SIRAJ

Despite the undeniable contributions of contemporary sociological and historical work to homosexuality studies, the impact of religion on the identity of homosexuals has been limited to Christianity (Rodriguez and Ouellette 2000; Yip 1997; Comstock 1993, 1996; Thumma 1991). For instance, only fragmentary evidence allows us insight into the lives of homosexual Muslims.[1] Homosexuality in Islam remains largely unexplored, principally because the Qur'an, Ahadith and Shari'a,[2] as heteronormative sources determining sexual morality, have stifled debate about the topic. Homosexual Muslims, until recently confined to a 'culture of invisibility', are now beginning to speak out to re-claim their identity and to reconcile their faith with their sexuality. My purpose is not to provide a generalized account of the experiences of Muslim homosexuals; rather, it is an attempt to unravel and illuminate the personal and collective processes the men go through to integrate their apparent incompatible identities. Further study of the religious identity of homosexual Muslims is therefore of considerable importance.

This chapter explores how some homosexuals combine a set of incongruent identities – homosexual, male and Muslim – and how they reformulate their understanding to reconcile them. Although 'Islam forbids homosexual practices (sexual relations between two men or between two women), regarding them a great sin' (Hewitt 1997: 29), the men in this study affirm both their Muslim identity and homosexual orientation. As a stigmatized minority, they contest the rigidity of heterosexual gender roles, call for changes to cultural attitudes and repudiate the idea of a divinely decreed heterosexuality. To give 'voice' to the respondents, this chapter draws upon the narratives of several homosexual Muslims from various London organizations.[3] Each respondent participated in a qualitative, semi-structured interview and, on average, the interviews lasted two hours. I assured the respondents of confidentiality because of the sensitive nature of the study and all respondents have been given pseudonyms. The respondents were all Muslims, aged between twenty-five and forty (median age 31.7), and all identified themselves as homosexual. Despite this, there were different degrees of openness regarding their sexuality (see Table 11.1).

TABLE 11.1 Respondents' demographic information

Name	Age	Ethnic background	Level of education	Occupation	Open about being homosexual	Relationship status
Omar	35	Kenyan	Master's degree	Therapist	Yes	Long-term
Sohail	29	Pakistani	Bachelor's degree	Theatre designer	Not with family	Single
Adil	25	Pakistani	Bachelor's degree	Ph D student	Not with family	Single
Imtiyaz	35	Pakistani	Bachelor's degree	Train driver	Yes	Long-term
Kashif	30	Pakistani	Bachelor's degree	Pharmacist	Yes	Long-term
Jamal	28	Somali	Bachelor's degree	Director of a HIV support organization	Yes	Single
Nasir	40	Pakistani	Bachelor's degree	Gay men's development worker	Yes	Single

One may question the degree to which my identity as a heterosexual female Muslim influenced the respondents. I was welcomed particularly by members of the support group Al-Fatiha[4] (who comprised the bulk of the sample), who were grateful that I, as a Muslim, was involved and interested in an issue that continues to be taboo in Muslim communities. Indeed, I had not anticipated such a high level of openness, and there was little, if any, inhibition on the part of the respondents. They appreciated the platform that the research was affording them to air their views, thoughts and concerns related to their sexuality and their faith. My religious background, if anything, contributed to their forthcoming attitude, as they were eager to initiate a discussion with the mainstream Muslim community, and I represented for them an opening to that discussion. In addition, the fact that several respondents and I were bilingual in the same languages (six of the respondents spoke either Urdu or Punjabi) and shared a similar ethnic background (Pakistani) heightened our connectedness.

Source of conflict

I typically began the interview with set questions on the importance of Islam in the respondents' lives. It was essential to address how the men shaped their identity as Muslims in light of the 'Qur'an – being very explicit in its condemnation, leaving scarcely any loophole for a theological accommodation' (Duran 1993: 181). The effect of such religious condemnation is detrimental, as 'many gay men and lesbians repudiate organised religion or at least maintain a healthy distance in order to survive in a hostile context' (Ellison 1993: 149). Despite this, the respondents placed, at least from the outset, a considerable importance on their faith. Kashif described the role that Islam plays in his life: 'being a Muslim means worshipping Allah and leading a decent and honest life. I try to be as human as possible from an Islamic point of view.' And Omar stated: 'Islamic values are a way of life to me, so that ultimately reflects on me as a person and how I relate to society.' In most cases, several of the men stated that they tried to pray regularly, to fast during the month of Ramadan and to give to charity. Nasir admitted that although in the past he used to pray, fast and celebrate Eid, 'the teachings of the Qur'an represent little importance to me', adding, 'I'm a cultural Muslim.' The determining factor behind his decision was Islam's condemnation of homosexuality. In renouncing his Islamic beliefs, he felt he no longer had to justify or rationalize his sexuality within an Islamic framework. As an openly gay man, he firmly believed that in avowing his sexual identity, he would for the same reason have to negate his identity as a Muslim. For Nasir, this was by no means detrimental: the impression given was a feeling of no longer being bound by religious doctrine.

Jamal, too, felt uncomfortable about his faith's denunciation of homosexuality: 'I feel upset about reading what the Qur'an and the Ahadith have to say about homosexuality. Anybody who has knowledge of the Qur'an knows that homosexuality is wrong. It's quite clear.' He dealt with the issue by separating the two identities and demonstrated this to me by depicting faith in one fist and sexuality in the other. However, he stressed that his homosexual feelings were too strong for him to suppress, and was therefore not able to renounce his gay self. Jamal appeared to have reached a compromise by separating rather than linking his two identities together. The question of reconciliation served as a painful reminder of Islam's rejection of him as a homosexual. Indeed, he commented, 'I don't like to talk about the issue; it upsets me.' Therefore, by dividing these discrete identities, he is able to live his life as a Muslim who also identifies as a homosexual. Adil expanded on the theme of conflict and conveyed the immense tension he felt between his faith and his sexuality: 'I find it very difficult to couple the two [Islam and homosexuality] together. The two are still quite exclusively at war, mutually destructive, I think is the word, or mutually conflicting – at least in my mind it's very conflicting.'

All the respondents had struggled to come to terms with their attraction to men at some point in their lives and this issue was a source of tremendous guilt and conflict. Reflecting on this, Kashif explains: 'I used to pray to God a lot to give me the understanding of why He has made me this way, if I'm not meant to be this way, then make me straight.' Similarly, Sohail stated that 'individually I used to feel inferior to myself; socially and emotionally I wanted God to make me straight'. Imtiyaz added: 'I was hoping I would change because I always thought there was something wrong with me.' Adherence to faith, then, not only provides a theologically sanctioned system of authority and a social framework with set practices and attitudes, but is also a source of condemnation and stigma of certain social and sexual practices (DeLamater 1981). From their tales of conflict, the men relate that they experienced a great sense of confusion and disorientation with their sexual feelings, creating an intense and prolonged period of 'self-harassment'. Their anguish was exacerbated by the fact that the prejudice against homosexuality is both culturally and religiously sanctioned. At the same time, in justifying their sexuality, several respondents resorted to a divine conceptualization to provide them with an explanation of their sexual feelings. Despite praying to God that their same-sex feelings would 'go away' in the hope that they, too, would eventually develop feelings for the opposite sex, the respondents no longer felt that their sexuality was 'abnormal' in any way. The grounds or catalyst for this change was perhaps the eventual acceptance that 'God had made them this way'. This was a profound issue, as it allowed the two identities to be integrated for the first time.

This connection, however, was not forged for all respondents. Jamal and Adil firmly held that homosexuality and Islam are exclusive categories and cannot forcibly be brought together. Despite the conviction of Adil and Jamal, for the following respondents, these two identities could co-exist and, in support of this, sexuality was held to be an innate characteristic of their personality: 'I was born gay and then I was born Muslim. When I was in the womb of my mother I believe I was gay' (Sohail). In a similar vein, Kashif stated: 'God has definitely made me this way; for me Islam is a natural religion; you're not supposed to be going against nature and for me my natural way of being is to be gay.' This 'devout' belief is essential, as the respondents are able not only to feel comfortable with their sexuality but also to rebuild their identity as Muslims. This is clearly highlighted by some of the men placing a particular importance in their relationship with God: 'For me, Islam is a personal search between me and my God' (Omar). The men thus attempt to renegotiate the boundaries of their Islamic identity, made possible by conceptualizing their sexuality within a religious context that emphasizes the concepts of love and compassion, characteristics fervently associated with God. It further emerges from the men's perspective that the oppression faced by homosexuals corrupts and taints the image of God as an all-loving and merciful deity. Thus, from this understanding, Islam's prohibition against homosexuality emanates not from a sacred decree but from societal norms and values. The intimate spirituality (Yip 1997) is used to affirm this homosexual identity as it deflects the attention away from their sexuality. Nevertheless, it was difficult to dismiss that 'homosexuality isn't something that is accommodated, so obviously it is not compatible' (Omar). This view accords with Sohail's remark that 'the general interpretation is that homosexuality is a sin: I know that I don't have support from the text'. These conflicting responses are related, on the one hand, to the disapproval of the wider Muslim community and, on the other, to the belief that God 'has made them this way' coupled with what they regard as their proclivity towards people of the same sex. As a result, some of the men account for their sexuality in the most natural of terms; that is, they feel that by understanding, accepting and justifying their sexuality using Islam, they deepen their religious attachment to their sexuality. Omar further points out: 'I feel entirely Muslim and my homosexuality doesn't come into question.' However, the ambiguity present in the comments of respondents should not be construed as a disagreement, but as evidence of the lack of theological discourse or accommodation that would enable them to delineate a position for themselves within Islam.

Indeed, the integration of contradictory aspects of the self has been an extremely tumultuous journey. Respondents described a common narrative concerning their homosexual identity: initially becoming cognisant of their homosexual identity; a period of prolonged silence about their sexuality, whereby they gradually came to terms with their same-sex attraction; learning to express their sexual identity; integrating a sexual identity with other aspects of self (Muslim identity); and refining that identity over time (Sandfort 2000).

The endeavour to rebuild and forge this identity was embodied by a support group called Al-Fatiha, a forum for exploring and discussing related religious and sexual identities for Muslims who are lesbian, gay, bisexual and transgendered. It was established specifically to promote and help homosexuals integrate their lifestyle with their religious identity. Membership in Al-Fatiha is an instrumental step in the pursuit of a gay Muslim identity. Indeed, being part of the group legitimates their new identity, that is, the members begin to internalize the homosexual Muslim identity, combining it into their self-concept. However, their personal effort at forging this new identity through Al-Fatiha lacks a wider theological accommodation. In their bi-monthly meetings, topics under discussion are geared towards understanding the areas in Islam which may allow them to foster a wider legitimacy for their sexuality. They challenge the rhetoric of the Qur'an and its traditional interpretation. The first issue considered is the source in which the condemnation of homosexuality is made: the parable of Prophet Lut[5] in the Qur'an. Although Lut's parable is considered important in imparting knowledge over the misuse of power and domination, Kashif introduces a view adopted previously by homosexual Christians (Boswell 1980; Scroogs 1983; Perry 1990) in reading the parable:

> The people of Sodom were not hospitable to travellers who were treated in a very inappropriate manner. It was because they were inhospitable that they were killed, but people have taken from that only the homosexuality part, the forced rape of the males as what was wrong. I am not forcibly raping any male person. I am not a rapist! The relationships that I enter into are consensual and loving.

Thus, both social context and interpretation are critical in a struggle for tolerance and acceptance by the wider Muslim community. Omar accentuates this point by contending that 'Sodom and Gomorrah were contextual so we can't relate to that society or what was said of the people'. Sohail elaborates: 'the Qur'an is a guidance, but remember it is a human interpretation of the Qur'an fourteen hundred years ago. The people of Lut not the people of Sohail.' This is a contentious issue and it reflects the tentative steps needed to revise contemporary Islamic thought on homosexuality. Further, the alternative interpretation would reformulate or more appropriately 'modernize' the traditional perspective in light of contemporary social changes. The idea that the Qur'an, its commentary and interpretation are context-based would therefore suggest that the homosexuality that is condemned in the Qur'an during a certain socio-cultural period is relative to that period, and should be open to reinterpretation to reflect contemporary society. Sohail gave particular prominence to the issue and was the main advocate for an attempt at reinterpretation: 'the interpretation is not the word of God; that's just human words, so why can't other human beings bring out another interpretation? It's like stories; it's references to incidents happening in that particular social set-up fourteen hundred years ago' (Sohail). The desire to reinterpret the Qur'an and the hadith arises from the fact that the interpretation and subsequent discourses have been exclusively undertaken by heterosexual males, thereby creating a hegemonic heterosexual context to analyse Islamic discourse. Indeed, Yip points out: 'unlike their Christian counterparts in the Western world, non-heterosexual Muslims do not have theological material that affirms their sexuality, which they could use to challenge the dominant Islamic discourse of sexuality' (Yip 2002: 4). There is a widely held belief that a challenge is imperative to confront the unwillingness of mainstream Muslim society to address the issue. Sohail believed that not only is this challenge necessary, as Muslims worldwide continue to rely on an archaic interpretation of the text, but also a requisite for contemporary society with changing norms and values. Closely related to this is questioning the authenticity of hadith. Among certain respondents, this was an issue of debate, since the Prophet Muhammad is reported to have castigated and set severe punishments for those caught committing sodomy.[6] By contending that the Ahadith are less than reliable, the men challenge the 'alleged' reported sayings of the Prophet on the subject of homosexuality. In response to this, Adil comments: 'I've got questions about Ahadith, because it's not a reliable source of information. It is purely descriptive and prescribed within a certain moral framework. Also, it does not contain factual statements or information about the issue that would guide one on that issue.' Adil's perspective was shared by the others. Omar believed that the accounts of the Prophet's life and sayings are coloured and biased and as such cannot be accepted as authentic. On the other hand, Jamal drew an explicit connection between the Ahadith and the Qur'an; he expressed disapproval at the thought of disregarding the Ahadith: 'you cannot have the Qur'an without Ahadith and you cannot have the Ahadith without the Qur'an.' It is evident then that for those who have reconciled their sexuality and faith, the importance of the Ahadith is not only questioned but also criticized. Indeed, the 'accommodation' of homosexuals within Muslim society would be possible only if, as Kashif points out, 'there is more discussion on the sources of hadith; only when we begin to discuss these issues will gay Muslims be able to go back into mainstream Islam'. For this 'accommodation' to take place a reinterpretation of the Qur'an (especially the verses relating to Prophet Lut) is required.

'Coming out'

The accommodation of 'deviant' identities is considerably more difficult if homosexuality is not discussed or debated. In countries such as Pakistan where Islam predominates (Murray and Roscoe 1997; Khan 1997), the subject continues to be clouded in ignorance and intentional neglect. Indeed, the traditional and continued silence on the issue prevents many with homosexual feelings from identifying themselves publicly. 'Coming out' – 'the dramatic quality of privately and publicly coming to terms with a contested social identity' (Seidman et al. 2002: 427), was overwhelmingly met with a lack of acceptance or violence: 'My father shouted at me, swore at me, spat on me, slapped me, and kicked me. It was the most disgusting behaviour I had ever seen. My uncle said it was a disgusting way of life, while my mum broke into tears and started screaming' (Kashif).

Not all respondents disclosed their sexuality: 'I wouldn't tell my parents; I wouldn't want this bit of information to destabilize the family environment. And frankly, I can't put my ageing parents through this; it would destroy them' (Adil). Sohail maintains that his parents are aware of his sexuality but, he explains, 'I haven't affirmed it'. His parents' awareness came from the knowledge of his affairs with older men and from being caught by his father in a sexual act with another boy. He recollects his treatment by his parents: 'I hated her [mother] so much! She used to call me *bhund marao* [bum basher]. I used to feel so bad inside. My father beat me up about four or five times really badly.' Imtiyaz described how he was shunned by his father, who no longer regarded him as his son: 'My father didn't talk to me for a whole year; he went berserk. He wouldn't want to go anywhere with me; if I went to visit them [parents], he would either ignore me or leave the room.' The situation for Jamal was significantly different when a confrontation with his father regarding his arranged marriage prompted a disclosure of his sexuality. Despite the freedom to live his life as a homosexual, a 'don't ask–don't tell' situation unfolded for him as there had never been any informal or formal discussion of his sexuality before. Omar's experience was perhaps the most positive. His parents' reaction was one of 'contemplation and understanding rather than sadness or regret'. He was thus able to devote less time and effort to appeasing his family; he explained, 'if you come beyond the stage of conflict and acceptance, you can begin to live comfortably as a person'. Spatial independence was also an important factor: 'parents are more concerned with what the extended family members think; you know, "what will people in society say?"' (Sohail). This was a frequent response since many of the men, while living at home, were severely restricted from pursuing relationships, sexual interests or leading a homosexual lifestyle. Evidently, moving away from the family home allowed them the sexual freedom and independence to experience and explore their sexuality. This independence also allowed the men to emotionally detach themselves from their family. This was particularly the case if their sexuality had created problems within the family: 'Every time I called my mother, she would go on about the gay issue, so I said to her, "this is no longer my problem to deal with; I'm happy with myself; this is something you have to understand and accept"' (Kashif). These observations illustrate the conflicts the men faced in coming to terms with their sexuality openly, although a few continue to grapple with this very issue in silence. Yet 'coming out' becomes a liberating process by which the oppression experienced is transformed in a positive light, in that it affirms and strengthens their homosexual identity.

Marriage

Socialization prepares individuals for the role they are to play, providing them with the necessary repertoire of values and beliefs. The social order prescribes a set of identities, roles and social ties for heterosexuals, which from an Islamic perspective concerns the sanctity of marriage.[7] Indeed, marriage serves to induce compliance with dominant social norms; concurrently, these heterosexist norms condemn homosexuality because it challenges and disrupts the dominant social structure: 'Islam remains violently hostile to all other ways of realising sexual desire, which are regarded as unnatural purely and simply because they run counter to the antithetical harmony of the sexes; they violate the harmony of life [...] homosexuality is a challenge to the order of the world as laid down by God' (Bouhdiba 1998: 31–2).

Society's expectation that its members will marry often overrides personal preferences. Its importance was remarked upon by Imtiyaz: 'Three things are important in society amongst Muslims: marriage, children and religion.' Such was the power of conforming to social, cultural and religious norms that Kashif, Imtiyaz and Nasir had all been married. As Kashif relates, 'I thought marriage would mean that my attraction to men would wither away'. Marriage gave the men a gender-appropriate role, which in turn allowed them the opportunity to try to relinquish (at least temporarily) their attraction to men. These three men had attempted to negotiate their sexuality in the face of the cultural and religious obligation of marriage. Although Kashif vehemently objected to marriage, he had very little choice. He relates that his wife was also pressured to marry and consequently the marriage ended in a relatively short period. He was divorced a year later without consummation. He disclosed his sexuality soon afterwards and his family members sought to rectify the 'problem': 'I was working in London at the time, and they told me to come back to Glasgow, to hand in my notice, so they could fix me. That is, they'd make me straight by getting me married again.' Marriage was held to be a remedy for the homosexual 'illness'. Imtiyaz attributed his marriage to the importance it held in his family: 'It [marriage] was a procedure because I always knew I was going to get married. At a young age, it was embedded in me that I was going to get married to my cousin, so we grew up knowing that.' Despite his attraction to men, Imtiyaz married at nineteen; he insists that he fulfilled his duties as a husband, providing and taking care of his wife financially. Indeed, Imtiyaz's life was compartmentalized to accommodate his double life. In the following extract, he recounts the lack of emotional support he provided for his wife and the 'balance' he maintained in holding his homosexual and heterosexual identity:

My wife was very jealous of the relationship I had with my female cousins, because I got on very well with them, but she couldn't understand why I wasn't like that with her, so, emotionally, I was never there for her. In the morning I would be either at work or at college; I would go back home in the evening and then at nights I would spend my time at gay clubs. I was spending so much time being straight that I needed to balance it out by being at gay clubs; it was only there that I was able to be myself. (Imtiyaz)

After thirteen years of marriage, he and his wife got a divorce, triggered, he recounts, because of his inability to have children. He insists that his marriage was simply a platform for him to 'play' out the role expected of men in society. However, the subsequent end of his marriage had a considerable impact on his identity as a homosexual; it has been a source of tremendous strength: 'This is the way I was meant to be; I tried to change but it didn't work, so I have no problem with calling myself a homosexual Muslim.' Although commitment to marriage was due to conforming to societal expectations, some of the men were also influenced by the desire to 'normalize' their sexual orientation, which, at the time, they thought was malleable.

The challenge to heteronormativity

Heterosexist norms construct heterosexual masculinity based upon a static binary of male/female; the antithesis of this construct is, in effect, the homosexual male. Indeed, the homosexual male as part of his self-identification challenges the dominant gender sexual paradigms and 'appropriate gender behaviour' (O'Donnell and Sharpe 2000). Risman and Schwartz corroborate this further:

> Power and equality are also significant issues for [gay] male couples and so equality may not be so much an issue for any couple where the authority patterns based on gender no longer apply. It may be that after the conventions of gender are removed, power inequalities are so unflattering to both that partners are intensely motivated to avoid the costs of greater power and powerlessness alike. For example gay men released from the family provider role do not reinvent it in their relationships; prefer a more egalitarian and mutually responsible allocation of economic responsibility. (Risman and Schwartz 1988: 135)

The quotation highlights how gendered roles are concretely entrenched within heterosexuality. Not surprisingly, the men's views reflected a need to base relationships on equality, as Omar tersely points out: 'There are no dichotomies for me at all.' Indeed, this emerged as a common theme and for several respondents the general use of the term 'gender roles' was regarded negatively. A closer analysis of the responses reveals that they shared a belief that masculine and feminine behaviours are in fact interchangeable. In some instances, the respondents were not able to define what for them was masculine or feminine or chose not to, although they easily provided the heterosexist definition of the two terms. Omar typified the view that 'one can't strictly compartmentalize the roles of men and women'. Nasir, in particular, resisted defining masculine and feminine behaviour. After several prompts, he argued that equality should characterize relationships, maintaining that men very often display 'feminine' traits while women display 'masculine' ones: 'I share a house with a lesbian; that doesn't mean that she does the dishes because she's a woman; if I need help putting up shelves she helps me because she is physically more capable than I am' (Nasir).

Rather than boxing people into specific roles, there is room for flexibility, as Omar explains: 'I can't tell you what is masculine or feminine behaviour because they are interchangeable roles which depend on the context.' Despite this, there was a realization that 'Islam certainly gives instructions; it gives positive guidelines as to what men's duties and women's duties are in the family' (Adil). In addition, the men felt that some heterosexual-based concepts would apply to homosexual relationships. Omar held the view that his family (composed of his partner and children) as compared to the traditional family unit would be Islamic because 'we would direct our lives in the way Islam wants us; it's the qualities of Islam which are important to me, not the actual role model of the family'. The men appeared to embrace the idea that there was little to prevent the social roles from being fulfilled, and a modification, Omar suggested, would quite easily be accommodated under the Islamic importance of the family. Interestingly, though, none of the respondents currently in a relationship had partners who were Muslims, as Sohail revealed: 'Islam is important to me as an individual, but it doesn't encompass my lover or partner.' Respondents frequently expressed the idea that within contemporary society they are able to reverse or 're-script' traditional gender roles. Many subverted the roles and felt they could play both: 'I play both parts: I cook for myself, I work for myself, and I provide for myself' (Imtiyaz). Omar took the point further: 'I play the role of both the man and the woman; I don't see any problem in washing up as a traditional mother would do and going out and earning a household income for the family as a father would be expected to do.' However, the expected or desired changes are not as straightforward; neither is the current climate as accommodating as they would wish. There is a recognition, as Omar notes, that, before changes can occur, 'a lot of working is required; it needs acceptance and conflict resolution by the Islamic society as a whole, coming to an understanding if not accepting and tolerating'. Sohail equally remained realistic about changes in thought and discourse:

> We have to start from scratch to find out what Islam says about homo-sexuality; we need more people from the *Ulema* [learned and knowledge-able people in Islam] to talk about it, and first they have to identify, yes, we have homosexuals, homosexuality does exist. The second thing is, is it a disease? Is it gender-orientated or is it their genes? You can imagine how many levels we have to go through, so guidelines are something that are way down on the list. It will take years or centuries to form guidelines.

Thus, despite their optimism regarding change, there was an acknow-ledgement that Islamic guidelines for homosexuals call for extensive dialogue and intellectual articulation from the mainstream Muslim com-munity.

Conclusion

This chapter is focused on the personal, sexual and religious journeys and conflicts experienced by some Muslim homosexual men. It examined the reconstruction of the religious identity to permit their previously held incongruent identity of homosexuality. In essence, the respondents argued for a legitimate expression of their sexuality, faith and spirituality and faulted the wider Muslim community for failing to address the issue. The accommodation of discrepant identities has been undertaken by groups such as Al-Fatiha, who offer support in preserving both identities. However, there is no definitive work on homosexuality in Islam, merely a series of cross-references that stress the 'abnormality' of homosexual individuals and their sexual relations (Doi 1996; Zafeeruddin 1996). The proscription of homosexual acts is grounded in the Islamic view that heterosexuality is natural and essential, and heterosexual marriage the only path to religious and personal fulfilment. Muslim homosexuals and human rights organizations (Amnesty International) have in recent years begun to question the underlying premise of traditional Islamic teaching on sexuality. Although their struggle is somewhat embryonic, their voices are gaining the attention of the media[8] and Islamic organizations[9] which, it has to be said, continue to be vociferous in their condemnation. Certainly, an argument can be made that by not discussing homosexuality, as is evident from the lack of support groups or Islamic scholarly literature, the Muslim community implicitly believes that it does not exist or that it is merely 'a symptom of westernisation' (Duran 1993), and thus poses no threat to Muslim communities.

What, then, are the tentative possibilities of 'accommodating' homosexuals within Muslim communities and societies? Although respondents foresee a positive future, there continues to be a tacit consent, which considers homosexuality a sin. Indeed, the Qur'an is clear in stating that men and women are divinely created creatures enjoined for many purposes, among them to provide security, companionship and to fulfil one another's sexual needs (Qur'an 30:21; 2:187). Homosexuality among Muslims and in Muslim countries continues to be taboo, although studies (Schmitt and Sofer 1992; Duran 1993; Murray and Roscoe 1997) indicate that knowledge of its existence is widely accepted, or, more appropriately, homo-sex is accepted as long as it does not lead to relationships of love. If there is an essential belief that humans have both a natural and divine purpose, then altering that 'way' is difficult to subvert. However, such subversion, or at least negotiation, is clearly being undertaken by a number of Muslim gay men.

Notes

1 Research on Gay, Lesbian, and Bisexual Muslims of South Asian origin (2001), funded by the ESRC, is currently being carried out by Nottingham Trent University researchers (at time of publication).

2 An Arabic word meaning the path to be followed, often interpreted as Islamic law based on the Qur'an and Sunnah (the practices of the Prophet).

3 Respondents were drawn from the following organizations: Al-Fatiha: a social support group for Muslim homosexuals; Al-Habaib: a service to support the mental health needs of homosexuals; LEAN: London East AIDS Network; and BILAN: Somalian group for people affected by or infected with HIV.

4 Al-Fatiha: taken from the first verse of the Qur'an; translates as the 'Opening' or the 'Beginning'.

5 The warnings given by Lut having been ignored by the people, Sodom and Gomorrah were destroyed by God because of the decadence and depravity of their inhabitants. 'We also sent Lut: He said to his people: "Do ye commit lewdness such as no people in creation (ever) committed before you? For ye practice your lusts on men in preference to women: ye are indeed a people transgressing beyond limits [...]" And we rained down on them a shower (of brimstone): Then see what was the end of those who indulged in sin and crime!' (Qur'an 7: 80–4). The parable is mentioned in four other chapters: 11:77–83; 21:74; 26:160–73; 27:54–8.

6 It is reported that the Prophet Muhammad said: 'if you find someone committing an act of the commitment of Lut kill the one on top and the one below'; and in another statement: 'kill the doer and the one with whom the act is committed' (Doi 1989: 243).

7 The Prophet said, 'When a man marries he has fulfilled half of the religion' (Bukhari Hadith).

8 'An Islamic Revolutionary', *Guardian*, 30 August 2001.

9 'Holy War Declared on Out-Gay Muslims', *Pink Paper*, 13 July 2001. The leader of the Al-Muhajiroun group, Sheikh Omar Bakri Mohammed, has issued a *fatwa* against Al-Fatiha. The press release stated that 'the very existence of Al-Fatiha is illegitimate (not Islamic) and the members of this organization are apostates. Never will such an organization be tolerated in Islam and never will the disease which it calls for be affiliated with a true Islamic society. The ruling for such acts is death. It is a duty of all Muslims to prevent such evil conceptions being voiced in the public or private arena.'

References

Ali, A. Y. (1990) *The Holy Qur'an: Translation and Commentary*. Birmingham: Islamic Propagation Centre International.

Boswell, J. (1980) *Christianity, Social Tolerance and Homosexuality*. Chicago, IL: University of Chicago Press.

Bouhdiba, A. (1998) *Sexuality in Islam*, trans. Alan Sheridan. London: Saqi Books.

Comstock, G. D. (1993) *Gay Theology without Apology*. Cleveland, OH: Pilgrim Press.

— (1996) *Unrepentant, Self-Affirming, Practising: Lesbian/Bisexual/Gay People within Organized Religion*. New York: Continuum.

DeLamater, J. (1981) 'The Social Control of Sexuality', *Annual Review of Sociology*, 7: 263–90.

Doi, A. R. (1996) *Woman in Shari'ah, Islamic Law*. London: Ta-Ha.

Duran, K. (1993) 'Homosexuality in Islam', in A. Swidler (ed.), *Homosexuality and World Religions*. Harrisburg, PA: Trinity Press.

Ellison, M. M. (1993) 'Homosexuality and Protestantism', in A. Swidler (ed.), *Homosexuality and World Religions*. Harrisburg, PA: Trinity Press.

Hewitt, I. B. (1997) *What Does Islam Say?* London: Muslim Education Trust.

Khan, B. (1997) 'Not-So-Gay Life in Pakistani in the 1980s and 1990s', in S. O. Murray and W. Roscoe (eds), *Islamic Homosexualities: Culture, History, and Literature*. New York: New York University Press.

Murray, S. O. and W. Roscoe (eds) (1997) *Islamic Homosexualities: Culture, History, and Literature*. New York: New York University Press.

O'Donnell, M. and S. Sharpe (2000) *Uncertain Masculinities: Youth, Ethnicity and Class in Contemporary Britain*. London: Routledge.

Perry, T. (1990) *Don't Be Afraid Anymore*. New York: St Martin's Press.

Risman, B. and P. Schwartz (1988) 'Sociological Research on Male and Female Homosexuality', *Annual Review of Sociology*, 14: 125–47.

Rodriguez, E. M. and S. C. Ouellette (2000) 'Gay and Lesbian Christians: Homosexual and Religious Identity Integration in the Members and Participants of a Gay-Positive Church', *Journal for the Scientific Study of Religion*, 39 (3): 333–47.

Sandfort, T. (2000) 'Homosexuality, Psychology, and Gay Lesbians Studies', in T. Sandfort et al. (eds) (2000) *Lesbian and Gay Studies: An Introductory, Interdisciplinary Approach*. London: Sage.

Schmitt, A. and J. Sofer (eds) (1992) *Sexuality and Eroticism Among Males in Moslem Societies*. New York: Harrington Park Press.

Scroogs, R. (1983) *The New Testament and Homosexuality*. Philadelphia, PA: Fortress Press.

Seidman, S. et al. (2002) 'Beyond the Closet? The Changing Social Meaning of Homosexuality in the United States', in C. L. Williams and A. Stein (eds), *Sexuality and Gender*. Massachusetts: Blackwell.

Thumma, S. (1991) 'Negotiating a Religious Identity: The Case of the Gay Evangelical', *Sociological Analysis*, 52 (4): 333–47.

Yip, A. K. T. (1997) 'Attacking the Attacker: Gay Christians Talk Back', *British Journal of Sociology*, 48 (1).

— (2002) 'Negotiating Space with Family and Kin in Identity Construction: The Narratives of Non-Heterosexual Muslims in the UK', Paper presented at the Annual Conference of the British Sociological Association, 'Reshaping the Social', University of Leicester, 25–27 March.

Zafeeruddin, M. M. (1996) *Islam on Homo-Sexuality*, trans Syed Azhar Ali Zaidi. Karachi: Darul Ishaat.

12 | 'The worms are weak': male infertility and patriarchal paradoxes in Egypt

MARCIA C. INHORN

Worldwide, between 8 and 12 per cent of couples suffer from infertility or the inability to conceive a child at some point during their reproductive lives (Reproductive Health Outlook 1999). However, in some non-Western societies, especially those in the 'infertility belt' of Central and Southern Africa, rates of infection-induced infertility may be high, affecting as many as one-third of all couples attempting to conceive (Collet et al. 1988; Larsen 1994; Ericksen and Brunette 1996). Unfortunately, the new reproductive technologies (NRTs) that may provide solutions to infertility for many Western couples are often unavailable in these settings, and modern healthcare services may themselves be of abysmally poor quality (Inhorn 1994a; Sundby 2002). Thus, it is not surprising that the infertile often turn to traditional remedies and healers (Inhorn 1994b), a pattern also found in the West (Van Balen et al. 1995).

A growing ethnographic literature also demonstrates that women worldwide bear the major burden of infertility (Abbey et al. 1991; Greil et al. 1990; Inhorn 1994b; Inhorn and van Balen 2002; Stanton et al. 1991; Van Balen and Trimbos-Kemper 1993). This burden may include blame for the reproductive failing; emotional distress in the forms of anxiety, depression, frustration, grief and fear (Greil 1997); marital duress leading to abandonment, divorce or polygamy; stigmatization and community ostracism; and, in many cases, bodily taxing, even life-threatening, forms of medical intervention. Infertility is a form of reproductive morbidity with profoundly gendered social consequences, which are usually more grave in non-Western settings than in the Western world (Inhorn and Van Balen 2002). In many non-Western societies, infertile women's suffering is exacerbated by strong pro-natalist social norms mandating motherhood. Yet policy-makers in these countries are often obsessed with curbing population growth rates, ignoring the sub-populations suffering because of their 'barrenness amidst plenty' (Inhorn 1994a, 1996).

Male infertility in global perspective

Infertility, like most reproductive issues, seems to be a 'woman's problem', and is conceptualized thus in indigenous systems of meaning and in global health policy discussions. However, the biological etiology of infertility does not reside solely or even largely in the female reproductive tract. The most comprehensive epidemiological study of infertility to date – a World Health Organization sponsored study of 5,800 infertile couples at thirty-three medical centres in twenty-two countries – found that men are the sole cause or a contributing factor to infertility in more than half of all couples around the globe (Cates et al. 1985; Reproductive Health Outlook 1999).

The causes are manifold: (1) low total volume of the ejaculate; (2) irregularities in the pH of the seminal fluid; (3) hyperviscosity of the seminal fluid or presence of pus (from infection) in the seminal fluid (so-called pyospermia, a problem in countries where sexually transmitted diseases go untreated); (4) low sperm count (oligozoospermia); (5) a complete absence of sperm (azoospermia) because of defects in the hypothalamo-pituitary axis or because a varicose vein in the scrotum (a varicocele) has raised the temperature of the testes; (6) poor sperm motility (asthenozoospermia), or movement, including problems of total motility or progressive motility (ability to sustain vigorous forward motion); (7) abnormal sperm morphology (teratozoospermia), involving sperm with deformed heads and tails (including microcephalic heads, double heads, coiled tails or multiple tails); (8) autoantibody formation against one's sperm, and the presence of male-derived protein complexes on the surface of the sperm that may act as antigens, inducing an immune response from the female partner leading to premature destruction of the sperm cell within the female reproductive tract; (9) defects in the proteins of the acrosome that reduce the sperm's ability to tunnel through the zona pellucida of the ovum and engage in fertilization; and (10) various obstructive conditions of the ejaculatory seminal ducts in the male genitals, due to congenital abnormalities or acquired testicular damage, which may prevent sperm from being ejaculated into the female reproductive tract (McConnell 1993; Wood 1994). Although some of these examples can be diagnosed, the underlying pathogenesis of most causes of male infertility remains 'idiopathic', or unknown (Irvine 1998). Furthermore, conventional therapies to treat male infertility, including hormonal drugs, surgical varicocele correction and intrauterine insemination, are largely unproven and mostly ineffective (Devroey et al. 1998; Kamischke and Nieschlag 1998). Thus, for many men, 'infertility' has, in fact, equalled 'sterility', or the permanent inability to conceive.

Male infertility problems may be compounded by so-called erectile dysfunction (ED), or impotence, whereby sexual performance problems prevent intercourse from being completed or undertaken. Although infertility and impotence are not synonymous, the two may be conflated in popular con-

218

ceptions of male reproduction (Inhorn 1994a; Webb and Daniluk 1999). Furthermore, impotence may be a product of and a contributor to infertility; many couples experience sexual dysfunction as a result of the infertility experience (including sexually demanding, 'timed' treatment regimes). Such dysfunction, when manifest in obstacles to successful ejaculation, may diminish the chances of conception (Rowe et al. 1993).

Given the various factors and the recalcitrance of male infertility to treatment, it is fair to say that men contribute significantly to global patterns of infertility.[1] It is surprising, then, that men do not bear more of the social burden for infertility. The reasons appear obvious: women's bodies bear the 'proof' of infertility through their failure to achieve pregnancy and childbirth, whereas men's bodies hide the evidence of reproductive defects. But a nuanced cultural analysis is required to account for this inequity, one that examines patriarchy as a system of gender oppression (i.e. male domination/female subordination) and that implicates patriarchy in the gendered asymmetry that accompanies infertility. Although arguments for 'universal' patriarchal oppression of women are difficult to sustain and have been rejected as ethnocentric in critiques of radical feminism (Elshtain 1981; Jaggar 1983; Tong 1989), it is clear that women's suffering over infertility is linked to patriarchal formations. Nevertheless, such patriarchal systems are often culturally diverse and locally informed; therefore, their expression is variable.

The case of male infertility in Egypt – where sperm are popularly referred to as 'worms' and male infertility is glossed as 'the worms are weak' – cannot be understood without reference to patriarchy in its local form. In Egypt, approximately 12 per cent of all married couples experience difficulties conceiving (Egyptian Fertility Care Society 1995), but women are stigmatized for infertility – even in situations of confirmed male infertility – because of entrenched patriarchal gender ideologies and relations (Inhorn 1994a, 1996). Male infertility provides an excellent example of the ongoing nature of patriarchy in Egyptian social life and a lens through which patriarchal gender and conjugal relations may be viewed. Following a discussion of methodology, I describe two cases of infertility among men of different social classes, focusing on how the husbands' infertility affected their wives. Using this material and more general findings from two research projects on Egyptian infertility, I then analyse a series of 'patriarchal' paradoxes whereby infertile husbands enjoy various forms of privilege in their marriages, social relations and treatment experiences, often to the disadvantage of the wives who love and support them.

Methodology

This chapter's findings and arguments are based on two periods of field research in Egypt, in which my focus of investigation was the problem of infertility. The first period lasted from October 1988 to December 1989 and involved mostly poor people living in and around Alexandria, Egypt's second largest city of more than five million inhabitants. Of the 190 women who formally participated in my study, 100 presented to the University of Alexandria's public ob/gyn teaching hospital for the treatment of infertility. There, I conducted in-depth, semi-structured interviews in the Egyptian dialect, eventually making my way into women's homes and communities, where I was then introduced to their husbands.[2] Forty per cent of husbands in this study had a diagnosed infertility factor, and an additional 10 per cent suffered from sexual dysfunction, which had led, in most cases, to procreative difficulties.

Returning to Egypt in 1996, I spent three months conducting participant observation and in-depth semi-structured interviewing in two private hospital-based in vitro fertilization (IVF) clinics located in elite suburbs of Cairo (Heliopolis and Maadi). In this study, involving sixty-six cases of infertility, most of my informants were educated, middle- to upper-class elites, who often presented to these IVF clinics as couples. Unlike my initial fieldwork, where women served as primary informants, the recent fieldwork involved male and female informants in nearly 40 per cent of cases. Of the male partners among these sixty-six couples, 70 per cent suffered from a diagnosed factor, including some severe cases (e.g. azoospermia).

This high percentage of male infertility cases in both studies reflects two sets of factors, one epidemiological and one clinical. With regard to epidemiological risk factors, Egyptian men are exposed to work and 'lifestyle' factors linked to increased rates of infertility. Manual and lower-class agricultural labourers are often exposed to high heat, pesticides and chemicals in their workplaces, all of which have been implicated in male infertility in Egypt (Inhorn and Buss 1994) and in other countries as well (Daniels 1997; Thonneau et al. 1998). Rural-born Egyptian men may also suffer the chronic effects of schistosomiasis, an endemic parasitic infection that affects reproductive function (Inhorn and Buss 1994; Yeboah et al. 1992). Finally, Egyptian men are heavy users of 'stimulants' like tea, Turkish coffee, high-nicotine cigarettes and tobacco-filled waterpipes (Inhorn and Buss 1994), all of which have been implicated in a reduced likelihood of conception (Curtis et al. 1997). These high numbers reflect the changing clinical nature of male infertility treatment in Egypt. With the introduction of new reproductive technologies over the past decade, some male infertility cases are now treatable in urban IVF clinics in Alexandria and Cairo.

Because my work was based in hospitals with IVF programmes, the number of male infertility cases is probably over-represented in my studies.

Nevertheless, the studies afforded me the opportunity to talk with men and women of various social classes. As with the rest of the world, male infertility in Egypt has been poorly investigated from a social science perspective. This chapter represents a first attempt to understand the gendered dimensions and consequences of male infertility in this patriarchal cultural setting, where this reproductive impairment is a profoundly emasculating and thus a delicate and 'invisible' subject.

Two cases of male infertility

Madiha and Ahmed Madiha[3] is a diminutive, attractive, and brave twenty-three-year-old, married to her infertile, twenty-eight-year-old husband, Ahmed, for five years. Both are uneducated and poor, as his carpenter's salary brings them only LE 40 a month.[4] Although Madiha worked in a textile factory before marriage and is willing to work again to improve their economic situation, Ahmed refuses this option, citing the problems of crowded transportation (with men who are 'strangers') and Madiha's potential neglect of the housework.[5] Madiha has been seeking treatment for infertility since the third month of her marriage, when her mother- and sister-in-law insisted on taking her to a physician. Since then, she has endured countless 'treatments', both ethnomedical and biomedical. Her mother-in-law has brought her vaginal suppositories of black glycerine to 'bring out' any infection she might have in her vagina. Traditional healers and neighbours have performed painful 'cupping' on her back to draw 'humidity' out of her womb. Spiritist healers have said prayers over her and asked her to perform various rituals of circumambulation at religious sites. During one Friday noon prayer, she was asked by a female spiritist healer to urinate on top of an eggplant to 'unbind' an infertility-producing condition known as *kabsa* or *mushahara*.[6]

Simultaneously, Madiha has pursued biomedical treatment, at the urging of Ahmed and his relatives, with whom she has lived for most of her marriage. Two of the doctors she has visited have performed a procedure called tubal insufflation, in which carbon dioxide is pumped into the uterus without any anaesthesia. One of the doctors told her that her cervix and uterus might be 'small' and that 'the smallest uterus can't get pregnant'; the procedure might 'widen', or 'dilate' her. The other physician offered no reason for performing the procedure. In fact, although tubal insufflation is widely practised as a money-making procedure by Egyptian gynaecologists with no specialized training in infertility, this technique, once used to diagnose tubal obstruction, has no therapeutic value and may

221

actually produce infertility by forcing pathogenic bacteria from the lower into the upper genital tract (Inhorn 1994a; Inhorn and Buss 1993).

Madiha also underwent an operation under general anaesthesia to correct a 'folded' uterus. As she explained, 'I didn't want this operation, but my in-laws pushed me and gave me the money.' When the operation failed, the doctor asked Ahmed to go to a particular doctor for an 'analysis'. Ahmed complied, and was asked to repeat the analysis twice and to take treatment.

According to Madiha, it was only then that 'I knew I'm all right and something is wrong with my husband'. Yet, Ahmed refuses to believe he is the cause of the infertility, and thus rejects treatment. His family, furthermore, refuses to believe that the first son in the family to marry is responsible for the infertility. As Madiha put it:

> Even my husband, when I tell him it's his problem, he doesn't answer me. When he went to the doctor for the first time, the doctor told him that he had pus and weakness in his *didan* [literally, 'worms' i.e., sperm]. But he never goes for treatment, even though he knows I want him to. Every time I tell his family that it's 'from him', they don't answer me. Instead, every time I tell them that I'm going to the doctor, they encourage me to, as if it's my problem. My family won't get involved. They know I'm not the reason and it's something wrong with Ahmed. They're 'relaxed' because they know it's his problem.

Concerned about her ongoing childlessness, one of Madiha's paternal uncles, who had read about the University of Alexandria's new infertility programme at Shatby Hospital, convinced her to go. At Shatby, Madiha underwent more tests, including laparoscopy, a surgical procedure to assess the condition of her fallopian tubes. There, the doctors told her that there was absolutely nothing wrong with her reproductive tract. Instead, another analysis showed Ahmed's sperm to be of 'poor quality' in terms of count and motility. The physicians encouraged Madiha to undergo artificial insemination using her husband's sperm (so-called AIH, because AID using donor sperm is religiously prohibited). The first attempt failed, but, at the time of my interview, she was mustering additional resources and nerve to try again.

She reported feeling sad and lonely, not only because she has no children to care for, but because she lacks support in her 'search for children', either from her husband, his relatives, or her family, who do not want to make trouble as long as there is no threat of divorce. 'One day,' she said, 'I got fed up. So I told him, "If you want to get married again, just go! I don't want any more treatments."' Although Ahmed does not admit to being infertile, she thinks some part of him must believe this, as he did not accept her offer of divorce and continues to be nice to her. Thus, even though Ahmed is a poor man, an unsatisfactory lover, and a traditional male who will not let Madiha work to fill her lonely days, Madiha believes that Ahmed loves her – more than she loves him – and that he will not divorce her, even if ongoing childlessness is 'God's will'. Madiha is literally *miskina* (a poor little thing) whose chances of becoming a mother remain slim because of the intractable infertility and truculent attitude of her husband.

Shahira, Mohammed and their ICSI twins Shahira is the twenty-five-year-old wife of Mohammed, a forty-three-year-old lawyer whose father was once a powerful politician. In addition to his legal practice, Mohammed rents a villa to a foreign embassy and owns a business centre run by Shahira. She is Mohammed's second wife, married to him now for ten months. Before this, Mohammed was married for seventeen years to Hala, a woman now in her forties, whom he divorced two years ago because of their childlessness.

Early in his first marriage, physicians told Mohammed that he suffered from severe male-factor infertility, involving low sperm count and poor motility. He underwent repeated courses of hormonal therapy, none of which improved his sperm profile. Ultimately, he and Hala underwent several cycles of artificial insemination using concentrates of his sperm, and five cycles of in vitro fertilization (IVF), three times in Germany and twice in Egypt. Each trial was unsuccessful.

It was obvious to the Egyptian physicians who undertook one of the trials that Mohammed and Hala's marriage was deteriorating during the course of therapy – a deterioration they implied had something to do with Hala's 'strong personality'. Shahira seemed to agree:

> In Egypt, if a man knows he doesn't get his wife pregnant, he's always upset. And if you're pushing him all the time, and he's the reason for the problem, he feels like giving up [on the marriage], because there are no children to keep in the house. In my husband's case, he preferred to divorce her because their relationship became bad. They had different attitudes and behaviours, and the major reason for the divorce was that he knows he's the reason for no pregnancy. He's kind, and she's nervous and always asking too many questions.

Although Hala has not remarried, Mohammed remarried in little over a year. He chose Shahira, a Christian, after knowing her for five months. Mohammed was less interested in Shahira's 'pedigree' (a college degree in tourism, with fluency in French and English) and in her religion (a Muslim man is allowed to marry a Christian woman), than in her youth, potential fecundity, acceptance of his infertility problem, and her willingness to try additional treatments with him. He told her, 'I want to marry you, but you are a young lady, and I'm sure you want a baby.' Shahira needed a 'father figure' and felt that Mohammed could be 'both a husband and a father'. (Her father works in the United Arab Emirates, and she has not seen him for eight years. Her mother died when Shahira was ten, and she has 'lived alone' with her younger brother and sister and two servants since their father emigrated in the early 1990s.) As Shahira stated:

> I need someone older, like a father, caring for me. And I'm sure he needs me, because he will think about pregnancy all the time, and he was bad, psychologically bad. And he needs someone to care for him as a wife. If I married a young man, he will ask first about himself. He wants to live with his wife alone. But my husband sees my case [i.e. she is like the 'mother' to her younger siblings], and he accepts my case. But I accept his [infertility]. He's feeling for me – I can't separate from them [her siblings] – and he loves this in me. Because he says, 'If you care for your sister and brother, you will care for me.'
>
> I took my decision in two months, without love before marriage, but with my mind. But love has grown – 100 per cent. An important thing in marriage is understanding, feeling secure. That's more important than love. He's kind and when I'm sick, he'll sit beside me and ask how I'm feeling. When I married him, I accepted 100 per cent that I will not have children, and I wouldn't push him. But since I knew his case before marriage, I told him I'd be willing to try [IVF] more than once because he's kind. I was afraid, but I'll try.

A few months into their marriage, Shahira went to a gynaecologist in Maadi, an elite suburb. The physician told her: 'You are young and you haven't anything wrong, but the lab report of your husband is bad.' She asked the physician about IVF, and he said: 'No way, because your husband is a very bad case.' Mohammed, meanwhile, underwent five months of drug therapy. His andrologist told him: 'Your wife is young. ICSI [intracytoplasmic sperm injection] may be successful, because she's young and has no problem. Don't hesitate. You should use any time you have.'

Mohammed took Shahira to one of the two Egyptian IVF clinics where he had also taken his first wife. The physicians confirmed that because Shahira was young, with no known reproductive impairments, their chances of conceiving with ICSI, the newest variant of IVF, were greater than in Mohammed's previous attempts. With ICSI, as long as a single viable spermatozoon can be retrieved from a semen sample or directly from the testicles, it can be injected through so-called 'micromanipulation' techniques into the ovum, thereby 'helping along' the fertilization process. Thus, with ICSI, men with severe forms of infertility – for which all other forms of therapy, including standard IVF, are unsuccessful – are able to conceive biological offspring. In other words, ICSI heralds a revolution in the treatment of male infertility, although it is accessible only to those who can afford it (at approximately £E10,000, or $3,000, per trial).

Mohammed was delighted that Shahira and he were candidates for ICSI, but Shahira's reaction was different: 'I'm afraid of any operation, or anything. I was so afraid, and I was not thinking it was going to be successful. But [the doctor] told me, "Don't be afraid. It's easy. A small operation. It will be successful."'

Shahira suffered uncomfortable side effects from the medication used to stimulate ovulation. Her gastric ulcer symptoms were exacerbated, and she felt abdominal cramping and pain throughout the treatment. 'It's too difficult doing this ICSI,' Shahira explained. 'I take all these injections, I come to the hospital every day, I prepare for the operation, I see the anaesthesia, the doctors. It's frightening. My husband – they just take the semen from him.'

Once the ICSI procedure was completed, Shahira was still unconvinced of its efficacy. Thus, when she was scheduled for a blood test to determine her pregnancy status, she refused. She was so intransigent that Mohammed finally called the laboratory and had a doctor sent to their home to draw the sample. The next day, Mohammed and Shahira went to the laboratory, where the physician told them: 'Congratulations. I wanted to tell you personally.' Repeated pregnancy tests, along with three ultrasounds, confirmed that Shahira was pregnant with twins, in separate amniotic sacs.

Now Mohammed is in a state of disbelief. Every day he looks at Shahira's expanding belly and says, 'Now I can't believe I will have children. I will believe it if I touch my son or daughter by myself.' Shahira hopes that the birth of his twins will make Mohammed stop smoking three packs of cigarettes a day. Shahira is also concerned about the potential difficulties associated with a twin pregnancy and caesarean childbirth,[7] and the demands of taking care of two infants simultaneously. She hopes that at least one of the infants will be a girl, although Mohammed hopes for a son he can name 'Ahmed'. If God wills, and the twins are born healthy, Shahira says, she won't do ICSI again: 'Once is enough. One operation, one delivery. It's too difficult and too frightening.'

Egyptian patriarchy

The cases of Madiha and Ahmed and Shahira and Mohammed illustrate the relationship of male infertility to patriarchy in Egyptian culture. In

Egypt, patriarchy involves relations of power and authority of males over females which are (1) learned through gender socialization within the family, where fatherhood gives men power; (2) manifested in inter- and intra-gender interactions within marriage, the family and other interpersonal milieus; (3) engrained in pervasive ideologies of inherent male superiority; and (4) institutionalized on legal, political, economic, educational and religious levels (Inhorn 1996: 3–4). Although I do not intend to suggest that Egypt is somehow more patriarchal than other societies, patriarchy operates on many levels in Egyptian society today. Furthermore, patriarchal ideologies cut across social classes, religious boundaries and household types. However, as seen in the case of Madiha and Ahmed, manifestations of patriarchy are often more pronounced among the rural and urban lower classes living in extended family households.

Indeed, as suggested by other feminist scholars (Kandiyoti 1988, 1991; Joseph 1993, 1994), patriarchy in the Middle East is operationalized in the classic patrilineal, patrilocally extended family household. There, the senior male has total authority. For young women, subordination to both men and senior women (the latter of whom 'buy into' patriarchy) is profound. This is particularly clear when young wives are unable to produce children, thereby threatening the social reproduction of the household and the husband's patrilineage at large. Exploring patriarchal relations in Middle Eastern households is thus crucial to understanding the social dimensions, inter- and intra-gender dynamics, and conjugal relations surrounding infertility. While it is clear why infertile women might suffer under such conditions of classic patriarchy, it is less clear what happens to women whose husbands are infertile. Yet, as shown in the case studies above, the condition of male infertility also threatens the happiness, health, security and lives of Egyptian women. I argue that women suffer over men's infertility because of the nature of Egyptian patriarchy and the kind of patriarchal support Egyptian men receive in their family lives, even when they are infertile. Male infertility in Egypt creates four main 'patriarchal paradoxes': (1) who gets blamed for infertility in a marriage; (2) whose gendered identity is diminished by infertility; (3) who suffers in an infertile marriage; and (4) who pays the price for infertility treatment.

Patriarchy and procreative blame

The first paradox is seen in the realm of procreative theory, or how Egyptians conceive of the 'coming into being' of human life (Delaney 1991; Inhorn 1994a). In contemporary Western reproductive biology,[8] procreation theories are 'duogenetic', in that men and women are seen as contributing equally to the hereditary substance of the foetus, formed through the union of a woman's ovum and a man's spermatozoon. However, even with the widespread penetration of Western biomedicine and education around the world in the past half-century, the globalization of such a duogenetic model is incomplete. Rather, in Egypt and in other parts of the Middle East (Crapanzano 1973; Delaney 1991; Good 1980; Greenwood 1981), lesser-educated people believe procreation is 'monogenetic', assigning men, the 'givers of life', primary responsibility for procreation. Specifically, most poor urban Egyptians believe that men are the creators of pre-formed foetuses, which they carry in their sperm and which are then ejaculated and 'caught and carried' by women's waiting wombs. In this scenario, women are not only marginalized as reproducers, but the products of their reproductive bodies, particularly menstrual blood, are seen as polluting to men and the foetuses they create. Although the notion of women's 'eggs' is beginning to gain credence, even some educated Egyptians argue that men's sperm are reproductively dominant to women's eggs in terms of biogenetic input into the foetus.

Given this ideology of male procreation, it is a true patriarchal paradox that women, rather than men, are blamed for procreative failure. In this masculinist pre-formation model, men cannot be blamed for failures of procreation, unless, because of impotence or premature ejaculation, they are unable to pass their worm-enveloped children into women's wombs. In other words, barring sexual inadequacy, men cannot fail reproductively so long as their bodies are the least bit spermatogenic. But women's bodies may be plagued by numerous problems that bar the facilitation of male procreation or result in an unsuitable gestational 'home' for the child that a man 'brings' in his ejaculate. This is why every act of sexual intercourse does not result in pregnancy. This is also why women are seen as suffering from many infertility conditions, both ethno- and biomedical (Inhorn 1994a, 1994c). These conditions are thought to impede women's ability to provide adequate reception and nurturance of the foetuses men make. In other words, just as men are seen as giving life, women are seen as taking it away because of wombs that fail to facilitate the most important act of male creation. Men, on the other hand, are seen as immune to infertility-producing bodily pathology. As long as a man can ejaculate his worm-borne foetuses into a woman's womb, he is deemed both virile and fertile.

With the advent of semen analysis in Egypt over the past three decades, however, the blame for infertility has shifted slightly. In fact, 'worm' pathology is a titillating topic of conversation among poor urban Egyptians. Virtually every Egyptian has now heard of the problem of so-called 'weak worms'. 'Weakness' is a common cultural illness idiom in Egypt (DeClerque et al. 1986; Early 1993) and is rife in popular reproductive imagery. Most

'The worms are weak'

227

Egyptians now accept the idea that men, too, may be infertile because the 'worms' are slow, sluggish, prone to premature death or absent altogether. Because men's worms are considered living animals, they are seen as suffering the problems of other animals, including excessive somnolence, natural death and even murder (by other microbes or by some substance in the woman's body). The problem of not having enough worms is also recognized as important. Some men are seen as having 'no worms at all', 'a low percentage of worms', 'too few worms' or, in a fusion of popular and biomedical imagery, 'a low worm count'.

Accepting male infertility in theory is not the same as accepting it in practice. Although Egyptians are willing to discuss the possibility of weak worms when a couple is childless, they are less willing to accept male infertility as the absolute cause of any given case. Even when men are acknowledged as having worm problems, such problems are seen as correctable through various medications thought to invigorate, even enliven, the most moribund of worms. The severity of many male infertility problems, which rarely respond well to drug therapy, remains unrecognized by most Egyptians.

Rather, women are blamed for the failure to facilitate male procreation. Women's reproductive bodies are seen as containing three types of 'equipment' – the uterus, fallopian tubes and ovaries – mechanically fragile and thus subject to injury and failure. Women are viewed as having 'many things that can go wrong' with their reproductive bodies, a view supported when women seek biomedical infertility treatment and are subjected to numerous diagnostic and therapeutic procedures. Women are usually blamed for having more severe, intractable infertility problems, and the degree to which Egyptian women view their reproductive bodies as fragile, potentially malfunctioning and difficult to treat is remarkable. Indeed, the persistence of women-blaming cannot be overstated. Women who are given a clean bill of health continue to be condemned as infertile by their husbands' relatives, neighbours and sometimes husbands themselves – even when the husbands suffer from serious male-factor infertility. Many women willingly accept and internalize patriarchal ideologies of reproductive blame, under the assumption that something must be wrong with them, too.

Among poor women unable to obtain high-quality, up-to-date infertility care, quests for conception typically involve painful and tortuous therapies that are obsolete in the West and that may create infertility problems where none existed. The quest is encouraged, even mandated, by husbands and husbands' families, who taunt a childless wife as 'useless', 'worthless', 'barren', 'incomplete', 'unwomanly'. As one woman explained: 'They always blame the woman and say she's like a tree without dates. Usually when it's known to be from the husband, they don't tell him anything, because it would make him feel embarrassed and his manhood would be shaken.'

Patriarchy and masculinity This brings us to the second paradox: whereas infertility always mars a woman's femininity, no matter which partner is the 'cause' of the problem, male infertility does not similarly redound on a man's masculinity. There are several reasons for this. First, there is widespread disagreement about the degree to which male infertility can be emasculating. The dominant view is that male infertility is profoundly emasculating, particularly given two major conflations: first, of infertility with virility or sexual potency; and second, of virility with 'manhood', the meanings of which are closely linked in North Africa (Ouzgane, personal communication). In Egypt, infertile men are said to 'not be good for women', to have their 'manhood shaken', or to be 'weak' and 'incomplete', not 'real men'. Thus, infertility casts doubt upon a man's sexual and gender identities – that is, whether he is a 'real' man with the normal masculine parts, physiological processes, requisite 'strength' of body and character, and appropriate sexual orientation. Furthermore, infertility threatens personhood itself or the acceptance of a man as a 'whole' human being with a normal adult social identity and self-concept. Indeed, infertility, a condition over which Egyptian men (like men everywhere) have no control, threatens 'norms of being' (Goffman 1963) – those attributes of a man felt to be so ordinary and natural that failure to achieve them leads to feelings of shame, incompleteness, self-hate and self-derogation. Given the threat of infertility to normative masculinity, it is not surprising that the condition is deeply stigmatizing and the source of profound psychological suffering for Egyptian men who accept their infertile status.[9] Because male infertility is glossed as spermatic 'weakness', many infertile Egyptian men seem to take this cultural idiom to heart, feeling that they are somehow weak, defective and even unworthy as biological progenitors. Many infertile Egyptian men seeking treatment at IVF centres bemoaned their 'weakness' and wondered out loud whether they would 'pass their weakness' on to their children.

On the other hand, an alternative view voiced by many Egyptians of all social classes is that 'a man is always a man', whether or not he is infertile, because having a child doesn't 'complete a man as it does a woman'. Indeed, whereas a woman's full personhood can be achieved only through attainment of motherhood, a man's sense of achievement has other potential outlets, including employment, education, religious/ spiritual pursuits, sports and leisure, friendship groups and the like. Egyptian men may delay marriage and parenting for many years as they pursue education, seek employment at home or abroad, and accrue resources to set up a household. Although more and more women in Egypt are entering the workforce (MacLeod 1991), the notion of a married 'career woman' who remains childless by choice is unthinkable. Thus, while men and women in Egypt, almost without exception, eventually marry and expect to become parents, the truly mandatory nature of parenthood is experienced much more keenly by women, whose other avenues for self-realization are limited and who are judged harshly when they are unable to achieve motherhood early in their married lives.[10]

Infertile men rarely receive the criticism and social scrutiny that infertile women experience. In fact, men who learn that they are infertile needn't fear much for their reputations, for male infertility is rarely exposed to others in Egyptian communities. Why? For one, semen analysis is fraught with difficulty in Egypt: some men refuse to undergo the analysis, others disbelieve the negative results, others hide their bad results from their wives and families, and some bribe laboratory technicians for false reports. Furthermore, infertility specialists bemoan the technical quality of semen analysis, which varies from lab to lab and may thus be unreliable.

Second, many women will go to great lengths to uphold their infertile husbands' reputations – shouldering the 'blame' for the infertility in public to avoid the stigma, psychological trauma and possible marital disruptions such disclosure is likely to instigate. Egyptian women, understanding all too well the androcentric norms of their society, are not inclined to undermine their husbands' authority or standing as potential patriarchs, whose ability to produce children must remain unquestioned, particularly by other men. Indeed, masculinity in the Middle East is largely a homosocial enactment performed before and evaluated by other men. Thus, at the core of masculinity in the Middle East is homosocial competition and hierarchy – men's needs to prove themselves to other men (Ouzgane 1997: 11–12). When male infertility does occur – wreaking havoc on a man's paternity, his ability to monogenetically procreate and prove his societal position as a patriarch, or father figure to his biological children – then such infertility is rejected as implausible, or hidden from public scrutiny by infertile men themselves and the women who share their 'secret'. So stigmatizing is male infertility to prevailing 'hegemonic masculinity' (Connell 1995: 76) that most Egyptian men would rather 'live a lie' – enforcing or tacitly accepting a cover-up on the part of their wives and families – than risk exposure of their emasculating 'defect' to their male peers. Themselves the victims of dominant masculinity norms, infertile Egyptian men thus pay the heavy price of diminished self-concept and profound psychic suffering over their 'secret stigma'. But, I would argue, the burden may be even greater for such men's wives: by feeling compelled to shoulder the blame, they ensure that male infertility remains 'invisible' and hegemonic masculinities remain intact. At the same time, such a 'patriarchal bargain' (Kandiyoti 1988) means that wives of infertile men must endure the social ostracism that comes with this stigmatizing condition, and the psychic and physical toll of medical treatment for a condition located outside their own bodies.

Patriarchy and infertile marriages That such women's marriages are threatened points to a third paradox: infertility stemming from a husband rarely leads to wife-initiated divorce and may, in fact, strengthen marital bonds. Yet, infertility may lead to husband-initiated divorce or polygynous remarriage, whether or not female infertility can be proven.

Egyptian men who acknowledge their infertility are unlikely to replace their wives in a futile attempt to prove their fertility. Knowledge of their 'secret failing' often makes infertile men extremely solicitous of their wives, largely because of the guilt they feel over depriving their wives of children. In turn, wives of infertile men typically express profound sympathy and care, and rarely deem the infertility a striking blow to their marriages. Indeed, marriages affected by male infertility are often some of the best. Infertile husbands are often reported by their wives to be exceptionally kind and loving. Women, for their part, often feel relief in knowing that their marriages are secure, and they generally (although not necessarily)[11] reciprocate their husbands' kindnesses with mutual affection and support, even 'babying' their husbands in the ways mothers do their children. Furthermore, wives' willingness to accept the blame publicly is often impressive to their husbands, cementing the marital bonds further.

Egyptian women are socialized to be care-givers, and they often boast of the superior compassion that comes with being a woman. Given the opportunity, women will play this role with their husbands, even if a husband's condition leads to permanent childlessness in the marriage. When a man's condition seems hopeless, some men take pity on their wives and offer to 'free' them from the childless union. However, unlike men known to leave their wives over childlessness, few women choose this route. Not only is a woman's decision to leave a marriage considered bad form, but many women feel profound sympathy for their husbands' plight and are even more loving as a result. As one woman explained:

> After the diagnosis, [my husband] told me, 'If you want to leave me, you can.' I was upset, and I went to talk to my mother – she's like my friend – and my mother wanted me to leave him! After thinking a lot, I refused. My mother got upset and told my brothers and sisters. They didn't – and can't – push me, but I felt all of them wanted me to leave my husband. And that's

up to me to decide. For example, my sister whose husband is sick has three children. I told her, 'Can you leave your husband because you know he's sick? My husband, too, is sick. It's a sickness. You leave your husband and I'll leave mine!' A few times [my husband] told me, 'If you want me to leave you, I will. I'll leave you the apartment and everything. I just don't want to upset you.' He said he'd go to live with his father. He feels he's depriving me. I act at home as if he's my son, and I cuddle him a lot. And if strangers ask me from whom it is, I say, 'Both of us are well and that's up to God.'

When a wife is known to be infertile, on the other hand, men at least consider their Islamically condoned options of polygynous remarriage or divorce – even though most men ultimately reject this option (Inhorn 1996). Husbands in Egypt typically experience significant family pressure to replace their infertile wives and perpetuate the patrilineage. Thus, even when men choose not to divorce their infertile wives, thereby resisting the patriarchal scripts engendered by Egyptian family life, a wife's infertility still leads to marital disruption and insecurity. Many infertile women live in fear that their marriages will collapse, for Islamic personal status laws consider a wife's barrenness as grounds for divorce. Although Islam also allows women to divorce if male infertility can be proven, initiation of a divorce continues to be so stigmatizing that women rarely choose this option unless their marriages are truly unbearable. Thus, as seen in the case of Mohammed and his first wife, Hala herself did not initiate the divorce. It was Mohammed who left the marriage to try his reproductive luck with a younger, more 'sympathetic' woman. Hala, meanwhile, was blamed for the divorce, by virtue of her 'strong' (qua emasculating) personality which further 'weakened' Mohammed's psyche and his commitment to his marriage. Hala was deemed by all to have 'brought the divorce upon herself' by reminding Mohammed too often of his diminished masculinity.

Patriarchy and new reproductive technologies Mohammed and Hala's case also points to the fourth paradox: the new reproductive technologies to treat infertility have actually increased the potential for divorce in Egypt. Thus, the final paradox involves the ways in which reproductive technologies themselves may serve particular patriarchal ends in this cultural setting.

The newest reproductive technology known as ICSI has now entered the Egyptian landscape; with ICSI, cases of seemingly intractable male infertility can be overcome, and the arrival of this revolutionary treatment has led to the flooding of Egyptian IVF clinics with male-infertility cases. But many of the wives who have stood by their infertile husbands for years arrive at

Egyptian IVF centres as 'reproductively elderly' women in their forties, too old to produce viable ova for the ICSI procedure. Unfortunately, because of declining success rates for IVF/ICSI in women aged forty and above, most Egyptian IVF centres refuse to accept these women into their patient populations. Some Egyptian IVF doctors argue that this is a compassionate restriction, since it prevents older women from suffering the economic, physical and psychic hardships of likely futile attempts.

However, these age restrictions have proven devastating for Egyptian wives of infertile husbands. Because contemporary Islamic legal opinion forbids ova donation, surrogacy and adoption, couples with a reproductively elderly wife face four difficult options: (1) to remain together permanently without children; (2) to raise orphaned foster children; (3) to divorce so that husbands can try their reproductive luck with younger women; or (4) to partake in a polygynous marriage. Polygyny is unacceptable to most Egyptian women; yet the first and second options are unacceptable to a significant portion of Egyptian men, including the highly educated, upper-class men presenting themselves for male infertility treatment to IVF centres.[12] Thus, cases of male-initiated divorce between infertile men in their forties and fifties and the once-fertile but now elderly wives who have stood by them for years, are beginning to grow.

For their part, Egyptian physicians performing ICSI realize this potentially untoward outcome, but remain divided in their approach. Some believe that these 'scientific developments' give infertile men the God-given, patriarchal right to conceive their biological children, regardless of the marital repercussions; thus, they inform their male patients about ICSI, regardless of a wife's age or marital vulnerability. Others argue for a less scientific but more 'compassionate' approach, refusing to inform either partner that ICSI is possible. But given the way such information quickly spreads, partly as a result of multimedia forces, men turned away at one clinic may simply seek another (there are now thirty-six in Egypt) with a new, more fecund wife.

That more and more affluent, educated men are choosing this route, with little consideration for their first wives' feelings or futures, is the latest sad twist to the male infertility story in Egypt. Thus, the gendered dimensions of this new reproductive technology reveal the ongoing nature of Egyptian patriarchy and the ways in which cases of male infertility serve to expose it.

Conclusion

I have focused on male infertility in Egypt, highlighting the patriarchal paradoxes posed by this condition. I have sought to demonstrate how

233

'The worms are weak'

women living under a particular patriarchal regime suffer over men's infertility. Not only are they blamed for the infertility, but their gender identities and marriages suffer as a result. Furthermore, women pay the price of male infertility treatment; not only the physically taxing embodiment of such treatment, but actual abandonment by husbands when such treatment is no longer an option for elderly wives.

Other stories could be told of how male infertility plays out in men's and women's lives in Egypt. Such stories must attend to infertile men's perspectives on their marriages, identities and experiences as members of a society in which men themselves are subject to stressful, competitive, hierarchical forms of hegemonic masculinity. Male infertility presents a crisis of masculinity for Egyptian men, one in which their manhood is shaken to its deepest core. But, as demonstrated in this chapter, the effects of such masculine crises do not end there: they redound in multiple, often profoundly detrimental ways on the lives of the women who, by virtue of marriage, must share infertile men's secrets and uphold their masculinity at all costs.

Notes

Reprinted from *Men and Masculinities*, 5.3 (January 2003): 236–56.

1 An ongoing debate in the clinical-epidemiological literature questions whether sperm concentrations have decreased globally over the past fifty years because of environmental toxins and global warming. While some investigators support the so-called 'big drop' thesis, others do not.

2 For further details of the study methodology and sample, see the appendices in Inhorn (1994b).

3 Names used here are pseudonyms.

4 In 1988, this was the equivalent of a little more than US$15, one of the lowest monthly household incomes in my sample of 100 women and their husbands.

5 Despite their poverty, many lower-class Egyptian men do not permit their wives to work. For a full explanation, see Inhorn (1996).

6 For full descriptions and interpretation of this cultural illness category, see Inhorn (1994a, 1994c).

7 Pregnancies with multiple foetuses are at greater risk of complications. In Egypt, all IVF and ICSI pregnancies result in caesareans, or 'surgical births'.

8 Although contemporary Western biological models of procreation are duogenetic, monogenetic models, including notions of foetal pre-formation in male sperm, have a long intellectual history in the West, dating from the time of Aristotle to the 1700s (Inhorn 1994a; Laqueur 1990).

9 Studies in the West have found that male infertility is more stigmatizing than female infertility (Becker, forthcoming; Van Balen et al. 1995).

10 Egyptian women may marry as early as their teens and usually by their twenties. Men often marry in their thirties, forties or even later.

11 Some Egyptian IVF physicians have expressed concern that my research does not reflect well enough the ways in which elite women may exert psychological power over their infertile husbands and generally make their lives miserable.

12 The permanent fostering of orphans, tantamount to 'adoption' in the West, is unpopular among Egyptians for several cultural reasons (Inhorn 1996). In my studies, middle- and upper-class Egyptians seemed less willing to entertain this possibility than did lower- and lower-middle-class infertile couples.

References

Abbey, A., F. M. Andrews and L. J. Halman (1991) 'Gender's Role in Responses to Infertility', *Psychology of Women Quarterly*, 15: 295–316.

Becker, G. (2002) 'Deciding Whether to Tell Children about Donor Insemination: An Unresolved Question in the United State', in M. C. Inhorn and F. van Balen (eds), *Interpreting Infertility: Childlessness, Gender, and New Reproductive Technologies in Global Perspective*. Berkeley: University of California Press.

Cates, W., T. M. M. Farley and P. J. Rowe (1985) 'Worldwide Patterns of Infertility: Is Africa Different?', *The Lancet*, 14 September 14: 596–8.

Collet, M., J. Reniers, E. Frost, F. Yvert, A. Leclerc, C. Roth-Meyer, B. Ivanoff and A. Meheus (1988) 'Infertility in Central Africa: Infection is the Cause', *International Journal of Gynaecology and Obstetrics*, 26: 423–8.

Connell, R. (1995) *Masculinities*. Berkeley: University of California Press.

Crapanzano, V. (1973) *The Hamadsha: A Study in Moroccan Ethnopsychiatry*. Berkeley: University of California Press.

Curtis, K. M. et al. (1997) 'Effects of Cigarette Smoking, Caffeine Consumption, and Alcohol Intake on Fecundability', *American Journal of Epidemiology*, 146: 32–41.

Daniels, C. R. (1997) 'Between Fathers and Fetuses: The Social Construction of Male Reproduction and the Politics of Fetal Harm', *Signs: Journal of Women in Culture and Society*, 22: 579–616.

DeClerque, J., A. O. Tsui, M. F. Abul-Ata and D. Barcelona (1986) 'Rumour, Misinformation and Oral Contraceptive Use in Egypt', *Social Science and Medicine*, 23: 83–92.

Delaney, C. (1991) *The Seed and the Soil: Gender and Cosmology in Turkish Village Society*. Berkeley: University of California Press.

Devroey, P., M. Vandervorst, P. Nagy and A. Van Steirteghem (1998) 'Do We Treat the Male or His Gamete?', *Human Reproduction*, 13 (Suppl. 1): 178–85.

Early, E. A. (1993) *Baladi Women of Cairo: Playing with an Egg and a Stone*. Boulder, CO: Lynne Rienner.

Egyptian Fertility Care Society (1995) *Community-based Study of the Prevalence Of Infertility and Its Etiological Factors in Egypt: (1) The Population-based Study*. Cairo: Egyptian Fertility Care Society.

'The worms are weak'

Elshtain, J. B. (1981) *Public Man, Private Woman*. Princeton, NJ: Princeton University Press.

Ericksen, K. and T. Brunette (1996) 'Patterns and Predictors of Infertility among African Women: A Cross-national Survey of 27 Nations', *Social Science and Medicine*, 42: 209–20.

Goffman, E. (1963) *Stigma: Notes on the Management of Spoiled Identity*. Englewood Cliffs, NJ: Prentice-Hall.

Good, M.-J. D. (1980) 'Of Blood and Babies: The Relationship of Popular Islamic Physiology to Fertility', *Social Science and Medicine*, 14B: 147–56.

Greenwood, B. (1981) 'Perceiving Systems: Cold or Spirits? Choice and Ambiguity in Morocco's Pluralistic Medical System', *Social Science and Medicine*, 15B: 219–35.

Greil, A. L. (1997) 'Infertility and Psychological Distress: A Critical Review of the Literature', *Social Science and Medicine*, 45: 1679–704.

Greil, A. L., T. A. Leitko and K. L. Porter (1990) 'Infertility: His and Hers', *Gender and Society*, 2: 172–99.

Inhorn, M. C. (1994a) *Quest for Conception: Gender, Infertility, and Egyptian Medical Traditions*. Philadelphia: University of Pennsylvania Press.

— (1994b) 'Interpreting Infertility: Medical Anthropological Perspectives', *Social Science and Medicine*, 39: 459–61.

— (1994c) 'Kabsa (a.k.a. Mushahara) and Threatened Fertility in Egypt', *Social Science and Medicine*, 39: 487–505.

— (1996) *Infertility and Patriarchy: The Cultural Politics of Gender and Family Life in Egypt*. Philadelphia: University of Pennsylvania Press.

Inhorn, M. C. and K. A. Buss (1993) 'Infertility, Infection, And Iatrogenesis in Egypt: The Anthropological Epidemiology of Blocked Tubes', *Medical Anthropology*, 15: 217–44.

— (1994) 'Ethnography, Epidemiology, and Infertility in Egypt', *Social Science and Medicine*, 39: 671–86.

Inhorn, M. and F. van Balen (eds) (2002) *Interpreting Infertility: Childlessness, Gender, and New Reproductive Technologies in Global Perspective*. Berkeley: University of California Press.

Irvine, D. S. (1998) 'Epidemiology and Aetiology of Male Infertility', *Human Reproduction*, 13 (Suppl. 1): 33–44.

Jaggar, A. M. (1983) *Feminist Politics and Human Nature*. Totowa, NJ: Rowman and Allanheld.

Joseph, S. (1993) 'Connectivity and Patriarchy among Urban Working-class Arab Families in Lebanon', *Ethos*, 21: 452–84.

— (1994) 'Brother/Sister Relationships: Connectivity, Love, and Power in the Reproduction of Patriarchy in Lebanon', *American Ethnologist*, 21: 50–73.

Kamischke, A. and E. Nieschlag (1998) 'Conventional Treatments of Male Infertility in the Age of Evidence-Based Andrology', *Human Reproduction*, 13 (Suppl. 1): 62–75.

Kandiyoti, D. (1988) 'Bargaining with Patriarchy', *Gender and Society*, 2: 274–90.

— (1991) 'Islam and Patriarchy: A Comparative Perspective', in N. R. Keddie and B. Baron (eds), *Women in Middle Eastern History: Shifting Boundaries in Sex and Gender*. New Haven, CT: Yale University Press, pp. 23–42.

Laqueur, T. (1990) *Making Sex: Body and Gender from the Greeks to Freud*. Cambridge, MA: Harvard University Press.

Larsen, U. (1994) 'Sterility in sub-Saharan Africa', *Population Studies*, 48: 459–74.

McConnell, J. D. (1993) 'Diagnosis and Treatment of Male Infertility', in B. R. Carr and R. E. Blackwell (eds), *Textbook of Reproductive Medicine*. Norwalk, CT: Appleton and Lange, pp. 453–68.

MacLeod, A. E. (1991) *Accommodating Protest: Working Women, The New Veiling, and Change in Cairo*. New York: Columbia University Press.

Ouzgane, L. (1997) 'Masculinity as Virility in Tahar Ben Jelloun's Work', *Contagion: Journal of Violence, Mimesis, and Culture*, 4: 1–13.

Reproductive Health Outlook (1999) *Infertility: Overview and Lessons Learned*. Website: <www.rho.org>

Rowe, P. J., F. H. Comhaire, T. B. Hargreave and H. J. Mellows (1993) *WHO Manual for the Standardized Investigation and Diagnosis of the Infertile Couple*. Cambridge: Cambridge University Press.

Stanton, A. L., J. Tennen, G. Affleck and R. Mendola (1991) 'Cognitive Appraisal and Adjustment to Infertility', *Women and Health*, 17: 1–15.

Sundby, J. (2002) 'Infertility and Health Care in Countries with Less Resources: Case Studies from Sub-Saharan Africa', in M. C. Inhorn and F. van Balen (eds), *Infertility around the Globe: New Thinking on Childlessness, Gender, and Reproductive Technologies*. Berkeley: University of California Press.

Thonneau, P. et al. (1998) 'Occupational health Exposure and Male Fertility: A Review', *Human Reproduction*, 13: 2122–5.

Tong, R. (1989) *Feminist Thought: A Comprehensive Introduction*. Boulder, CO: Westview Press.

Van Balen, F. and T. C. M. Trimbos-Kemper (1993) 'Long-term Infertile Couples: A Study of Their Well Being', *Journal of Psychosomatic Obstetrics and Gynaecology*, 16: 137–44.

Van Balen, F., J. E. E. Verdurmen and E. Ketting (1995) *Caring about Infertility: Main Results of the National Survey about Behaviour Regarding Infertility*. Delft: Eburon.

Webb, R. E., and J. Daniluk (1999) '"The End of the Line": Infertile Men's Experiences of Being Unable to Produce a Child', *Men and Masculinities*, 2: 6–25.

Wood, J. W. (1994) *Dynamics of Human Reproduction: Biology, Biometry, Demography*. New York: Aldein de Gruyter.

Yeboah, E. D., J. M. Wadhwani and J. B. Wilson (1992) 'Etiological Factors of Male Infertility in Africa', *International Journal of Fertility*, 37: 300–7.

Contributors

Durre S. Ahmed has master's degrees in psychology (Pb), sociology (Columbia), communication (Columbia) and a doctorate in communication and education (Columbia). She is director, graduate program in communication and cultural studies, National College of Arts, Lahore, where she is also professor of psychology and communication and chairperson, Department of Academics. She is the author of *Masculinity, Rationality and Religion: A Feminist Perspective* (Lahore ASR, 1992) and editor and contributing author of *Gendering the Spirit: Women, Religion and the Post-colonial Response* (London, Zed Books, 2002).

Mohammed Baobaid has his doctorate in psychology and criminology from the Erlangen-Nuremburg University, Germany. Dr Baobaid was the head of research department of the women studies centre at the University of Sana'a, Yemen. Currently, he works as a men's counselor with abusive men at Changing Ways in London, Ontario, and is the coordinator for the Muslim Family Safety Project. He is also a research associate at the centre for research on violence against women and children at the University of Western Ontario, Canada.

Rob K. Baum, a senior lecturer at Monash University, has degrees in performance studies with a concentration in anthropology. Since completing her post-doctorate in gender, gesture and ritual in the Middle East, she has taught in Israel, New Zealand and Australia. Her phenomenological research includes the book *Female Absence: Women, Theatre and Other Metaphors* and articles on Palestinian ritual, race/gender issues and identity politics. Currently completing a book on the influence of the Shoah, Rob performs in improvisational movement, theatre and circus.

Don Conway-Long is an assistant professor of anthropology and sociology at Webster University in St Louis, Missouri. In 1978, he was a co-founder of RAVEN, a program designed to end men's physical and sexual violence against women through education and activism. He has been teaching courses on the critical analysis of men and masculinities since 1982.

Banu Helvacioglu has received her PhD in politicalstudies at Queen's University and taught at Queen's and Ryerson Polytechnical University. She was a research associate at CERI (Paris). She is currently teaching political theory in the Department of Political Science at Bilkent University. She has publications on postmodernity, American New Right, religious and nationalist constructios of contemporary Turkish politics. Her current research is on 'deconstucting masculinity in Turkey'.

Marcia C. Inhorn is director of the Center for Middle Eastern and North African Studies at the University of Michigan, where she is professor in the Department of Health Behavior and Health Education, School of Public Health, the Program in Women's Studies, and the Department of Anthropology. A medical anthropologist specializing in Middle Eastern gender and health issues, she has conducted research on the social impact of infertility and assisted reproductive technologies among Muslim populations in Egypt, Lebanon, and Arab America over the past 20 years. She is the author of three books on the subject, including *Local Babies, Global Science: Gender, Religion, and In Vitro Fertilization in Egypt* (Routledge, 2003). Her current research project focuses on male infertility and masculinity in the era of assisted conception.

Daniel Monterescu received his PhD in anthropology from the University of Chicago (2005). His publications feature articles in *Journal of Mediterranean Studies, Theory and Criticism, Israeli Sociology* and contributions to numerous edited volumes. He is currently co-editing a volume entitled *Mixed Cities/Trapped Communities: Historical Narratives, Spatial Dynamics, Gender Relations and Cultural Encounters in Palestinian-Israeli Mixed Towns* (forthcoming at Ashgate Publishing). He is an assistant professor of sociology and anthropology at the Central European University in Budapest

Lahoucine Ouzgane is associate professor of English and film studies at the University of Alberta, where his teaching and research interests focus on postcolonial theory and literature, composition and rhetoric, and masculinity studies. His recent publications include *Crossing Borderlands: Composition and Postcolonial Studies* (University of Pittsburgh Press, 2004) and *African Masculinities: men in Africa from the late 19th century to the present* (Palgrave Macmillan, March 2005). He is Consultant Editor for *The Routledge International Encyclopedia of Men and Masculinities*.

Najat Rahman is assistant professor of comparative literature at the University of Montréal. She is co-editor of a forthcoming critical volume on the poetry of Mahmoud Darwish (Interlink 2005). She has published serveral articles on gender and Islam as well as translated selected poetry of Mahmoud Darwish and of Abd al-Wahab al-Bayyati. Her research interests include exploring cultural and political enactments of myths; the nexus between masculinity, nationalism, and patriarchy; current discourses on terror; cultural globalization in the Arab world.

Ruth Roded, of the Hebrew University of Jerusalem, deals in the social and cultural history of the Middle East; her PhD and subsequent research was on Ottoman Syria and for two decades she has focused on gender. She has published a study of *Women in Islamic Biographical Collections From Ibn Sa'd to Who's Who* (1994), and an introductory reader on *Women in Islam and the Middle East* (1999). In recent years, she has been working on a rather ambitious project on 'Twentieth-Century Gendered Perceptions of the Life of the Prophet Muhammad,' chapters of which have appeared as articles.

Achim Rohde studied at Hamburg, Tel Aviv and Birzeit Universities, received an MA in Middle Eastern studies from Hamburg University (2000). His areas of interest include Israel/Palestine, Iraq, Muslim immigrants in Europe and the history of German oriental studies. In 2002–03 he was a researcher at the Center for Interdisciplinary Women and Gender Studies at the Carl-von-Ossietzky University, Oldenburg. He is currently completing his PhD at the Institut für Islamwissenschaft at the Free University of Berlin with a thesis entitled 'Facing Dictatorship. State-Society Relations in Ba'thist Iraq'.

Celia Rothenberg is an assistant professor at McMaster University in the Department of Religious Studies and the Health Studies Programme. Her book, *Spirits of Palestine: Gender, Society, and Stories of the Jinn* (2004), looks at stories of the jinn among women and men in the Palestinian village of Artas. Her interests include diaspora studies, spirit possession, women in the Middle East, and the interrelationships among religion, health, and illness.

Asifa Siraj is a doctoral student at the University of Glasgow. Her current research examines the relationship between religion, masculinity and femininity amongst heterosexual couples in Scotland. The chapter in this volume is drawn from her PhD research, concerned with the role of sexuality in the construction of masculinities in Islam.

Index

General Federation of Iraqi Women (GFIW), 184, 196
Ghoussoub, Mai, with Emma Sinclair, *Imagined Masculinities*, 1
glass, breaking of, at weddings, 115, 116
God, 25
Golcuk, earthquake in, 36

hadith, questioning of, 208
Hagar, 81; exile of, 74; repudiation of, 73, 82
Hala, wife of the Prophet, 232
Hallaj, 18
Hamad, Mahmud, 194
Hamit, Halil, 49
Hanim, Zeyneb, 49
Haykal, Muhammad Husayn, 64; *Life of Muhammad*, 64–5
healthcare services, 168
Hebrew language, 101, 105, 106, 109; knowledge of, 97–8
Hebron, violence in, 79
heretical communities within Islam, 21
heteronormativity, 214; challenging of, 212–13
hijab, 1, 152
Hillman, James, 12, 17
Hizbullah (Turkey), 52
Holy, Ladislav, 112
home, as woman's place, 147
homeland, 81
homoeroticism, 2
homosexuality, 2, 5–6, 26, 177; and marriage, 210–11; banned in Islam, 202, 205, 206, 208; coming out, 209–10; Islam and, 202–16; Islamic guidelines for, 213; negation of, 129; seen as symptom of Westernization, 214
honour: family, 169, 176 (ideology of, 186); killings for, 169, 174, 176; of women, protection of, 52
Horney, Karen, 152
horse, 117; wild, image of, 113–14; woman's translation as, 113
hostage-taking, 162

husbands: failed, 95; responsible for wage, 95; weakness of, 100
Hussein, Saddam, 190, 193, 196, 197
hybridity, as third space, 128
hysteria, 14

Ibn al 'Arabi, 16, 19
Ibn Sa'd, 57
'Id el fitr, 136
identity, 126
ijtihad, intellectual activity, 73
illiteracy, 169
imams, female, 41
impotence, 29, 119
Imru' al-Qais, 81
in vitro fertilization (IVF), 220, 223, 229, 232–3
infertility: blaming of women, 226–33; burden of, rests on women, 217; infection-induced, 217; lifestyle factors of, 220; male, 6 (in Egypt, 217–37; invisibility of, 231); men's contribution to, 219; men's refusal of responsibility for, 222, 228; relation to manhood, 229; relation to patriarchy, 225–6; seen as women's problem, 217–18
inheritance, rights of women, 166, 171, 174
initiation, role of, 17
International Crime Victimization Survey, 164
Intifada, 106, 108, 110
Intifada literature, 90
intracytoplasmic sperm injection (ICSI), 224–5, 232–3
Iran-Iraq War, 185, 188, 190, 192
Iraq, 5; masculinity and love in, 184–201; Personal Status Law, 184
Isaac, 74, 75; attempted sacrifice of, 77
Ishmael, 74, 81, 82
Islam, 156–7; and gender, 19–21; and homosexuality, 202–16; as category, 2; as revealed religion, 59; as terrain of political struggle, 47; attitudes to women, 11; different traditions within,